RACIAL CRISIS
IN AMERICAN EDUCATION

RACIAL CRISIS IN AMERICAN EDUCATION

Edited by Robert L. Green

Professor of Educational Psychology
and Director of the Center for Urban Affairs
Michigan State University

Follett Educational Corporation • Chicago

LA
210
. G72

"Education and Redistribution: The Limits of a Strategy"
is reprinted with the permission of Integrated Education
Associates, Chicago.

Editor: LaVerne Hosek
Designer: Lowell Richardson

To my wife Lettie and my sons Vince, Kurt, Kevin
and to Martin Luther King, Jr., and his family,
and to those who have contributed to the struggle
for social justice in America. It is my sincere hope
that the forces of good will will unite to make America
a just nation for all. A nation in which skin color,
race, or religion will not be used to determine
the worth of a man or woman. Finally, it is my hope
that America will work to eradicate poverty, war,
and racism and to share its technological skill,
wisdom, and resources with newly independent and
developing nations throughout the world.

R.L.G.

CONTENTS

RACE AND EDUCATION: AN INTRODUCTION

Robert L. Green
Frederick Howe

Dr. Robert L. Green is Professor of Educational Psychology and Director of the Center for Urban Affairs at Michigan State University. In 1963, Professor Green collected data and conducted research pertaining to the educational and social status of school deprived black children in Prince Edward County, Virginia. He was formerly Director of the Chicago Adult Education Project, a job placement program for the urban unemployed, and Educational Director for the Southern Christian Leadership Conference under Dr. Martin Luther King, Jr. Professor Green's primary responsibility with the Southern Christian Leadership Conference was the structuring of educational programs for southern urban and rural blacks.

Dr. Green is also Urban Education Advisor to the Committee on Economic Development and Educational Consultant for Project Read in the Washington, D.C. public school system and Ocean Hill-Brownsville school community in New York City. He is co-author of the *Famous Negro American Series* and has written extensively on factors that affect the educational, economic, and social status of the disadvantaged in American society.

Mr. Frederick Howe is Assistant Professor of Educational Psychology at Eastern Michigan University and has conducted research on the educational status of disadvantaged youth.

About ten years ago, the white school board in Prince Edward County, Virginia, voted to close the public school system in that county rather than comply with court-ordered school integration (Green, *et al.,* 1964). The court order was precipitated by black parents who felt that school integration was the quickest route to quality education. In November, 1968, the black residents of Hyde County, North Carolina, took to the streets, demonstrated, and refused to allow black schools to be closed in order to integrate white schools in that county. These two significant educational incidents are symbolic of how the objectives and mood of the black community have changed regarding the education of their children. Yet, the major issue within the black community remains essentially the same: How can academic programs be designed to meet the educational needs of black youngsters?

The current press on the part of black parents for a meaningful educational program for their children is not limited to any geographic section of the country. The recent crisis in New York City over community control of the schools and the efforts of the black citizens of Roxbury District in Boston to write a proposal seeking funds for a Central Cities project with the advice of school officials are indicative of the concern of black parents for the education of their children.

Chicago recently established a 21-member governing board for a Central Cities project with equal representation from the city's central school board, the University of Chicago, and a community group known as the Woodlawn Organization. A group of black teachers in Pontiac, Michigan, recently organized themselves, *not* with the objective of seeking better pay and shorter working hours, but of working toward the development of a comprehensive educational program that will increase the academic achievement of black students in Pontiac.

Black high school students in Detroit, Philadelphia, and Chicago have openly expressed their displeasure with the current status of urban education. The recent confrontations between college administrators and college students, both black and white, at Columbia University, Howard University, Grambling College, and San Francisco State College are all manifestations of disgust with an educational system that has failed to respond to the problems of race and poverty in America.

These events all point to the significance of the current crisis confronting American education. Without a doubt, race is a significant factor. Indeed, race has always been a significant factor in the education of blacks in America.

Witness the historical development of the United States. During slavery, laws were enacted which made it a crime to teach blacks how to read and write (Romano, *et al.*, 1968). Although some slaves and "free Negroes" were educated during the Revolutionary Period, particularly due to the efforts of the Quakers, most blacks were not given formal instruction for fear that this might lead to slave insurrections. Virtually no educational program existed for blacks as slave labor became a principal factor in the economy of the United States. With the rise in value of slave labor and the fear of slave insurrections, black codes were put into effect throughout the South which prohibited the teaching of blacks.

Following the Civil War, education for blacks came about only on a piecemeal basis. Many black schools were bombed, and blacks were forcibly prevented from attending school throughout the South (Franklin, 1967). In addition, separate school facilities that were grossly unequal were maintained for blacks and whites. This pattern continued de jure in the South and de facto in the North.

Despite the landmark Supreme Court decision in 1954, which held that the "separate but equal" school doctrine was no longer tenable, schools throughout the United States are still separated along racial lines. The report of the U.S. Commission on Civil Rights entitled *Racial Isolation in the Public Schools* (1967) stated that the degree of school segregation rose sharply from 1950 to 1965. Since 1965, the racial composition of American schools has become even more tightly drawn along racial lines. Racial separation, poor school facilities, inadequately trained teachers, and the unwillingness of school systems and teachers to act in the best educational interests of black students have led to a situation that can only be described as volatile today.

The *Report of the National Advisory Commission on Civil Disorders* (1968), more popularly known as the Kerner Report, states:

> Education in a democratic society must equip the children of the nation to realize their potential and to participate fully in American life. For the community-at-large, the schools have discharged this responsibility well. But for many minorities, and particularly for the children of the racial ghetto, the schools have failed to provide the educational experience which could help overcome the effects of discrimination and deprivation.
>
> This failure is one of the persistent sources of grievance and resentment within the Negro community. The hostility of Negro parents and students toward the school system is generating increasing conflict and causing disruption within many school districts.[1]

The Kerner Report suggests further that the most dramatic evidence of the relationship between race and educational practices lies in the high incidence of riot participation by poor youth who have dropped out of high school.

There are many indices of the failure of the public school system to educate minority youth who are black, Mexican-American, Puerto Rican, or poor white. If academic achievement alone is used as the criteria of success in educating black youth, then the record is most unfortunate. As pointed out in the Kerner Report, in the two most critical academic areas, verbal and reading ability, black students fall consistently behind whites as they increase in age or years of school completed:

> In the metropolitan northeast, Negro students, on the average, begin the first grade with somewhat lower scores on standardized achievement tests than whites, are about 1.6 grades behind by the sixth grade, and have fallen 3.3 grades behind white students by the twelfth grade.[2]

The recent *Report of the Detroit High School Study Commission* (Cushman and Keith, 1968) substantiates the findings mentioned in the Kerner Report regarding the academic achievement of black youth. The Commission, attempting to discover why black high school students in Detroit decided to boycott their classes, found that one out of every three students fails a course each school semester. Further, the study reveals that although white students steadily improve academically as they progress through the city schools, black youngsters tend to fall farther and farther behind. Both the Kerner Report and the efforts of the Detroit High School Study Commission document the critical status of urban education.

The most obvious educational problems can be found in our urban communities, both North and South. The low academic achievement of many urban youth, the growing reluctance on the part of many teachers to accept assignments in urban schools with large percentages of minority students, and the growing controversy over issues such as corporal punishment and community control of black schools are all indications of a system that needs restructuring. A basic restructuring of the educational system should provide "a redistribution of power with a set of exclusive powers being assigned to the local community and its representatives."[3]

Many black parents and educators are now saying, in effect, "If you are going to keep all-black schools and all-white schools, then it is time that blacks have a say in the operation of black schools." Black parents have asked themselves whether people who have established and supported segregated, inferior educational opportunities for black youth for years can be expected to take the necessary steps to ameliorate these wrongs; whether people who fear blacks and believe them to be intellectually inferior can be expected to structure the educational system so that it provides quality education for black youth.

Thus, decentralization and community control are efforts on the part of the community to hold the schools accountable for the education of their children. The movement is a direct response by black parents to their lack of decision-making power to positively affect the education of black children. White communities have exercised this kind of local power throughout the history of the educational system, and they are still exercising it. That is the reason why all public schools are still training children toward a "white middle class" bias. For black children, this direction is highly questionable.

What, precisely, is community control? Here is what one writer, Preston Wilcox (1969), has to say. The urban black communities are asking for:

1. Control over hiring, firing, training, and programming of school staff. The local governing board should have the power to establish a staff with knowledge of the community and a commitment to the education of children in that community. Evaluation of the staff should be based on pupil performance.
2. Control over site selection and naming of schools. The local governing board should have the power to determine school location within the black community and have an effect on any associated housing relocation. In addition, schools serving predominantly black youth should be allowed to name their schools for famous black people.
3. Control over expenditure of funds—local, state, and federal. The local governing board should have the power to employ local people, develop programs, and direct money toward locally-owned businesses through its purchasing power.
4. Control over design and construction of schools. The local governing board should have the power to award contracts permitting the employment of skilled black people present within the community.

However, despite the necessity for restructuring the educational system, the forces of society that have produced segregated, inferior schools may be expected to block this restructuring.

Seriously complicating the issue is the increasing conflict between teachers and the community in urban areas. In a recent article, Wallace Roberts states that "the ultimate question of control comes down to whether a semi-autonomous school board has the right to hire and fire its teachers at will."[4] For many years teachers have been struggling to regulate their own profession, and they see community control as an agent which attempts to take away their newly-won bargaining power. Community control also threatens the familiar system of education as it challenges teachers to innovate in their classrooms, to make up new curricula, and to redesign teacher qualifications and regulations for tenure. Thus, the struggle between teachers and the community can be a bitter one. However, if teachers can be brought into the early stages of decentralization and involved directly in curriculum planning, this bitterness probably can be avoided.

The controversy in the Ocean Hill-Brownsville district of New York City during 1968 provides an excellent example of the conflict between black parents demanding quality education for their children and the forces opposing the changes which black parents and educators feel are necessary. In Ocean Hill-Brownsville, the community is predominantly black and Puerto Rican while the school administrative and teaching staff is predominantly white.

With financial aid from the Ford Foundation, this district and several others were designated for an experimental program in local control of the schools. In February, 1967, a broadly based community planning council began to outline the duties of the new local governing board. It was soon felt, however, that the city board of education was reluctant to give authority to the local board and to define its powers. Due to the ambiguity existing as to the authority of the local governing board, a rift developed between this body and the teachers in September, 1967. Teachers complained that the local governing board was ignoring established hiring procedures, and the United Federation of Teachers called a city-wide strike.

During the course of the 1967-1968 school year, local administrators and teachers directed their energies toward abolishing decentralization plans in a campaign which too often carried explicit racial overtones. The attempted experiment ended in chaos through the failure of the central board of education to adequately define the authority of the local governing board and through the opposition of the New York United Federation of Teachers to community control.

The Ocean Hill-Brownsville controversy is exemplary of the racial crisis in American education.

Throughout this book, the authors will delineate the educational issues in urban school communities. Factors such as the curriculum, the urban school child, the language patterns of disadvantaged black children, teacher training, compensatory education, administrative leadership, community control of the schools, and educational separatism will be analyzed systematically. However, the consistent theme throughout this book is that (1) minority group children can learn; and (2) the public school system must search for strategies that will lead to educational success for *all* students.

It is stated that we must search for ways to reform the present educational system as well as focus on pupil behavioral change. Much of the dysfunctional educational behavior that we observe within minority school populations is related to the educational environment in which they are placed.

It is also important to note that much recent data supports the view that environmental modification will often lead to behavioral modification or change. The research of Woodyard, Harrell and Gates (1965), Deutsch (1968), Bloom (1964), and Green (1966) documents the importance of early environmental stimulation upon later educational growth. Educational efforts such as Project Head Start and Follow Through are designed to provide disadvantaged children with optimal academic stimulation. Preschool programs should be expanded, focusing particularly on language development, and including medical and dental services and diet supplementation as integral aspects. Finally, preschool programs can educate urban mothers to lead their children toward academic success.

It is also demonstrated that students from disadvantaged urban backgrounds can experience academic success when we arrange the environment in a manner that is appropriate to their needs. Arranging the environment to meet the needs of disadvantaged youth may mean providing them with tutorial or personal counseling services. It will require an understanding of the social environment from which the student comes. It could well mean rewriting aspects of the curriculum (which undoubtedly would benefit all students).

Throughout this book, it is recommended that the urban school be redesigned to interest all children and to reflect life as urban children observe it. Textbooks must adequately reflect the positive contributions of minority Americans. Innovation and experimentation with new reading and math materials must be implemented since success in school depends almost totally upon these areas. Most important of all, experimental programs must be carefully assessed in order to determine their effectiveness.

Rearranging the environment may require different reinforcers for academic striving. It has been argued that disadvantaged children should be paid in cold, hard cash for exhibiting achievement-oriented behavior (Green and Stachnik, 1968). Since the acquisition of achievement-oriented attitudes does not develop without proper reinforcers, efforts must be made to develop meaningful reinforcers for school-related behavior.

This book stresses the need for quality education in the schools that are most depressed. Improving the quality of teachers is critical. The Teacher Corps may succeed in establishing a model program for training teachers for urban assignments. The Education Professions Development Act provides grants and fellowships in an effort to retrain and provide advanced training for teachers in urban areas. More immediately, however, colleges should prepare courses which will sensitize future teachers to the history and culture of urban youth. Teachers who are successful in teaching urban youth should function as master teachers and supervise the field placement of education students. Master teachers could teach methods courses in our teacher preparation programs. Too many teacher-training personnel are unfamiliar with the modern classroom. The urban master teacher could serve as a special resource person and close this significant void.

Every urban classroom should make extensive use of paraprofessionals who are residents of the community. The use of paraprofessionals would provide community people with jobs and provide students with the model of a minority group adult in a position of responsibility. Not only would parents benefit from working with the schools, but children would benefit from having informed parents. The involvement of parents with the school inevitably leads to greater interest on the part of the student. There may be additional benefits. In P.S. 144 in New York City, the inclusion of parents in the classroom during a community control controversy resulted in a decrease in disciplinary problems!

Racial imbalance or isolation is cited as a major social-educational problem facing the urban school. Although the majority of white

American educators posit school desegregation as a necessary aspect of quality education, the American educational system is still tightly drawn along racial lines. Black parents have recognized the unwillingness of school officials to move towards developing a multiracial school community designed to educate all children, and they are now pressing for quality education in predominantly black schools. If we are to strive toward building a multiracial society in which race and class lines are minimized, then our schools must set an example for the larger society. In short, racial segregation and racist practices in the American public school system must be abolished. Until then, we must strive to provide quality education in uniracial schools. However, the goal of a multiracial school system must not be abandoned if the greater society is to eventually reflect the many faces of America.

The Ocean Hill-Brownsville crisis demonstrated the vital concern felt by urban parents for the education of their children. It is clear to all Americans that academic achievement is a necessity in our society. However, the existence of hostility between the school and the community it serves can only indicate that education is not effective in that setting. The urban schools must relate to the broader problems of the cities and their children. Parental participation in educational practices and decisions must be encouraged. Power must be dispersed and parents must have the authority to tell administrators what they expect from the schools. This means:

> . . . creating whole new mechanisms for bringing parents and teachers together, for allowing people with little formal education to work in classrooms and offices, and as liaison workers with the community.[5]

The schools must be as open for today's urban parents and as responsive to their expectations as they were for the immigrants of the 1920's.

Finally, it is stressed that without a major effort to eradicate racist practices from the American educational system, many of our current problems will accelerate.

In essence, a total commitment must be made by school board members, administrators, teachers, and teachers' unions to upgrade the quality of urban education. Our educational system is one of the most important institutions in American life. If our public schools continue to miseducate a large segment of American children, our nation will be confronted with even greater social problems during this generation and in the future.

The chapters that follow attempt to provide guidelines for the establishment of democratic educational institutions that will serve the best interests of all American children.

Notes

1. *Report of the National Advisory Commission on Civil Disorders.*
2. J. S. Coleman, *et al.*, *Equality of Educational Opportunity* (Washington, D.C.: U.S. Government Printing Office, 1966), p. 20.
3. P. Wilcox, "The Meaning of Community Control," *Foresight* (1969), 1, p. v.
4. W. Roberts, "The Battle for Urban Schools," *Saturday Review* (November 16, 1968), p. 97.
5. *Ibid.*, p. 101.

References

Bloom, Benjamin S. *Stability and Change in Human Characteristics.* New York: John Wiley and Sons, 1964.

Cushman, Edward and Damon, Keith. *Report of the Detroit High School Study Commission,* Detroit Public Schools, Detroit, Mich., 1968.

Deutsch, Martin. "Patterns of Perceptual Language and Intellective Performance in Children With Cognitive Deficits," *Research and Evaluation.* Institute for Developmental Studies, New York University, November, 1968.

Franklin, John Hope. *From Slavery to Freedom: A History of the American Negro.* New York: Alfred A. Knopf, 1967.

Green, Robert L., Hofmann, Louis J., Morse, Richard J., Hayes, Marilyn E., and Morgan, Robert F. *The Educational Status of Children in a District Without Public Schools.* Study of Prince Edward County, Va., U.S. Office of Education Cooperative Research Project No. 2321. Washington, D.C.: U.S. Government Printing Office, 1964.

Green, Robert L., Hofmann, Louis J., Morse, Richard J., and Morgan, Robert F. *The Educational Status of Children During the First School Year Following Four Years of Little or No Schooling.* Prince Edward County, Va., Study, U.S. Office of Education Cooperative Research Project No. 2498. Washington, D.C.: U.S. Government Printing Office, 1966.

Green, Robert L. and Stachnik, Thomas J. "Money, Motivation and Academic Achievement," *Phi Delta Kappan,* 1968, 50: 228-230.

Racial Isolation in the Public Schools. U.S. Commission on Civil Rights. Washington, D.C.: U.S. Government Printing Office, 1967.

Report of the National Advisory Commission on Civil Disorders. U.S. Riot Commission Report; also called the Kerner Report. Washington, D.C.: U.S. Government Printing Office, 1968.

Roberts, Wallace. "The Battle for Urban Schools," *Saturday Review* (November 16, 1968), 52: 97-98.

Romano, Louis, Georgiady, Nicholas, Green, Robert L., and Tall, James F. *Famous Negro American Series.* Milwaukee: Franklin Publishers, 1968.

Wilcox, Preston "The Meaning of Community Control," *Foresight,* 1969, 1:v.

Woodyard, Ella, Harrell, Ruth, and Gates, Arthur. *The Effect of Mothers' Diets on the Intelligence of Offspring.* New York: Columbia University Press, 1965.

1 | THE EDUCATION AND EMPLOYMENT STATUS OF BLACKS AND WHITES SINCE 1946: THE GROWING DISPARITY

Daniel H. Kruger

Dr. Daniel Kruger presents a critical examination of the economic and educational status of American blacks since World War II. There are two distinct approaches which can be used to evaluate the progress of blacks during the past twenty years, and they lead to entirely different conclusions. In terms of the absolute approach, blacks have shared in advances in the American economy. They have made gains in employment and education. In terms of the relative approach, the author demonstrates that blacks have made no significant economic advances, their status in relation to whites is generally unchanged, and the civil rights activities of the past few years have failed to stimulate significant progress.

Because of this socioeconomic gap, a policy of equal opportunity will not bring about the changes needed to improve the status of blacks as a group. What is urgently needed is a policy aimed at achieving equal results. Achieving equal results will require a massive effort by all segments of our society, both public and private, with the prerequisite that white Americans *want* to bring blacks into the mainstream of American life.

Dr. Kruger is a professor in the School of Labor and Industrial Relations and Associate Director of Manpower Service at Michigan State University. He was assisted in the preparation of this chapter by James Van Tassell, a graduate student in the College of Education, Michigan State University.

This chapter will focus on the economic phase of civil rights for blacks and the prerequisites to full participation in American society. The economic status of the nonwhite population will be examined in terms of income levels, types and levels of employment, and rates of unemployment in an effort to demonstrate clearly that blacks have made *no significant* economic advances in relative terms since World War II, that their status in relation to the white population is generally unchanged, and that the increased civil rights activities of the past few years have failed to stimulate any significant economic advances. It is postulated that economic improvements and the press for civil rights are highly interrelated.

In the recent history of the American Negro, World War II was an extremely important catalyst which brought about dramatic alterations in American societal patterns that enabled blacks to vastly upgrade many facets of their environment. One of the most significant changes was in the economic base of blacks as a group. The war brought unprecedented demands for industrial manpower. Negro workers in large numbers were able to enter many industries and occupations from which they had been excluded previously. In response to these increased opportunities, they migrated from the rural South to cities in industrialized sections of the country. During the 1940's, over 1,500,000 blacks shifted both their place of residence and their means of earning a livelihood. Both income and living conditions were improved by these moves.

Data for the postwar years are often contrasted with prewar data in attempts to demonstrate that the war years truly mark the boundary between two distinct eras of Negro socioeconomic history. The implication of these analyses is that the great improvements of the early 1940's enabled many blacks to recover from the severe economic conditions of the Depression. It was reasoned further that the black sector of the American economy would continue to expand rapidly in the postwar period since an adequate base had been created for the first time. As a result of the impressive gains made by blacks in civil rights, employment, and earnings during the past twenty years, one could conclude that this has been a period of enormous growth. The purpose of this chapter is to examine critically the economic status of the American Negro population since World War II in order to assess this growth.

In this study, comparisons will be made between blacks and whites, using data from government sources. The federal government uses a white and nonwhite racial classification, but this is not viewed as a limiting factor. Negroes account for about 95 percent of the nonwhite group. The remaining proportion consists of Orientals and American Indians.

In a sense, these two groups cancel each other in that they represent the two extremes in economic status. Thus the data for the nonwhite population may be considered representative of Negroes as a group.

The Changing Environment of American Blacks

Blacks living in the South declined from 77 percent in 1940 to 55 percent in 1966 as about 3,700,000 left for other regions.[1] This is one of the major social upheavals that has affected the social and economic status of Negroes. In most instances, blacks moved to industrial cities, while the white population was gradually leaving the cities for the suburbs. Thus, blacks in 1966 were more urbanized than the white population, with 69 percent living in metropolitan areas as compared with 64 percent of the white population.

Mass Negro migration from the rural South to urban centers and to other regions of the country is of significant importance. As an isolated sharecropper or farm laborer in the rigidly segregated and stratified culture of the South before World War II, the Negro had little acquaintance with the way of life of most Americans. His relatives and neighbors lived under conditions of poverty that approximated his own, and the living standards of rural white southerners, although only slightly superior, were unobtainable. Even though the Negro aspired for a better life, he often was powerless to bring about changes in his economic status.

When he left the South, the Negro entered an entirely different environment in which many more choices were open to him—although he was still a victim of discrimination. His earnings exceeded the amount needed for basic subsistence, often for the first time, and he had money for some of the luxuries of modern living.

Often he found employment that brought him into daily contact with white workers and he became acquainted with a new standard of living that contrasted with his own existence. As his earnings and social awareness increased, he began to aspire and agitate for the same type of life that his white peers enjoyed. This is not to imply that Negroes were not interested in improving their socioeconomic status prior to the migrations of 1940-1960, but rather that changes in residence and occupation greatly enlarged the Negro's awareness of the need for improvements among the Negro population. Thus, the degree of social change necessary to satisfy Negroes and whites has become a dominant issue in Negro-white relations. One measurement of this social change can be applied to the economic status of Negroes.

Two Views of Living Standards Among Blacks

Blacks have shared in advances in the American economy in the postwar period. They have made gains in employment, and their income has more than doubled. In fact, nonwhite family income has increased at a slightly higher proportional rate than the income of white families. (See Table 1.)

Why then are blacks so discontented? Why aren't they satisfied with their rate of economic advancement? The answers to these complex questions can be discovered in the same data that list the economic gains of blacks. The problem is that there are two distinct approaches which can be used to evaluate the economic status of blacks during the past twenty years, and they lead to entirely different conclusions. One is the *absolute approach,* and the second is the *relative approach.*

In the absolute approach, the current status of blacks is compared with past attainments. Here is a typical press article that demonstrates this line of reasoning:

> The economic situation of the Negro again shows striking progress in historical terms. In the last twenty years the median income of Negro families has multiplied by more than six, while the figure for whites has gone up a little more than four times.[2]

Andrew F. Brimmer, a member of the Board of Governors of the Federal Reserve System, echoes this view:

> The last several years of economic expansion have been the best years in our history for the American Negro . . . the Negro worker has shared at least proportionately in the overall advance. In fact, in the aggregate, Negroes have shared better than average . . .[3]

Those who support the absolute point of view generally conclude that the Negro is doing very well for himself in economic terms. They are willing to evaluate any aspect of the economic environment, including housing, types of employment, earnings, education, and mortality rates, in terms of the ratios between present and past data.

Table 1 — Median Income of Urban and Rural White and Nonwhite Families in the United States

Year	All Families			Urban			Rural Non-Farm			Rural Farm		
	Total	White	Non-White	Total	White	Non-White	Total	White	Non-White	Total	White	Non-White
1947	3031	3157	1614	3349	3465	1963	2826	2922	1446	1963	2156	1026
1949	3107	3232	1650	3486	3619	2084	2763	2851	1240	1587	1757	691
1952	3890	4114	2338	4249	4484	2631	3720	3842	2075	2226	2473	1170
1955	4421	4605	2549	4840	5069	3118	4328	4451	2029	2111	2339	972
1958	5087	5300	2711	5469	5679	3392	5048	5211	2361	2747	3025	1123
1961	5737	5981	3191	5924	6189	3395	NA	NA	NA	3241	3500	1276
1964	6569	6858	3839	6755	7045	4021	NA	NA	NA	3558	3868	1750
1966	7436	7722	4628	7582	7868	4765	NA	NA	NA	4841	5150	2008

Calculated from *Current Population Reports: Consumer Income* (U.S. Bureau of the Census) Series P-60, Nos. 1-53.

While these absolute gains are unquestionable statistical measures, their validity as measures of social change may be questioned. Absolute gains may be very superficial, and they are often misleading since they ignore the concurrent advances of the white population. Further, it may be argued that today's Negro is not living in the society of 1947 or any other previous year. Times have changed for both blacks and whites. The American standard of living has risen dramatically since World War II. Since blacks have a right to share equally in these improvements, why compare him today with the black of any past time in history?

A more realistic comparison is the relative approach in which blacks are compared with whites at a given point in time. To what extent do blacks' earnings and living conditions approximate those of his white peers? Blacks are and always have been below white Americans on every known economic yardstick. Proponents of the relative approach are interested in the economic and social distance, or the gap, between the two groups.

Whitney Young, Jr., executive director of the National Urban League, pointed out the conclusions derived by using the relative approach to analyze improvements in Negro earnings and other economic measures:

> In spite of what we wishfully like to think and feel, there have been few strides for the American Negro in this country during the last ten years. . . . From the standpoint of the basic needs of life—food, shelter, health—there has been very little gain in closing the gaps.[4]

This is certainly a less optimistic view of the changing status of blacks during the past two decades.

The relative approach is a more realistic appraisal. It provides a better understanding of why so many blacks are discontented in today's society. It provides a partial explanation for the social unrest which has been expressed by blacks through rebellions and demonstrations in recent years.

Family Income

Median nonwhite family income rose steadily from $1,614 in 1947 to $4,628 in 1966, an increase of 187 percent. White families improved their income from $3,157 to $7,722 during the same period, a gain of about 145 percent. (See Table 1.) A comparison of percentage gains does not present a realistic interpretation, since a smaller base requires a smaller dollar gain to attain a higher percentage increase. Dollar increases in nonwhite family income during the twenty years amounted to a net gain of $3,014, while white families gained $4,565. In 1947 there was a $1,543 differential between white and nonwhite family incomes. Despite the gains of nonwhites, this gap had increased to $3,094 by 1966. In the period 1947-66 the income of nonwhite families ranged from 50 to 60 percent of white families. (See Table 2.)

Table 2 — Income of Nonwhite Families Expressed as a Percentage of White Family Income

Year	All Nonwhite Families	Urban Nonwhite Families	Rural Nonwhite Families
1947	51.1	56.6	47.6
1949	51.1	57.6	39.3
1952	56.8	58.7	47.3
1955	55.4	61.5	41.6
1958	51.1	59.7	37.1
1961	53.5	54.8	36.5
1964	56.0	57.1	45.2
1966	60.0	60.5	39.0

Calculated from *Current Population Reports: Consumer Income* (U.S. Bureau of the Census) Series P-60, annual editions.

During the 1950's, nonwhite families made only slight gains toward attaining parity with white families. Glenn (1963) calculated that at the rate of improvement evidenced during this decade, parity would be obtained in 805 years. In 1966, nonwhite family income was 60 percent of white families, as compared with 51 percent in 1947. Thus, in twenty years Negro families as a group improved their relative position by nine percentage points.

In absolute dollars, however, Negro families are farther behind white families than they were in 1947. It is the dollar difference that is most important since it is dollars that Americans spend and save.

What have been the economic differences between blacks living in the rural South and those who have migrated to the industrial cities? When family income is examined by place of residence and by color, the data (see Table 1) indicate the following:

1. The relative earnings of all American farm families have declined since 1947 compared with urban families. Clearly, the farm population has lost ground in absolute terms and has failed to improve its relative position in the postwar era. In 1947, the income of the nonwhite farm family was 48 percent of the white farm family; in 1966, it was 39 percent.

2. When the dollar earnings of nonwhite farm families are compared with those of white farm families, an even more dismal economic picture emerges. In 1947, a gap of $1,130, or 52.4 percent, existed. During the next nineteen years, black farmers rapidly lost ground. In 1966, a gap of $3,142, or 67 percent, existed.

3. In 1947, nonwhite farm families earned $1,026 compared with $1,963 for urban nonwhite families—a gap of $937, or 48 percent. By 1966, urban nonwhite families were earning $4,765 compared with only $2,008 for farm nonwhite families, and the earnings gap had increased to $2,757, or 58 percent. Thus, it can be seen that urban nonwhites improved their earnings much more rapidly than did their rural peers.

4. A comparison of urban families shows that in 1947 nonwhites trailed whites by $1,502, a gap of 43.4 percent. By 1966 the dollar difference had increased to $3,103, or 39 percent. Between 1947 and 1966 the dollar gap doubled. In 1947, the nonwhite urban family income was 57 percent of the white urban family income, and in 1966 it was 60.5 percent. Therefore, urban nonwhite families not only maintained their relative economic position, but gained in absolute dollar earnings.

These data suggest that blacks who moved to the cities did improve their economic status, both in absolute and relative terms. The earnings of urban nonwhite families rarely exceeded 60 percent of the earnings of their white peers, but even these humble circumstances were far above the economic status of farm-dwelling nonwhite families.

Part-time employment is another factor that reduces the earnings of nonwhite workers. U.S. Department of Labor data for the period 1957-67 indicate that in each of these years a disproportionate number of nonwhite workers who usually worked full time could find only part-time employment. Furthermore, a disproportionate number of nonwhite workers usually work part-time.[5] The high rate of part-time employment not only limits nonwhite incomes, it is a gross example of underemployment.

Number of Workers Per Family

Family earnings data can be misleading unless the number of workers within the family is known. Drake (1965) reports that in 1960 about half of white families were supported entirely by the husband's earnings, while only about a third of nonwhite families depended on a husband for support. In 60 percent of nonwhite families, two or more persons worked; this was the case in fewer than one-half of the white families.

The percentage of nonwhite females who participate in the labor force is consistently higher than that of white women (except during the teenage years). The differences are apparent across income lines and regardless of the age and presence of children in the home.

Negro women have a different role in providing earnings for their families than do white women. Because of the lower employment levels of Negro men, or the absence of a male head of the household, women are more likely to help support the family. They often work at low-paying jobs. In 1967, for example, half of all nonwhite female workers were employed as private household and service workers.

Incidence of Poverty

Another measure of nonwhite economic status is the incidence of poverty (as defined by the U.S. Census Bureau). Census data on income for the period 1959-1966 show that the incidence of poverty in the total population is decreasing and that whites are benefiting more from the decline than nonwhites.[6] Between 1959 and 1966, the incidence of poverty among whites declined from 18 percent to 12 percent. During the same period, poverty among nonwhites declined from 55 percent to 41 percent. While poverty has declined, the proportion of nonwhites among the poor has increased from 28 percent in 1959 to 32 percent in 1966. These data show that in 1966 a nonwhite person was almost four times as likely to be poor as a white person.

Census data also show that, in 1965, 35 percent of nonwhite families had incomes under $3,000 as compared with 14 percent of white families. Forty-one percent of nonwhite families had incomes of $3,000 to $6,999; whereas one-third of white families were in this income bracket. The proportion of families earning between $7,000 and $11,999 was 18 percent for nonwhites and 36 percent for whites. Sixteen percent of white families and 6 percent of nonwhite families earned $12,000 or more a year in 1965.

The Effect of Education on Income

It is generally believed that lack of education is part of the vicious cycle of despair that prevents blacks from attaining equality. Comparing the incomes of white and nonwhite groups with different levels of education reveals that education alone does not improve the economic status of nonwhites. (See Table 3.) Whites add an increment to their earnings each time they complete an additional level of schooling. But for nonwhites, the picture is not so clear. Apparently it makes no difference whether the nonwhite drops out of school after elementary school or after a few years of high school. If he attends college or at least graduates from high school, he stands a reasonable chance of earning as much as a white worker who has completed only elementary school. It is not until the nonwhite student graduates from college that he is able to improve his earnings significantly.

Table 3 — Comparison of White and Nonwhite Family Income by Level of Education of Family Head

Year	College Grads		1-3 years College		High School Graduates		1-3 years H. S.		Elementary School	
	W	NW	W	NW	W	NW	W	NW	W	NW
1958	8202	NA	6568	NA	5742	3929	5226	3288	4487	3167
1961	9315	NA	7344	5525	6390	4559	5882	3449	4911	3338
1963	9857	7295	7895	5000	6997	4530	6244	3518	5454	3629
1964	10678	9353	8235	5907	7297	5039	6512	3927	5386	3931
1965	11075	9084	8547	6294	7665	5621	6861	3951	5602	3896

Source: *Current Population Reports: Consumer Income* (U.S. Bureau of the Census) Series P-60, annual editions.
Not Available — the Census Bureau does not include any population group numbering fewer than 200,000.

In interpreting the earnings of nonwhite college graduates, it must be kept in mind that this is a small, highly select group. The U.S. Census Bureau did not publish data until 1963 because the sample was so small. One could conclude that all nonwhite children must become college graduates if their incomes are to approximate those of white workers.

An overall conclusion is that black family income has not improved relative to white family income. There has been hardly any proportional gain. Furthermore, the income gap between blacks and whites has increased significantly at all levels. The income of blacks is not very high in relation to whites—no matter what the criteria used in evaluation. Perhaps the best statement that can be made is that some blacks do better than others. This is particularly true for urban-dwelling blacks with a high level of education, but this group is not very large when compared to whites of similar educational background.

The sections following will examine some of the reasons for the low income status of blacks in the United States.

Employment

There are considerable differences between the occupations of black workers and white workers. These differences affect the Negro's income in both absolute and relative terms. In order to understand the concept of occupational status and to interpret meaningfully its effect upon Negro workers, some system of evaluation must be used. Glenn (1963) has developed an index of occupational status (I.O.S.) computed from the following formula:

$$\text{I.O.S.} = \frac{(a/A + b/B) \times 100}{2}$$

a = median income of experienced workers in the occupational group.

A = median income of entire experienced labor force.

b = median years of school completed by experienced workers in the occupational group.

B = median years of school completed by the entire experienced labor force.

By applying this formula to data obtained during the 1960 national census, the relative values shown below were obtained:

Professional, technical, and kindred workers	147
Farmers and farm managers	72
Managers, officials, and proprietors	140
Clerical and kindred workers	111
Sales workers	109
Craftsmen, foremen, and kindred workers	114
Operatives and kindred workers	96
Private household workers	55
Other service workers	79
Farm laborers and foremen	58
Laborers other than farm	83

Table 4 shows the distribution of white and nonwhite workers among occupational classifications in 1950 and 1960. With the exception of farmers and farm managers, nonwhites are over-represented in all of the lower ranking occupations and under-represented in all of the higher ranking groups.

The absolute data versus relative data controversy that clouds the understanding of white and nonwhite income patterns also applies to employment. Blacks have scored small absolute gains in many of the desirable occupational groupings and token entry in others from which they were previously excluded; but the relative gains have not been impressive. It must be emphasized that the relative approach is not only more realistic but more meaningful as well. One of the problems with using absolute data is that the number of blacks employed in the higher occupational groups is so small compared with white workers that a relatively insignificant increase in numbers tends to inflate the data. It might also be argued that it is not as important to measure the raw gains of blacks over a period of time as it is to determine whether or not they are adequately represented within a particular group.

Nonwhites are concentrated in the lower status, lower paying occupations. (See Table 5.) Although they have almost doubled their representation in the white-collar group since 1950, the proportion of white workers employed in white-collar jobs in 1967 was still more than double nonwhite workers.

Between 1950 and 1967, the proportion of white blue-collar

Table 4 — Ratio of White to Negro Workers by Occupational Field
and Sex, 1950 and 1960
(Relative to Their Numbers in Total Work Force)

Sectors	Male 1950	Male 1960	Female 1950	Female 1960
All Sectors	1.0	1.0	1.0	1.0
Nonfarm, total	1.1	1.1	1.1	1.0
White-collar, total	3.8	2.9	4.5	3.4
Professional, kindred	3.1	2.8	2.3	2.4
Proprietors, managers, and officials	5.1	5.5	3.4	2.9
Clerical, sales	3.4	2.0	6.9	4.0
Manual and service	.8	.7	.5	.5
Skilled workers, foremen	2.4	2.2	2.5	1.6
Semiskilled workers and operatives	1.0	.8	1.3	1.0
Laborers	.3	.3	.5	1.4
Service workers	.4	.4	.3	.3
Farm, total	.6	.6	.3	.5

Source: Dale L. Hiestand, ·Economic Growth and Employment Opportunities for Minorities (New York: Columbia University Press, 1964), p. 48.

workers declined from 39.3 percent to 36.0 percent; whereas nonwhite blue-collar workers increased from 37.5 percent to 42.4 percent. During these years, the proportion of nonwhite private household
workers declined from 17.7 percent to 10.5 percent; and nonwhite
farm workers declined from 18.4 percent to 5.3 percent. Although
there has been movement of nonwhites to better jobs since 1950, in
1967 over two-fifths of nonwhite workers were laborers, farm laborers,
private household workers, and other service workers. By comparison,
about one-sixth of white workers were in the same occupational
groups.

The fact that nonwhite workers are over-represented in lower
paying occupational groupings tends to negate the value of many of
the breakthroughs in employment that blacks have made in recent
years. Often they have greatly increased their representation in industries or occupational groups that are remaining constant, declining, or
not expanding at the same pace as the general economy. Many more
blue-collar jobs are filled by blacks than ever before, but the total
labor force requirement in this occupational area is declining gradu-

Table 5 — Comparison of Employed Persons by Major Occupational Group and Color 1950 and 1967 (Percentage Distribution)

Occupational Group	1950 W	1950 NW	1967 W	1967 NW
White-collar	40.3	10.2	48.8	22.9
Professional, technical and kindred	8.0	3.0	14.0	7.4
Managers, proprietors and officials	11.6	2.5	11.0	2.6
Clerical and kindred	13.8	3.5	17.2	11.2
Sales workers	6.9	1.2	6.6	1.7
Blue-collar	39.3	37.5	36.0	42.4
Craftsmen and foremen	13.7	4.8	13.9	7.7
Operatives and kindred	20.6	18.6	18.1	23.5
Laborers	5.0	14.1	4.0	11.2
Service Workers	8.5	33.8	10.5	29.4
Private household workers	1.6	17.7	1.4	10.4
Other	6.9	16.1	9.1	19.0
Farm Workers	11.7	18.4	4.7	5.3
Farmers and managers	7.3	7.5	2.8	1.3
Laborers and foremen	4.4	10.9	1.9	4.0

Source: Bureau of Labor Statistics, U.S. Department of Labor.

ally. It would appear that white workers are moving on to better jobs, especially those with growth potential, in other areas of the labor market—leaving dead-end factory and service jobs for black workers. It is unrealistic to view gains of this type as permanent advances, even though the jobs may be comparatively well paid.

Education and Employment

With technology changing rapidly, quality education is of extreme importance in locating and holding a well-paying job in today's labor market. The quality of education for Negroes in the South and in the northern ghettos is not the same as for whites. Negroes have been affected adversely by two related sets of circumstances—length of schooling and quality of education.

First, blacks lag behind the white population in years of schooling completed. (See Tables 6 and 7.) In 1967, the proportion of white college graduates in the labor force was over twice that of nonwhites.

Table 6 — Years of School Completed by the Civilian Labor Force 18 Years Old and Over by Color (Percentage Distribution)

Year		Elementary School 1-4 yrs.	5-8 yrs.	High School 1-3 yrs.	4 yrs.	College 1-3 yrs.	4 yrs.
1952	White	5.2%	29.3%	18.7%	28.3%	8.8%	8.5%
	Nonwhite	26.7	38.7	15.9	10.8	3.7	2.6
1957	White	4.3	25.8	19.0	30.8	9.0	9.7
	Nonwhite	21.2	34.9	19.3	14.8	3.9	3.4
1962	White	3.3	21.4	18.8	33.5	11.3	11.8
	Nonwhite	15.4	29.8	23.2	21.0	5.7	4.8
1967	White	2.2	16.9	18.1	37.7	12.4	12.8
	Nonwhite	10.4	25.5	23.7	27.5	7.2	5.8

Source: *Manpower Report of the President and a Report on Manpower Requirements, Resources, Utilization, and Training* (U.S. Department of Labor, 1968), p. 259.

Table 7 — Comparison of Median Years of School Completed by the Civilian Labor Force 18 Years and Over by Color

Year	White	Nonwhite	Difference
1952	11.4	7.6	3.8
1957	12.1	8.4	3.7
1959	12.1	8.7	3.4
1962	12.2	9.6	2.6
1964	12.2	10.1	1.8
1965	12.3	10.5	1.8
1967	12.3	10.8	1.5

Source: *Manpower Report of the President and a Report on Manpower Requirements, Resources, Utilization, and Training* (U.S. Department of Labor, 1968), p.259.

While 62.9 percent of all white workers had completed at least high school, 40.5 percent of the nonwhite group were high school graduates. At the bottom of the distribution, almost twice as many nonwhites had gone no farther than elementary school.

The educational gap, according to these data, is narrowing. In 1952, the median years of school completed by whites in the civilian labor force was 11.4 years as compared to 7.6 years for nonwhites. By 1967, it was 12.3 years for whites and 10.8 years for nonwhites.

Educational comparisons based upon years of schooling completed are misleading. The assumption is made that a year of schooling for a black child equals a year of schooling for a white child. This assumption is certainly not warranted in most American communities. It obviously is false in the case of the many black students in the segregated schools of the South.

Conditions in many of the black schools of our major northern cities leave much to be desired. Many are rigidly segregated. Education of teachers, pupil-teacher ratio, expenditures, and other measures are often used as yardsticks, but it is extremely difficult to evaluate a given school objectively. In 1962 the Chicago schools were analyzed in these terms, comparing white, integrated, and Negro schools:[7]

Indices of Comparison	Type of School		
	White	*Integrated*	*Nonwhite*
Total appropriation per pupil	$342	$320	$269
Teacher's salary per pupil	$256	$231	$220
Percent uncertified teachers	12%	23%	49%
Number of pupils per classroom	30.95	34.95	46.80
Library books per pupil	5	3.5	2.5
Expenditures per pupil other than teachers' salaries	$86	$90	$49

If the above measures are reliable indicators of quality, it can be concluded that a year of schooling for a black child in Chicago does not equal the experience of his white peers.

Ginzberg and Bray (1953) demonstrated the regional weaknesses of American education in a very comprehensive study aimed at identifying the reasons for the rejection of 700,000 men for military service in World War II on the grounds of "mental deficiency."

Since the Negro rejection rate exceeded the white rate in every region of the United States, it might seem to be evidence of racial superiority. However, Negroes in three regions did better than whites from two other regions. When this was coupled with extreme variance in the rejection rates of both blacks and whites, education was identified as the primary influence. Since large numbers of blacks now in the labor force were educated in the South, it is not difficult to understand the severe educational deficits they possess.

Since most blacks enter the blue-collar and service industries, it would seem that vocational schools would be of prime importance in their education. Wachtel (1965) reports that this need is not being met. In the South, segregated vocational schools are the rule—with blacks receiving only inferior training in cleaning, pressing, and sewing as preparation for traditional "Negro jobs" such as cooks, seamstresses, and laundry workers.

In the North, there are not enough vocational schools in the black districts, and other vocational schools, practicing a type of "cooperative racism," refuse to accept black students. Notions and myths about jobs that are suitable for blacks persist. Often whites decide which jobs are suitable for Negroes, whites construct the tests used to measure Negroes, and when black students graduate, whites may refuse to refer these students to employers because they assume that employers do not want them.

Many blacks cannot gain entrance to quality colleges and universities because they lack the finances. And a vicious circle exists for the large group of blacks who attend all-Negro colleges. Because of the poor educational background of most blacks, the coursework is often "watered down." Consequently, the black college graduate tends to be less informed than his white counterpart.

To a certain extent, the same situation exists at elementary and high school levels. Blacks are usually the poorest students—but they attend the poorest schools with the poorest materials and facilities, and they usually have the poorest teachers. It would appear that any serious attempt to improve the economic position of blacks must focus on improving the quality of education for them.

The data show that often blacks are less prepared educationally than their white peers, but educational background is not always the best predictor of success on the job. There are numerous occasions when blacks are denied employment or entry into apprenticeship or other training programs for reasons that have little or nothing to do with their potential ability to perform a specific job.

Aptitude Tests

Aside from outright discrimination, one of the major devices that excludes blacks is the preemployment aptitude test that is administered to all applicants as a matter of company routine or as a screening technique. Such tests often discriminate against members of minority groups because they reflect middle class norms or because they place great emphasis upon culturally-acquired knowledge. The Equal Employment Opportunity Commission has called attention to how these tests discriminate against minority groups:

> An aptitude test that fails to predict job performance in the same way for both Negroes and whites, or fails to predict job performance at all is not a valid test. If such a test is weighted to differentiate between Negroes and whites, it is similarly invalid and similarly discriminatory. Tests may be held to discriminate in the *social sense* if they deny equal opportunity for consideration. [8]

While it is most difficult, if not impossible, to construct a *culture-free* test, it is possible to build a *culture-fair* test by utilizing items equally familiar to all population groups. There are reasons related to learning theory, psychometry, and social psychology to expect that blacks and other minorities will do poorly on traditional, "paper and pencil" tests. If the use of testing as an exclusion device is to be eliminated, better testing devices must be developed.

Tests are often used in another way that acts to the detriment of blacks and others from culturally and educationally deprived environments. Advancement within a firm or within an occupational classification is often based upon successful completion of a test or battery of tests. Oddly enough, governmental units are among the major offenders since they often rely upon civil service tests and rigid administrative codes in filling vacancies and advancing employees from grade to grade. The Post Office Department, for example, employs a large number of well-trained, college-educated Negroes in hundreds of communities who work at jobs below their skill levels and potential abilities. At the same time, other governmental agencies are attempting to fill higher grade vacancies with little success (Sheppard and Striner, 1966). Presumably, similar situations exist in industry. Underemployment of this type is a waste of manpower and an inhibiting factor that could easily be eliminated.

Unemployment

Unemployment is a major factor in the American Negro's inability to earn an adequate income or to close the income gap between himself and the white American. Blacks are out of work more often and for longer periods of time than white workers. A general rule of thumb has proven to be very accurate in the years since World War II: nonwhite unemployment rates are double those of white workers. (See Table 8.) In view of this disturbing relationship, national unemployment statistics must be closely examined, for the nonwhite proportion of the labor force is so small that overall figures do not reflect the true picture of their unemployment.

Unemployment rates that are considered to be unduly high for the labor force as a whole are the norm for nonwhites, except in the peak years of employment. For example, since World War II, white unemployment rates have exceeded five percent only three times; while nonwhite unemployment rates have been under five percent only once. For six straight years (1958-1963), nonwhite unemployment rates were over ten percent. For the twenty years 1948-1967, mean unemployment for white workers was 4.3 percent; for nonwhites it was 8.7 percent.

Of particular importance to an understanding of the racial disturbances of the 1960's are the data for teenagers and young adults. (See Table 9.) The nonwhite unemployment rate for teenage males has not been *below twenty percent* since 1957. The rate for young females has hovered around thirty percent since 1960. Data for this age range are especially important since the Negro population is relatively young compared to the white population. Furthermore, black young people, in most cases, have no alternative to work since they do not attend college or trade schools to the same degree as white youth.

Table 8 — Comparison of Rates of Unemployment by Color and Sex

Year	Both Sexes			Male			Female		
	Total	White	NW	Total	White	NW	Total	White	NW
1948	3.8	3.5	5.9	3.6	3.4	5.8	4.1	3.8	6.1
1951	3.3	3.1	5.3	2.8	2.6	4.9	4.4	4.2	6.1
1954	5.5	5.0	9.9	5.3	4.8	10.3	6.0	5.6	9.3
1957	4.3	3.8	7.9	4.1	3.6	8.3	4.7	4.3	7.3
1960	5.5	4.9	10.2	5.4	4.8	10.7	5.9	5.3	9.4
1963	5.7	5.0	10.8	5.2	4.7	10.5	6.5	5.8	11.2
1965	4.5	4.1	8.1	4.0	3.6	7.4	5.5	5.0	9.2
1967	3.8	3.4	7.4	3.1	2.7	6.0	5.2	4.6	9.1

Source: *Manpower Report of the President and a Report on Manpower Requirements, Resources, Utilization, and Training* (U.S. Department of Labor, 1968), p. 234.

Table 9 – Unemployment Rates of Males and Females 16 to 24 Years Old by Color (Percentage Distribution)

Year	Males 16-17 W	NW	18-19 W	NW	20-24 W	NW	Females 16-17 W	NW	18-19 W	NW	20-24 W	NW
1948	10.2	9.2	9.4	10.5	6.4	11.7	9.7	11.8	6.8	14.6	4.2	10.2
1951	9.5	8.7	6.7	9.6	3.6	6.7	9.6	13.0	6.5	15.1	3.9	8.8
1954	14.0	13.4	13.0	14.7	9.8	16.9	12.0	19.1	9.4	21.6	6.4	13.2
1957	11.9	16.3	11.2	20.0	7.1	12.7	11.9	18.3	7.9	21.3	5.1	12.2
1960	14.6	22.7	13.5	25.1	8.3	13.1	14.5	25.7	11.5	24.5	7.2	15.3
1963	17.8	27.0	14.2	27.4	7.8	15.5	18.1	40.1	13.2	31.9	7.4	18.7
1965	14.7	27.1	11.4	20.2	5.9	9.3	15.0	37.8	13.4	27.8	6.3	13.7
1967	12.7	28.9	9.0	20.1	4.2	8.0	12.9	32.0	10.6	28.3	6.0	13.8

Source: *Manpower Report of the President and a Report on Manpower Requirements, Resources, Utilization, and Training* (U.S. Department of Labor, 1968), p. 237.

A slight business recession has a much greater effect on Negro employment:

> Just before the 1961 recession, 937 out of every 1,000 white males 25 to 54 years old were working, and it took two more years for the figure to rise above the prerecession rate. Nonwhites fared much worse. The prerecession employment rate for nonwhites was 861, and not until four years later did it rise above that rate. Nonwhite males thus experienced greater losses in employment during a recession, and they take longer to recoup such losses, as compared to whites of the same age group. Besides, they start from a lower base, a lower employment percentage.[9]

Thus the workers who can least afford a reduction in their incomes are hit hardest by business slumps.

Another factor affecting the income of nonwhites is the duration of unemployment. Although nonwhite workers represent about 11 percent of the labor force, they experience long term unemployment disproportionately. (Long term unemployment is defined as 15 weeks or more.) Between 1957-1967, 20 percent of the labor force who were unemployed 15 or more weeks were nonwhites.[10] The percentage of nonwhite workers who were unemployed for 15 to 26 weeks was more than double the proportion of nonwhite workers in the labor force during this period. Furthermore, approximately one-fourth of all workers with 27 or more weeks of unemployment were nonwhite.

Negro unemployment rates have two basic effects upon the lives of the workers and their families. Obviously, annual earnings are reduced by erratic employment patterns. This is one of the major reasons why blacks have been unable to reduce the income gap and why they are falling farther and farther behind the white population in dollar earnings. Perhaps a more important effect is the role of potential unemployment as a threat to the basic economic security of the Negro family. Not only is it more difficult to plan for the future because of the greater uncertainty that a steady income level can be maintained, but there is a continuing need for extra money.

Perhaps these are the reasons why Negro families tend to have more workers on an average than do white families. Multiple sources of income are important in terms of absolute dollars, but they are even more desirable as a type of insurance against sudden reversals due to unexpected layoff or dismissal.

The lack of a steady employment record may hinder the Negro family in other ways. They are likely to have extreme difficulty in other ways. They are likely to have extreme difficulty in arranging for credit—particularly if they need long term credit as in the case of a home mortgage. If they obtain credit, they may be forced to pay higher interest rates. Thus, unemployment is a major threat to blacks. The incidence and duration of unemployment affect them more adversely than whites.

Summary

It is often misleading to judge the Negro's economic position today by comparing him with Negroes of any other time in American history. An objective approach requires that his achievements and levels of attainment be compared with white persons of the same educational background, employment skills, occupational classification, place of residence, age, or sex.

In developing comparisons of this type, a dismal picture of Negro life emerges. An analysis of the data on income, occupations, employment, and unemployment clearly shows that blacks are at the bottom of American society economically—and their relative status is not improving. Although blacks are improving their economic status in absolute terms, they are not narrowing the economic gap which exists between them and the whites to any significant degree. The persistence of this gap is contributing to social unrest in the United States.

The status of Negro youth is perhaps the most disturbing. Many youth are starting their employment ill-equipped and ill-trained to compete with white youth in a society that is becoming increasingly competitive. Ill-trained white youth do appear to have a better break in their bid for a job. The color of one's skin does make a difference. White youth do have an advantage.

Since the Negro population is younger as a whole than the white population and since lower income Negro families have more children, the employment problem of the teenagers and young adults cannot be overemphasized. Any meaningful improvements for Negroes as a group must be directed towards Negro youth. They have been locked out of active participation in the mainstream of American life. Conditions will deteriorate unless there are some immediate and drastic changes—there will be more riots. But more important, these youths represent a tragic waste of human resources. They must be given the opportunities to be useful, productive citizens.

One solution to the problem of low income in the Negro population—aside from the obvious need for reducing discrimination and segregation—lies in upgrading the vocational skills of blacks. Massive improvements are necessary from primary school education to on-the-job training if the Negro is to gain parity with the white population.

There are two approaches to the black's problems. One calls for extending to blacks—and all other disadvantaged Americans—the same quality schools, housing, medical care, and other environmental factors that are now reserved almost exclusively for middle class white Americans. Such a change might enable blacks to start life with the same potential as the general population and afford them the same opportunities. While this might enable blacks to maintain the same levels of growth as the white community, it would do little to close the gap between the two population groups, since whites would be advancing at the same rate.

Therefore, equal opportunity as a policy is insufficient. Such a policy would not bring about the changes needed to improve significantly the economic status of blacks as a group. The emphasis must be on equal results. This means that there must be a redistribution of community resources to enable blacks to catch up with their white peers. To put it another way, what is needed is preferential treatment that would enable the blacks to improve their economic status at a rate which exceeds the increments for whites. This would bring about a narrowing of the economic gap between blacks and whites and would eventually result in parity.

To bring about significant improvements in the socioeconomic status of blacks will require not only massive federal financial assistance but significant involvement by state and local governmental units. It must be stressed that all levels of government must assume critically important responsibilities, from the Federal government, to the local school district. The school board makes decisions as to the allocation of educational resources. It decides where new schools are to be located, where teachers are to be assigned, and how educational materials are to be distributed.

All other basic institutions in the United States must become more involved in helping to narrow the gap between whites and blacks. Employers, both public and private, should intensify recruitment efforts, critically reexamine their hiring qualifications, provide orientation and training programs, train foremen and supervisors in interpersonal and intergroup relations, and provide supportive services to hasten the acculturation of black workers.

Finally, white Americans must want to bring blacks into the mainstream of American life. Their attitudes and actions will, to a large measure, determine the rate of progress that blacks will make in closing the socioeconomic gap which is so striking between the two groups. Whites have the power to determine what kind of society there will be in the United States. It is, therefore, imperative that this power be used constructively to build a society where all men are equal.

Notes

1. As used in this context, the South includes the following states: Alabama, Arkansas, Florida, Georgia, Kentucky, Louisiana, Mississippi, North Carolina, South Carolina, Tennessee, and Virginia.
2. A. Lewis, "Washington: Administration's Commitment to Negro Rights Has Resulted in Major Gains," *New York Times* (September 30, 1962).
3. A.F. Brimmer, "The Quests for Economic Stability and Equal Employment Opportunity." Speech at National Urban League Equal Opportunity Day Dinner, New York, 1966.
4. W. Young, Jr. Address to Columbus, Ohio Urban League, 1962, in A.B. Batchelder, "Decline in the Relative Income of Negro Men," *Quarterly Journal of Economics* (1964), 78, p. 526.
5. *Manpower Report of the President* (Washington, D.C.: U.S. Government Printing Office, 1968), p. 247.
6. "Current Population Reports," Series P60, No. 53, 1967, Bureau of the Census, U.S. Department of Commerce.
7. St. C. Drake, "The Social and Economic Status of the Negro in the United States," *Daedalus: The Negro American* (1965), 94 p. 783. Reproduced by permission.
8. P. Wallace, B. Kissinger, B. Reynolds, *Testing of Minority Group Applicants for Employment* (Washington, D.C.: U.S. Government Printing Office, 1966), p. 4.
9. H.L. Sheppard and H.E. Striner, *Civil Rights, Employment, and the Social Status* of *American Negroes* (Kalamazoo: The W.E. Upjohn Institute for Employment Research, 1966), p. 7.
10. *Manpower Report of the President, op. cit.*, p. 247.

References

Drake, St. Clair. "The Social and Economic Status of the Negro in the United States," *Daedalus: The Negro American*, 1965, 94: 784-785.

Ginzberg, Eli and Bray, D.W. *The Uneducated.* New York: Columbia University Press, 1953.

Glenn, Norval D. "Some Changes in the Relative Status of American Nonwhites, 1940 to 1960," *Phylon: The Atlanta University Review of Race and Culture*, 1963, 24: 118.

Rutzick, Max A. "A Ranking of U.S. Occupations by Earnings," *Monthly Labor Review*, 1965, 88: 254-255.

Sheppard, Harold L. and Striner, Herbert E. *Civil Rights, Employment, and the Social Status of American Negroes.* Kalamazoo: The W.E. Upjohn Institute for Employment Research, 1966.

Wachtel, Dawn. *The Negro and Discrimination in Employment.* Institute of Labor and Industrial Relations, University of Michigan and Wayne State University, 1965.

2 | EDUCATION AND REDISTRIBUTION: THE LIMITS OF A STRATEGY

S. M. Miller and Pamela Roby

Miller and Roby provide a searching examination of the role of education in reducing the poverty that exists in the United States. The authors find four major limitations to this strategy. First, it neglects many poor people. Second, the goals are difficult to achieve, requiring a radical redistribution of resources and enough first-rate teachers to make the educational experience effective for a high proportion of students. The third limitation is that this strategy is only partially effective for youths who do obtain an education. Lack of know-how, racial discrimination, and uneven rewards restrict the value of education for many minority group members. Fourth, our schools are not a humanizing or an educational force as much as they are a credentialing agency, sorting out people who do not fit into the regular channels of educational development.

In light of these limitations, the schools cannot be assigned the entire burden of reforming the social structure of America. We would be asking too little of the rest of society.

Dr. S.M. Miller is Professor of Education and Sociology at New York University. He has been a program advisor and is now a consultant for the Ford Foundation. Dr. Miller is author of *Comparative Social Mobility: A Trend Report* and co-author of *Social Class and Social Policy.*

Pamela Roby is an advanced doctoral student in the Department of Sociology at New York University.

Journalists, economists, proponents of government poverty programs, and educators frequently proclaim that the answer to poverty is simply more education for the poor. After all, the facts are striking: the lower the level of education, the higher the rate of unemployment and the lower the level of income. The growth of the American economy, some leading economists argue, is largely due to investing in human resources, in the education of the labor force. Therefore, increasing the education and skill levels of the labor force will solve many American problems by stimulating economic growth, a prerequisite for better living.

> The best long term bet (for combating poverty), we think, is simply education. Despite some unencouraging studies of compensatory programs, experience suggests education is a better engine of social advancement than any alternative. And partly because too much energy has been wasted arguing other things, the nation's cities have yet to evolve a truly comprehensive and coordinated school program for slums. Such a program would require spending more money on slum schools than even on suburban ones. . . .[1]

Manpower strategists also support the conclusion that education is the answer to the needs of the poor. They point to "structural unemployment," the mismatch of available people and jobs. The total number of jobs, they contend, is not insufficient; rather, the unemployed lack the skills and education to fill the available jobs. Therefore, they conclude, education will reduce poverty by enabling formerly unskilled individuals to fill jobs in the American economy.

The Limits Of Education

Despite its importance, education is not the simple panacea for deepseated American ailments that it first appears to be. Educational programs alone clearly cannot solve all problems of poverty. The educational strategy for poverty reduction suffers from four major limitations: the strategy neglects many poor people; its goals are difficult to achieve, requiring a radical redistribution of resources; the strategy is only partially effective for those youth who do obtain education because discrimination and other factors intervene between education and income; its heavy emphasis on education damages individuals and society by constricting alternative channels of occupational mobility and by restricting the pluralism of social values. In the following sections, we will discuss each of these limitations.

Scope

From the perspective of human resources, education is viewed as an investment enabling individuals to support themselves. In this approach to poverty, education is aimed at improving the prospects of the young. By working directly with youth rather than with their families, these strategists hope to cut the relationship between the position of the family and that of its offspring. It is important to recognize that the strategy not only neglects the families of the youngsters, but it overlooks others living in poverty: the aged, the working poor who do not receive enough to maintain their families, and those families which must depend upon transfer income (welfare). It also neglects those youngsters who are unable to succeed in school because their families are living on low income wages, with the resulting consequences of poor housing facilities and the lack of adequate medical attention.

Implementation

The goals of the educational strategy are difficult to achieve. Their implementation requires both redistribution of educational resources and recruitment of personnel who can improve education in low income areas. Today the issues of poverty are essentially questions of inequality (Miller, *et al.*, 1967; Miller and Roby, 1967). If, as the poor extend their educational attainment, those who are better off extend theirs, the gap between the two may not be reduced. Therefore, educational resources must be redistributed as well as increased if poverty is to be reduced. If the poor are to catch up, they must get proportionately more of the new resources moving into education. Politically, this is extraordinarily difficult to achieve. Only a minority of the policy makers who now support education as a human resource are asking that it be used as a means of redistributing national resources. Because all groups are striving to improve their education so as to improve their economic prospects, redistribution is unlikely to take place in the near future.

The history of recent years is not reassuring about the redistribution of educational resources. A Syracuse University study of school expenditures shows that in 1962, in thirty-five of the largest metropolitan areas, expenditures in the central cities—where there are many children of low income families—were $145 per pupil less than in the contiguous suburbs—where there are fewer children of low income families. One of the most disturbing findings in this investigation is that more state funds go to the suburbs than to the cities; in state aid, suburban schools receive $40 more per pupil than city schools. Even more disconcerting, the gap between cities and suburbs is growing: the 1962 difference did not exist in 1958, for then the two areas were spending the same amount.

The objective of the Elementary and Secondary Education Act of 1965 was to insure that more federal resources went to the poor than to higher income people. We lack statistics on who really did benefit from the ESEA money, but we have been told that many school superintendents channeled the funds to children whose conspicuous talents would reflect well on themselves and the children of community influentials rather than to the poorest youth in their districts.

After questioning the level and distribution of educational resources, we must also ask: "If we had adequate monetary resources, would we have the capacity to implement our educational goals in the way we know they should be implemented?" The answer is probably "No." Not only money, modern school buildings, and technological equipment such as teaching machines, but *people*—teachers and administrators—are required for effective education. Like so many other things, the capacities of teachers and principals are distributed roughly along a normal curve. Only a few are very effective, a few are very ineffective, and most are average. Money devoted to new methods of training and guiding teachers and administrators may improve the effectiveness of the poor and the average teachers, but it is doubtful whether any technique can make all teachers as effective as those few talented and concerned individuals who stand out in our minds as great. These outstanding individuals are the most important educational need of low income youth in Appalachia, Harlem, or Watts. The need is not easy to fill.

Thus, increasing expenditures does not guarantee the availability of a staff adequate to the challenge of improving the educational performance of the disadvantaged. Educational strategy cannot be evaluated abstractly; the capacity for effective operations must also be considered.

Education and Income

A one-to-one relationship does *not* exist between education and income. Therefore, even if we could meet the educational needs of all youth, education would only have a limited effect on the future income of youth. The know-how which is required in addition to education for many positions, the racial discrimination which occurs in the recruitment and selection of employees, and the uneven rewards of various levels of educational attainment intervene between education and income.

Manners, style of life, and know-how are considered in selecting individuals for many jobs. Educational credentials or no credentials, knowledge or no knowledge, the man who speaks ungrammatically, who wears an outdated suit, who has spent several years without a job (unless he was a student or a millionaire's son seeing the world), who does not have the right words for the right situations, or whose "good hours" do not fall on a regular schedule—preferably nine to five—is at a definite disadvantage in today's occupational world. Most social learning takes place outside of school and depends upon one's friends or family.[2]

For some persons, behaving the "correct way" means following the family's traditions, the family's culture; for others, the "correct way" means breaking with the family's way of life. The anguish of such a break has been frequently described in psychological and sociological literature.[3]

Discriminatory practices continue to intervene between education and income and thereby limit the educational strategy. The following survey of educational, occupational, and income data demonstrates that education alone does not produce income and occupational equality for Negroes.

Negro mothers, fathers, and students have *already* embraced the educational strategy because they consider education the most effective, if not sure, means of advancement. Dorothy Newman, who has summarized the findings of several studies, reported that among poor families, Negro parents tend to be more interested in their children's schooling and more ambitious for their children than white parents.[4]

Not only do black parents value education, but their offspring are obtaining more education than heretofore. Since 1960, young Negroes have radically narrowed the education gap which traditionally existed between nonwhites and whites. Between 1960 and 1967 the difference in median educational attainment of white and nonwhite males 25 to 29 years old shrank from 1.9 years to .5 years. The difference separating the percentage of nonwhites and whites possessing high school diplomas also declined. However, the gap separating the percentage of whites and nonwhites graduating from college remained unchanged, for while the number of nonwhites completing college increased, the number of whites increased at an equivalent rate.

To date, blacks have not reaped the monetary or occupational rewards which education delivers to whites. At every educational level, nonwhites earn less than whites. A portion of the discrepancy between Negro and white earnings may be accounted for by differences in the quality of Negro and white education. Another fraction may be attributed to the higher concentration of Negroes working in the South where wages are low. Unfortunately, discrimination is the only factor which can account for a major portion of the difference. As Duncan (1967) has noted, a survey of the equality of educational opportunity shows that a wide variety of measures of school quality do "not vary by race as much as most analysts had hitherto assumed." Siegel (1965) has also found that differences in white and nonwhite occupational and regional distributions accounted for only 37 percent of the mean 1959 earnings differential between white and nonwhite high school dropouts and high school graduates, 45 percent of that between college dropouts, and 16 percent of that between college graduates.

Sharp differences exist not only between the earnings but also between the occupational distributions of Negroes and whites. Even college graduation does not completely protect blacks from being treated differently than whites in the occupational arena. Differential treatment applies to the younger as well as the older cohorts. Only eight percent of nonwhites as opposed to 30 percent of white high school graduates 16 to 21 years old who had not enrolled in college were able to obtain clerical and other white collar jobs in 1964.[5]

Nonwhites at every educational level were not only employed in lower paying, less prestigious occupations than whites, but their chance of even obtaining work was considerably lower than that of whites. The unemployment rates of Negro college alumni and high school graduates in all but the 35 to 44 age group were two to three times those of white college alumni and high school graduates.[6]

These data indicate that discrimination continues to intervene between education and income, between education and occupation, and between education and chances for employment. Education is important for Negroes' advancement—we do not wish to be interpreted as arguing otherwise. With education, nonwhites do gain higher incomes, more prestigious occupations, and a smaller risk of unemployment. But, unfortunately, the roots of Negro poverty lie in the discriminatory practices of the larger society as well as in Negroes' lack of education. As long as discrimination exists, education alone will not solve the problems of redistributing incomes and occupations between whites and nonwhites.

The relationship between education and income for whites as well as nonwhites is further complicated by the upward movement of the tipping point where the "payoff" for education is greatest. For poverty reduction, the issue is not more years of education, but moving people toward the point where the level of education makes a difference. More and more, the significant cleavage in society is between college graduates and noncollege graduates. For example, Duncan (1967) has noted greater dissimilarity in the occupational distribution of white and nonwhite high school graduates and college dropouts than among college graduates. Although Negroes rapidly increased their median educational attainment during the 1960's, the difference between the percentages of nonwhite and white males graduating from college remained constant and the gap between females increased.

Because the gap between the occupational rewards whites and nonwhites gain from education is greater at the level of high school graduation and some college short of graduation than at the level of college graduation, Negroes, given present educational trends, are likely to suffer increasing deprivation despite their educational progress.

Further, the educational strategy assumes that the economy will absorb and recompense those who have a higher education. At the present time, this assumption seems to be undebatable. Highly educated people do get higher incomes in the United States. However, if all people improve their education, is there an automatic guarantee that they will be absorbed at higher level jobs than before? They may be rapidly absorbed today when there is a shortage of highly educated people and a reservoir of less educated people, but they may not be absorbed when this reservoir disappears and all people have a higher educational level.

Style of life preference, discriminatory practices, and uneven rewards at various levels of educational attainment intervene between education and income. The educational strategy must be supplemented by other efforts.

Dysfunctions of Education

America's recent "degree worship" has negative consequences for society as a whole as well as for individuals.

The emphasis on education has the unanticipated effect of stressing social control and a limited range of values. Schools today are not a humanizing or an educational force as much as a credential agency, sorting people out who do not fit into the regular channels of educational development. Because our schools function to certify that individuals are not harmful rather than to develop the potential of all, the educational strategy tends to limit the pluralism of society's values and institutions (Miller, 1968). Education socializes the young to certain values and warehouses them by keeping them out of the labor market and out of mischief. In part, mandatory education (through law or threat of poverty) conditions low income youth and strengthens established values. The educational strategy is aimed at helping people to fit into the existing occupational structure rather than at constructing new policies which would aid the poor directly by changing the income stream through improving the transfer system or the wage structure. Many objectives for education obviously appeal to those who do not want to change significantly the present structure of American society and economic life.

Not only does our overemphasis on education frequently restrict the creative growth of society, but it hurts millions of individuals. Schools tend to be "feminine" institutions as Patricia Sexton has pointed out in an analysis of a national school study. She observed:

> [Schools] seem particularly unsuited to the needs and temperament of the more masculine (generally lower socioeconomic) boys. . . To the extent that the system rewards the less masculine boys, it seems to encourage two opposite tendencies in the more masculine boys: resistance and submission. With the growing importance of schools in the society, the effect in the long run, logically, would be to diminish some of the masculine qualities of boys and make them more submissive. In effect, then, schools do in a real sense make "sissies" of boys, honoring the least masculine and encouraging the more masculine, through the increasing value of school honors, to emulate the more feminine.[7]

By forcing all persons to enter the occupational world through the school gate, we have drastically underestimated and underutilized the potential of many low income youth. Today over one-fourth of white and nearly one-half of Negro youth are dropping out of school before they complete high school. In ghetto communities the proportion is higher. Many youth whose cultures stress the importance of masculinity need alternative routes into the occupational world rather than "better schools." Individuals who may have outgrown the issues which propelled them out of school continue to be economically disenfranchised. With our increasing emphasis on academic credentials, our Chinese walls of exclusion grow ever higher for persons who are ignored because they lack the magical diploma although their occupational experience and performance prove them qualified. An overemphasis on credentials is society's loss as well as the individual's.

Implications

Education can become a slogan, an escape from the wider responsibility of aiding the poor. Although education is very important, it cannot solve all the problems which produce poverty in American society. If educational strategies are not viewed in perspective, an overemphasis on education may lead to neglect of economic assistance programs and be self-defeating.

Education as we conceive of it today is essentially a youth strategy. It is unlikely to improve the situation of the aged or many mothers who are receiving welfare. Therefore, when we consider educational spending from the point of view of the poor, we must weigh the value of this approach against that of other strategies for reducing poverty. Should more money be spent, for example, providing cash income to families that are poor in the hope that the increased income will lead to improvement in the school performance of youth? This is a question of whether to emphasize families or youth, and a question of whether investment in families or in schools affects educational performance most.

Although education partially improves the economic prospects of Negroes and helps them to deal more effectively with agencies and bureaucracies which dispense services, rising levels of education do not insure the reduction of gaps in income and occupation which persist between whites and blacks in this country. Nor does education insure the transfer and transformation of power, which is a growing issue as Negroes struggle for equality in the late twentieth century. We must fight discrimination more directly.

For education to enrich rather than constrict, men must be free to choose to use or not to use it. It is one of the paradoxes of our time that education, considered to be a liberating force, has become a prison for many. The current emphasis on academic credentials by employers forces individuals to remain in school and makes education a form of coercion; when youth do not follow mandates of the schools, they are sentenced to unemployment, uselessness, and poverty. Until youth are offered alternative entries into the occupational world, the pressure of *having* to make it through the educational system will continue to be debilitating to many.

Conclusion

In the 1930's and 1940's, education was charged with a wide range of tasks extending beyond the narrow confines of developing skills and knowledge. Education was to develop the "whole child"—which meant socializing him so he fit more easily into American society, developed good manners, was patriotic and a good citizen. In the 1950's and early 1960's, the burden of desegregating American society was left to the children and the educational arena rather than to adults who were wary of the task they displaced on their offspring. In the late 60's, the reduction of inequalities has been given largely to the schools of America. Obviously, they can make an important contribution, and perhaps they have already done so, but they cannot be assigned the entire burden of reforming the social structure of America. We ask too much of the schools and too little of the rest of society.

Notes

1. *The Wall Street Journal*, November 15, 1967.
2. For one example, see Hall, 1948.
3. See Douvan and Adelson, 1958; Douvan, 1956; Hollingshead, *et al.*, 1954; Sexton, 1968.
4. See Newman, 1965; Glenn, 1963; Lewis, 1960; Rose, 1962; and Rosen, 1959.
5. *Education and Race* (New York: National Urban League, 1966), p. 17.
6. H.R. Hamel, "Educational Attainment of Workers," in *Monthly Labor Review* (June, 1967), p. A-15.
7. P.C. Sexton, *School Adjustment and Maladjustment of Boys of Lower Socioeconomic Status* (New York: New York University, 1968), p. 1. Reproduced by permission.

References

Douvan, Elizabeth. "Social Status and Success Strivings," *Journal of Abnormal and Social Psychology*, 1956, 52: 219-223.

Douvan, Elizabeth and Adelson, Joseph. "The Psychodynamics of Social Mobility in Adolescent Boys," *Journal of Abnormal and Social Psychology*, 1958, 56: 31-44.

Duncan, Otis Dudley. "Discrimination Against Negroes," *The Annals*, 1967, 371: 102.

Duncan, Otis Dudley. "Inheritance of Poverty or Inheritance of Race?" Unpublished report, Symposium on Poverty, American Academy of Arts and Sciences, 1967.

Glenn, Norval D. "Negro Prestige Criteria," *American Journal of Sociology*, 1963, 68: 645-657.

Hall, Oswald. "The Stages of a Medical Career," *American Journal of Sociology*, 1948, 53: 327-336.

Hollingshead, A. B., Ellis, R., and Kirby, E. "Social Mobility and Mental Illness," *American Sociological Review*, 1954, 19: 577-584.

Lewis, Hylan. "The Changing Negro Family," in E. Ginsberg (ed.), *The Nation's Children*. New York: Columbia University Press, 1960.

Miller, S. M., *Breaking the Credentials Barrier*. Ford Foundation, 1968.

Miller, S. M., Rein, Martin, Roby, Pamela and Gross, Bertram M. "Poverty, Inequality, and Conflict," *The Annals*, 1967, 373: 16-52.

Miller, S. M. and Roby, Pamela. "Poverty: Changing Social Stratification." Unpublished report, Symposium on Poverty, American Academy of Arts and Sciences, 1967.

Newman, Dorothy K. "The Negro's Journey to the City," *Monthly Labor Review*, 1965, 88: 505-506.

Rose, Arnold M. *The Negro in America*. Boston: Beacon Press, 1962.

Rosen, Bernard C. "Race, Ethnicity, and the Achievement Syndrome," *American Sociological Review*, 1959, 24: 47-60.

Sexton, Patricia C. *School Adjustment and Maladjustment of Boys of Lower Socioeconomic Status*. National Institute of Mental Health. New York: New York University, 1968.

Siegel, Paul M. "On the Cost of Being a Negro," *Sociological Inquiry*, 1965, 35: 41-57.

3 | THE BLACK REVOLUTION AND EDUCATION

Donald H. Smith

Dr. Donald Smith is Executive Associate of the Urban Coalition, Washington, D.C. He is also a member of the President's National Advisory Committee on Vocational Education and a consultant to Project Follow Through and the National Teacher Corps.

The author sees the revolt that is taking place in the schools as a reflection in microcosm of the revolt of black people in American society. Black pupils are discovering that direct action often must be taken in the schools in order that the educational system will become responsive to their needs.

Dr. Smith outlines the history of the civil rights movement from quiet revolution toward open revolt. The hope-despair syndrome has led to black nationalism and the use of force by some black militants.

In the schools, there are three things that black students want: teachers who believe blacks can learn and who expect them to learn; a curriculum that will release blacks from psychological captivity; and models with whom blacks can identify and from whom they can derive feelings of pride and worth.

To correct the ills that deny black pupils their chance for educational participation, Dr. Smith introduces several proposals. Administrators and teachers must examine and understand their biases. They must learn more about the historical, cultural, and educational characteristics of minority pupils. They must be willing to abandon traditional curricular approaches which are questionable for the white middle class and almost criminally inappropriate for nonwhites. The schools must exercise deliberate and systematic efforts to provide equal educational and social opportunities *within* each school. Also, teachers must understand and accept all children as human beings. They must be sensitive enough to the black experience to help black children appreciate themselves and their people. Whether a school system decides to integrate or to upgrade all-black schools, it must address itself to the issues expostulated in this chapter.

A*ll I wanted was to be a man among other men. I wanted to come lithe into a world that was ours and to help to build it together. . . . I wanted to be a man, nothing but a man.*[1]

Frantz Fanon

In the autumn that followed the great summer revolt of 1967, a new black student entered America's schools. His likes had never been seen before, and his coming was devastating. Public schools that had hardly known how to deal with his forerunners found him unfathomable.

His haircut and the ebony tiki around his neck were strangely African. Strange for a boy who in the recent past had rolled his eyes in embarrassment and looked away at the mention of Africa or blackness. During that fiery summer he had worn sandals and thought "Black is Beautiful," "I am my Black Brother's Brother," and "It's So Beautiful to be Black." If he lived in Newark or Detroit or even one of the less scorched cities, he may have hurled bottled fire. Whether or not he participated in the riots, he is likely to have experienced a feeling of power and pride as he watched his peers lash out at society and its agents, the police and the fire fighters.

In their way, speaking to society with the only means they could discover, dispossessed black youth signaled their desperate determination to strike down the ghetto walls. And further, they signaled the assertion of their selfhood. Denied dignity and acceptance by the white society that had promised equality in exchange for assimilation, these youngsters were reversing the psychology of rejection and self-abnegation with the counter-psychology of beautiful blackness and self-love.

These young people, who burned and looted during the summer of 1967 and during the emotion-wrought period following the assassination of Dr. Martin Luther King, Jr., were attempting to survive. They fought for their lives in the only way they knew how. They enraged a nation that did not even know they existed. By some standards, the behavior of these young people is considered delinquent and dysfunctional. Others, however, label these disruptive responses as "normal" in an "abnormal" society, as healthy in a sick society. Kenneth Clark, for instance, has written the following:

> The Negro delinquent, therefore, calls attention to the quiet pathology of the ghetto which he only indirectly reflects. In a very curious way the delinquent's behavior is healthy; for, at the least, it asserts that he still has sufficient strength to rebel and has not yet given in to defeat.[2]

The schools of the nation that watched Watts, Newark, and Detroit burn without perceiving the true message of the flames have been equally imperceptive about the emergence of the new angry black students, the children of revolt, in their own corridors. Many urban schools have become battlegrounds for the open revolt of black pupils. Student uprisings have jolted schools and communities from their complacent attitudes about race relations. Schools throughout the nation have experienced open hostility in the form of violence between black and white students and between black students and school personnel. In all-black schools, students have declared war upon school personnel, mostly white, but including some black teachers. In some biracial schools, hostilities have erupted as a result of open conflict between individuals or groups of black and white students. In others, mere rumors of racial conflict have been sufficient to create the fact.

At first, the complaints of black students fell into two categories: denial of the opportunity to become homecoming queen or king and nonrepresentation on cheering squads. Two seemingly minor issues, they were the catalysts that sparked black student revolts.

But another issue has come to the surface: in all-black and biracial schools black students are demanding the inclusion of their own history and culture in textbooks and curriculum. But these issues— determination to participate in significant school activities and insistence upon the recognition of black culture and achievement—are part of a larger and more fundamental problem. *The revolt in the schools is a microcosm of the revolt of black people in American society.* And this revolt has changed from a nonviolent direction to one that includes violent conflict.

The Quiet Revolution

Black America has always been angry with white America (Kardiner and Ovesey, 1964; Lomax, 1963). Until quite recently, most blacks managed to sublimate their hostilities into channels that would not bring direct confrontation with the dynamite stick or the lynch rope. But an oppressive environment offers a limited number of responses: withdrawal, acquiescence, accommodation, and confrontation (Pettigrew, 1964).

Poor blacks who came into daily contact with whites and whose livelihood, to say nothing of life and limb, depended upon the continued approval of whites frequently accommodated themselves by grinning and scratching and mouthing the expected platitudes of survival. Still others built protective walls of apathy.

Blacks who were more secure financially, the teachers, professors, and physicians, particularly in the South, found their psychic survival in withdrawing from direct interaction with whites. Yet, when necessity dictated, they, too, swallowed pride and dignity and bowed to the vaunted intimidation of whites who are able to give jobs but also take away life (Frazier, 1957).

In spite of the protest activities of black militants such as Denmark Vesey and Nat Turner, who led slave insurrections, and in spite of hundreds of slave revolts, there had never been a sustained, united black confrontation with the social order prior to the 1950's.

The Montgomery bus boycott of 1955-56 provided the first opportunity for American blacks to confront oppression directly and massively. During the Montgomery confrontation, Dr. Martin Luther King, Jr., emerged as the nonviolent apostle whose philosophy and tactics dominated civil rights activities for over a decade.

Dr. King's philosophy of the social gospel was undergirded by the thinking of two men: Thoreau, who believed that men have a moral obligation to resist unjust laws and to accept the penalty for breaking such laws; and M. K. Gandhi, whose own practice of nonviolent "Soul Force" exacted India's freedom from the British.

The courageous victory won by Montgomery's blacks gave hope to their people all over the country, and Dr. King emerged as the most powerful black leader in American history. His work and that of his colleagues in the Southern Christian Leadership Conference forged important achievements during the 1960's, in terms of legislative accomplishments and positive shifts in the attitudes of white people (Hyman and Sheatsley, 1964). Following the demonstrations in Birmingham and the historic march on Washington in 1963, President Kennedy sent the strongest civil rights bill of all time to Congress and a year later President Lyndon Johnson guided the bill to passage.

One of the provisions of the civil rights bill of 1964 attempted to abolish school segregation for the second time in a decade. This, coupled with multi-billion-dollar education bills, promised to improve substantially the educational opportunities of Afro-American children. Other provisions of the civil rights acts of 1964 and 1965 had promised improved job opportunities and political power, but they failed to be effective; and, thus far, the education bills have failed to register any significant impact upon so-called "target area" schools. Measured by almost any standard—achievement scores, dropouts, window breakage, or attacks on teachers—life in urban schools grows worse, not better.

In spite of the inspirational leadership of Dr. King, the civil rights acts, the education bills, and the Economic Opportunity Act, the lives of poor people, like the lives of their children in the schools, have become more frustrating, more unbearable.[3]

Civil rights bills that are not enforced, poverty programs that fail to build self-determination and self-support, and the existence of institutional racism which relegates black citizens to the bottom of the heap—all combine to produce a strange mixture of anger and hatred, hope and despair, expectation and defeat.

The Move to Violence

The hope-despair syndrome, created by the great promises of legislation and the frustrating results, gave rise to the leadership of Malcolm X and the new black militants, typified by young revolutionaries Rap Brown and Stokely Carmichael. Curiously enough, Brown and Carmichael as young boys were under the tutelege of Dr. King and the SCLC. In Mississippi in 1964, Carmichael with much compassion schooled young blacks and whites in the philosophy and tactics of nonviolence. But that was before Carmichael, Brown, and the other young members of SNCC had endured the virtually unpunished murders of Medgar Evers, Viola Liuzzo, Jonathan Daniels, of Cheney, Schwerner and Goodman, and before Carmichael was committed to Parchman Farm, the state penitentiary, for daring to encourage Mississippi blacks to register to vote. Such experiences can turn idealistic, compassionate young men into hardened realists. Such experiences can cause followers of nonviolence to take up the sword, rhetorically or sometimes in deed.

The black militants have given up on America's capacity to do what is right out of noble, humane motives. Instead, they believe that the nation must be forced to live up to its professed ideals. Corollary to forcing white America to deal justly with blacks, they believe the blacks must unite themselves into a self-protecting, self-determining, self-promoting group. Carmichael and Hamilton have called this process the closing of ranks:

> By this we mean that group solidarity is necessary before a group can operate effectively from a bargaining position of strength in a pluralistic society.[4]

Other militants move beyond the sound economic and political strategies suggested by Hamilton and Carmichael in *Black Power* and into the realm of violent revolt, subscribing to the ideas of Frantz Fanon, the black psychiatrist from Martinique. Fanon believed that enslaved, colonized people must free themselves through violent revolution. As Fanon wrote in *The Wretched of the Earth:*

> Violence is a cleansing force. It frees the native from his inferiority complex and from his despair and inaction; it makes him fearless and restores his self-respect.[5]

Following the assassination of Dr. King, the poor-affluent, black-white schism was widened and the battle lines hardened. As Black Panther leader Eldridge Cleaver wrote:

> The assassin's bullet not only killed Dr. King, it killed a period of history. It killed a hope, and it killed a dream. That white America could produce the assassin of Dr. Martin Luther King is looked upon by black people—and not just those identified as black militants—as a final repudiation by white America of any hope of reconciliation, of any hope of change by peaceful and nonviolent means.[6]

White America has not been completely unconscionable and unconcerned about the plight of black America. Attempts have been made to redress some of the grievances, to bridge part of the gap, to repair some of the damage. Unfortunately, most of these efforts have been planned and administered by whites, and occasionally by blacks, who have not represented the best interests of lower class blacks. Never have commitments and funds been anywhere near the requirements; almost never have lower income blacks, or concerned middle class blacks, been in control. The contemporary black mood asserts that blacks are determined to take control.

Malcolm X, one-time Muslim minister and assassinated leader, is the martyred hero and inspirational symbol of the new black quest for self-determination. His philosophy of black nationalism is the guiding force of black militancy. As Malcolm X announced in 1964:

> Our political philosophy will be Black Nationalism. Our economic philosophy will be Black Nationalism. Our cultural emphasis will be Black Nationalism.[7]

In explaining the substance of tripartite black nationalism, Malcolm X stated:

... the political philosophy is that which is designated to encourage our people, the black people, to gain complete control over the politics and the politicians of our community.

Our economic philosophy is that we should gain economic control over the economy of our own community, the businesses and other things which create employment so that we can provide jobs for our own people instead of having to picket and boycott and beg someone else for a job. . . . our social [cultural] philosophy means that we feel that it is time to get together among our own kind and eliminate the evils that are destroying the moral fiber of our society, like drug addiction, drunkenness, adultery. . . . We believe that we should lift the level or the standard of our own society to a higher level wherein we will be satisfied and then not inclined toward pushing ourselves into other societies where we are not wanted.[8]

Revolution in the Schools

Within the last decade, the civil rights movement has forced considerable attention upon the plight of Americans who hunger in a land of plenty. Puerto Ricans, Mexican-Americans, American Indians, and poor southern whites have been thrust into the national spotlight along with black Americans. Since the early 1960's, verbiage in great profusion has described the characteristics of the dispossessed poor, their world views, and their pathology. Believing the old cliche that "education will cure the nation's ills," Congress has appropriated billions of dollars to save the children of poverty.

Tragically, the sum total of these efforts has left America's blacks and our other poverty-stricken children still outside of the educational mainstream and outside of the social mainstream. The panacea—compensatory education—has proved to be a colossal failure. Like so many efforts to help, or at least to placate the poor, compensatory education never had a chance. It is ludicrous that white teachers and administrators could believe themselves capable of devising special compensatory programs to do the job they were incapable of doing in the far more lengthy regular program (Smith, 1968).

However, failure has not discouraged whites from continuing to dominate and control the education of blacks; it has not prevented large cities from continuing to appoint white school superintendents to administer black and Spanish-American majorities.

Some whites are interested, perhaps deeply, in the educational needs of the nation's twenty-two million blacks. However, it is the belief of this writer, supported by the compelling evidence of nonperformance, that however well-meaning whites may be, they lack the social perception to penetrate the mass of white racism that permeates the American school but is almost imperceptible to them. Instead of addressing themselves to the real source of the failure to educate blacks, white educators have busied themselves with methods, techniques, and special curricula for "motoric" children.

The President's Commission on Civil Disorders has correctly identified white racism as the corrosive force which is rotting the American fabric. In the words of the commission:

> What white Americans have never fully understood . . . but what the Negro can never forget . . . is that white society is deeply implicated in the ghetto. White institutions created it, white institutions maintain it and white society condones it.

> Race prejudice has shaped our history decisively; it now threatens to affect our future. White racism is essentially responsible for the explosive mixture which has been accumulating in our cities . . .[9]

Nowhere is the effect of white supremacy more pervasive and more debilitating than in the American school. Whether it takes the form of textbooks which promulgate white supremacy by excluding the lives and accomplishments of blacks and other minorities, whether it takes the form of white teachers who have double standards of expectation, reward, and punishment, or whether it takes the form of self-hating black teachers who despise black children—white racism has poisoned the American school. White supremacy has left many black teachers and white teachers paralyzed in its wake, and it has been most deadly when they are unaware of their social sickness.

At last, black pupils have begun to discover that they must force the schools to serve their needs by taking the same kind of chaotic action within the schools that others are taking in the larger society.

The demands and actions of the black students confront the racism that has always been present in the schools and is finally being unmasked. The view of many administrators and teachers that student revolts are deleterious is refuted by others who see the efforts to attack and destroy racism as a positive force that will benefit both blacks and whites.

As Dr. Martin Luther King wrote in his last book, *Where Do We Go From Here: Chaos or Community?*:

The value in pulling racism out of its obscurity and stripping it of its rationalizations lies in the confidence that it can be changed. To live with the pretense that racism is a doctrine of a very few is to disarm us in fighting it frontally as scientifically unsound, morally repugnant and socially destructive. The prescription for the cure rests with the accurate diagnosis of the disease. A people who began a national life inspired by a vision of a society of brotherhood can redeem itself. But redemption can come only through a humble acknowledgement of guilt and an honest knowledge of self.[10]

How incredible it is that young people have to threaten and sometimes bring about destruction to get the attention of society outside and inside the schools. Their goals are so amazingly simple, so undeniably just, that rational men must wonder about the wisdom, the morality, even the sanity of those who would deny their goals because the means by which they are communicated are discomforting.

What Do They Want?

First, what black pupils want and need are teachers who believe they can learn, who expect them to learn, and who teach them. Teachers whose naivete and cultural biases have conditioned them to believe that blacks, Indians, poor whites, or Spanish-speaking children are inferior can never teach them. It is extremely difficult for most teachers to understand how their own perceptions of the worth and ability of their students actually affect the emotional development and achievement of the children.

The research of Rosenthal and Jacobson (1967) suggests the critical relationship between teacher expectation and pupil achievement. In this study, involving an experiment with rats, graduate students received information that certain rats were "abnormal." As a result, the students failed to teach these rats to perform expected tasks, even though some of the rats so labeled were actually normal. Yet with groups of rats alleged "normal," the graduate students were successful in teaching the same tasks. The labels themselves became determinants of how the rats were perceived and of the subsequent behavior of the experimenters in attempting to teach their subjects.

Rosenthal and Jacobson's work with the children of Oak School in the South San Francisco Unified School District bore similar results. Based upon an achievement test and the random selection of certain children as "spurters" in achievement, Rosenthal and Jacobson were able to convince classroom teachers that the children so designated would undergo significant achievement spurts during the forthcoming year. The children labeled as spurters actually did excel because, as Rosenthal and Jacobson conclude:

> ... one person's expectation of another's behavior may serve as a self-fulfilling prophecy. When teachers expected certain children would show greater intellectual development, those children did show greater intellectual development.[11]

A teacher need not be an avowed advocate of race or class supremacy to damage the emotional or intellectual growth of minority pupils. It is very possible for a well-intentioned teacher to succumb unwittingly to thinking that children who live in housing projects or slum tenements, who are supported by public assistance, whose skins are dark, or whose language is nonstandard are not able to learn. Such beliefs may cause teachers to despair at the hopelessness of it all or cause them to engage in the curious rationalization that because such pupils are unlikely to succeed, they would waste effort trying to teach them.

Let it be clearly understood that all children want to learn in school. Further, all mothers and fathers in the black ghetto want their children to receive a good education. Parents often are unable to communicate this desire, and frequently the horror of their lives forces them into acts which appear neglectful and unconcerned. The children themselves enter school eager to learn, in love with their teachers, with policemen, with firemen, with everybody. Sometimes they, too, lack the signs by which their desire to learn might be communicated to teachers whose own culture has taught them how to detect readiness and willingness to learn.

Dr. Helen Redbird tells a classic story that underscores the absurdity of concepts such as "school-oriented children" and "readiness to learn." Dr. Redbird, professor at the Oregon College of Education, visited an elementary school to inquire about the progress of a little American Indian boy. She was told by the boy's teacher that he was doing poorly in class. The teacher explained that he appeared disinterested in learning, perhaps unwilling to learn. Dr. Redbird, who is an Indian, asked to remove the boy from the classroom for a few days to see if she couldn't get him "ready to learn." The teacher granted permission, and after a few days of "motivating" the student, Dr. Redbird returned him to his class.

About a week later Dr. Redbird inquired about the boy's progress. Not to her surprise, he was doing excellently and his teacher was amazed with the results. Unknown to the teacher, Dr. Redbird had taught the little boy two things: *to smile and to nod his head in response to his teacher.* When the boy had mastered these two acts of accommodation, his teacher was convinced of his willingness to learn! Neither smiling nor nodding was part of the little boy's culture, but until he was taught to behave in ways that signaled his desire to learn, he was abandoned. How many children are lost because they don't know or are unwilling to play the school game?

Second, black pupils need a curriculum that will release them from psychological captivity. The literature is replete with studies that reveal the psychological damage that slavery and post-slavery racism have imposed on black people. In spite of the growing "Black Power, Black Pride" movement, millions of blacks are trapped in the delusion of worthlessness so carefully engineered by an exploitative larger society.

When black children do not see themselves in their textbooks, when they are denied the chance to read of their people's accomplishments, when all about them they see only maids and porters, high rises and run-down tenements, when they perceive in the mass media only a replication of the black meniality and degradation that are their daily companions, they are trapped by self-doubt and self-rejection. Black children must have proof of their own worth. They must learn about their own worth as a derivative of the worth of their forebears. Black children must. be taught to understand and appreciate their cultural heritage by teachers who understand and appreciate that heritage. Black children must know who they are and they must learn about the racial accomplishments of which they can be very proud.

Dr. Frantz Fanon, a victim of the "black is worthless" philosophy, came to realize that he had been seeking the wrong thing when he desired the approval of whites. He learned after much emotional turmoil that the only acceptance that has any meaning is self-acceptance:

> I resolved, since it was impossible for me to get away from an *inborn complex,* to assert myself as a BLACK MAN. Since the other hesitated to recognize me, there remained only one solution: to make myself known.[12]

As a concomitant to curriculum which is meaningful and inspiring, black pupils want to be taught and administered by models with whom they can identify and from whom they can derive feelings of pride and worth. Black pupils need to be taught and administered by educational personnel who are proud of black culture. They need to see their own people in control of their schools, not playing second or third man to "Mr. Charlie."

Proposals for Change in the Schools

Obviously, many readers of this chapter will be in agreement with it. However, many readers will find the ideas difficult to understand and even more difficult to accept. Some may dismiss the writer's interpretation of the contemporary black mood; others may agree with the interpretation but deny that white racism and oppression are responsible for black deprivation and subsequent anger and bitterness; still others may accept the interpretation, concur with racist causation, but believe that black nationalism is white racism in reverse.

For those who are convinced that the assertions in this chapter are invalid, the proposals that follow will have little meaning. For those who agree or are willing to suspend disbelief temporarily, these proposals may have positive impact.

The rationale for these proposals is based upon the following assumptions:

1. Racism is pervasive in all American institutions.
2. Racism in the American school is destroying black children and other minority youth, and little reversal appears likely without systematic counter-efforts.
3. American schools have served the interests and needs of the white middle and upper classes. Blacks, poor whites, Amerindians, and the Spanish-speaking minority have never been full members in the American school or the American way of life.
4. Black people have suffered deep psychological injury which has resulted in self-abnegation and group rejection.
5. Black students and their elders are justified in their anger, and they should be supported in their determination to gain equitable treatment.
6. The new wave of "Black Consciousness" and "Black Pride" is a positive psychological affirmation of the worth and dignity of Afro-Americans.

7. Ignored and denied approved channels to redress their grievances, black pupils have had no recourse but to be disruptive.
8. There are large numbers of educational personnel who are the unwitting agents of school systems that fail blacks and other minority pupils.
9. Given the opportunity, these educators would align themselves with other educators who possess the know-how and have the desire to educate minority pupils.

If the foregoing assumptions are valid, then the following proposals may be viewed as viable approaches for correcting the ills that deny black pupils their chance for equal participation in education.

1. Administrators, teachers, and other school personnel should undergo intensive sensitivity training to be able to engage in meaningful self-introspection. Hopefully, educational personnel would be helped to understand themselves and to discover how their own biases, stereotypes, and cultural limitations inhibit the emotional and intellectual growth of black pupils.

2. In addition to self-analysis, school personnel need to learn more about the historical, cultural, and educational characteristics of blacks and other poor. Courses such as the History and Culture of Afro-Americans and other disadvantaged people should be requirements for undergraduate, graduate, and in-service training of educational personnel. Certainly these courses should have greater substance than the study of heroes and their deeds. They should come to grips with the fundamental issues of exploitation, oppression, and racism and various individual and group responses to those issues.

3. School personnel must be willing to abandon traditional curricular approaches that are questionable even for the white middle class and are totally inappropriate for nonwhites. By means of curriculum changes to include relevant political, economic, historical, cultural, and environmental experiences and materials, schools will succeed in the motivation of poor blacks, heretofore alleged as not possible. Nat Turner, Frederick Douglass, Ida B. Wells, Malcolm X, and Martin Luther King, Jr., should be the heroes of young black students. Their lives and deeds and those of other outstanding Afro-Americans must provide the philosophy and psychology for black liberation. The politics and economics of social change must become the tools of physical liberation.

4. The schools must exercise deliberate and systematic efforts to provide equal educational and social opportunities *within* each school. Blacks who attend so-called desegregated schools must be afforded the opportunity and encouraged to participate in all academic and extracurricular activities. Even within an all-black school, if middle class or "nice" conformist youngsters are most likely to be selected for activities, care must be taken to include children of the lower socioeconomic class.

5. Black youngsters need to be taught and administered by models of black manhood and black womanhood who have been released from white psychological captivity. In many central city areas, it is possible for black pupils to be taught by staffs that are predominantly black. The more difficult problem is for blacks to be administered and supervised by their own people. Big city school systems are not yet willing to bestow the control and high salaries of administrators upon many Afro-Americans.

6. In school systems where black pupils are a very small minority, it is probably unrealistic to expect a substantial number of black pupils to have black teachers. Obviously, for a number of years to come, some blacks will continue to be educated by white people, particularly when they live in integrated housing patterns. Such pupils will desperately need teachers who have been taught to understand and accept them as human beings and who are sensitive enough to the essence of black culture and the black experience to help black children appreciate themselves and their people.

7. Whether a school decides to integrate or to upgrade substantially the existing all-black schools, it must address itself to the issues expostulated in this chapter.

Considerable attention must be given to changing the attitudes of school personnel toward black pupils. This is true for black as well as white personnel, for a great many black teachers have been and remain the victims of a vitiating white racism which causes them to demean and reject black children.

Summary

After many years of being pushed out of schools, or dropping out of irrelevant, often hateful schools, black students are taking hold of their own destinies. They are in open rebellion against society and its agents, including the schools, that have kept the doors of opportunity closed and have treated them as a subhuman species. These young people are determined that they will be respected, that they will be taught, that they will have access to the same opportunities available to whites.

Whether the American schools recognize it or not, their black pupils are in revolt. They demand just treatment as well as relevant school experiences. Their anger and determination will be assuaged by nothing less than revolutionary responses—by nothing less than drastic changes in administrative and pedagogical attitudes and practices. Schools, like the greater society, cannot be maintained by positioning armed guards outside the doors. The schools and society must acknowledge their criminal neglect of black citizens, and they must take radical and forthright measures of correction. We must assume that the chaos in our school buildings and in our streets is a portent, not a final judgment. But we must understand that failure to act in massive and positive ways may be, in Dr. King's words, "mankind's last chance to choose between chaos and community."

Notes

1. F. Fanon, *Black Skin, White Masks*, (New York: Grove Press, 1967), p. 112-113.
2. F. B. Clark, *Dark Ghetto* (New York: Harper and Row, 1965), p. 88.
3. This conclusion has been reached by many, particularly the poor. See the *Report of the National Advisory Commission on Civil Disorders*, 1968; Cloward, 1965.
4. S. Carmichael and C. V. Hamilton, *Black Power, The Politics of Liberation in America* (New York: Random House, 1967), p. 44.
5. F. Fanon, *The Wretched of the Earth*. Translated from the French by Constance Farrington (*Presence Africaine*, 1963; New York: Grove Press, 1966), p. 73.
6. From "Requiem for Nonviolence" in R. Scheer (ed.), *Eldridge Cleaver* (New York: Random House, 1969). Reproduced by permission.
7. Malcolm X, Announcement at Press Conference, March 12, 1964.
8. Malcolm X, Speech on Black Revolution, New York, April 8, 1964.
9. *Report of the National Advisory Commission on Civil Disorders*, pp. 2, 10.
10. M. L. King, Jr., *Where Do We Go From Here: Chaos or Community?* (New York: Harper and Row, 1967), p. 83. Reproduced by permission.
11. R. Rosenthal and L. Jacobson, *"Self-Fulfilling Prophecies in the Classroom,"* 1967.
12. F. Fanon, *Black Skin, White Masks* (New York: Grove Press, 1967), p. 115.

References

Cloward, Richard A. "The War on Poverty: Are the Poor Left Out?" *Nation*, 1965, 201: 55-60.

Frazier, E. Franklin. *Black Bourgeoisie*. Glencoe, Ill.: Free Press, 1957.

Hyman, Herbert H. and Sheatsley, Paul B. "Attitudes Toward Desegregation," *Scientific American*, 1964, 211: 14, 16-23.

Kardiner, Abram and Ovesey, Lionel. *Mark of Oppression.* Cleveland: World Publishing Co., 1964.

Lomax, Louis E. *When the Word is Given.* New York: New American Library, 1963.

Pettigrew, Thomas. *A Profile of the Negro American.* New York: Van Nostrand, 1964.

Report of the National Advisory Commission on Civil Disorders. U.S. Riot Commission Report; also called the Kerner Report. Washington, D.C.: U.S. Government Printing Office, 1968.

Rosenthal, Robert and Jacobson, Lenore. "Self-Fulfilling Prophecies in the Classroom." Unpublished paper presented at the American Psychological Association, September, 1967.

Smith, Donald H. "Changing Controls in Ghetto Schools," *Phi Delta Kappan,* 1968, 49: 451-2.

4 | THE URBAN SCHOOL CHILD

Robert L. Green

The fact that many youths in our urban centers are minority group members who have been raised in educationally and economically handicapped environments presents schools and teachers with problems they have not handled well.

In this chapter, Dr. Green examines the forces which affect the educational performance of urban youth. He cites research findings that contribute to an understanding of the urban school child—his personal values, his self-concepts, his levels of aspiration. An understanding of both present and past points of reference is essential: the extraschool environment of home and neighborhood and the child's geographic, racial, national, and ethnic background.

Dr. Green proposes that the urban teacher needs sound "first aid" methods to deal with disruptive behavior in the classroom. A working knowledge of the students and how their background can be tied into classroom instruction is essential. Urban children are eager to learn material that will build on their past experiences, but they are antagonistic or inattentive when confronted with irrelevant instruction.

The urban school is faced with the problem of educating urban youth to cope with life in a society that is growing in complexity. However, the task will be hopeless unless the process of American education is restructured. The challenge of educating disadvantaged youth is one that the teacher in the urban community cannot avoid.

It is important to understand the past and present background of the urban school child if we are to assess realistically the needs of the child and the school. Most teachers would readily acknowledge the importance of the child's immediate environment. The neighborhood and home environment of the child and available adult models play an important role in shaping the child's classroom behavior and academic performance. Geographic and racial background is significant. In addition, the patterns of migration of our highly mobile population guarantee that a large segment of the student population in today's urban school will be a racial minority, often black or Spanish-speaking, who may experience difficulty in coping with the current urban school curriculum.

The shifting points of origin, rural to urban, have been well documented (Ravitz, 1963; Wayland, 1963). The rural to urban and the urban to suburban shifts will continue for some time. Thus, while a majority of the nation's children go to urban schools, there is still a large rural population that will continue to shift into urban communities in an attempt to structure a new way of life. The new urban residents are often poor blacks, whites, and Puerto Ricans. However, the urban to suburban shift is overwhelmingly white and middle class. If this trend continues, our cities will become storehouses of the black and the poor.

As a result, the urban teacher is faced with the loss of many school-oriented students from families that emphasize school-related tasks. In their place, the teacher is presented with educationally disadvantaged children, some of whom have problems in behavior and in learning. In addition, educationally disadvantaged students often share characteristics that are negatively perceived by the teacher. Also, it must be remembered that black children with southern antecedents often have been nurtured in a climate of intolerance and rejection as well as educational deprivation.

Throughout America's past, most urban immigrants settled in tightly ethnocentric neighborhoods. It is only within the past few decades that American blacks have become a more important factor in migration than these extra-national groups. Our restricted immigration quotas over the past forty years have decreased foreign immigration. Sloan Wayland (1963) considers the influence of foreign immigrants on today's urban scene as short term and minor. This may not always be the case, for Presidents Kennedy and Johnson strongly suggested liberalization of immigration quotas.

Within the context of a specific city, political refugees and other migrating national or ethnic groups can have a profound effect on the urban scene. Newly-arrived groups of Mexican-Americans in San Antonio, Cubans in Miami, and Puerto Ricans in New York make knowledge of a second language a prerequisite for many teachers in these cities. On the other hand, established residents of the urban community who do not belong to the incoming groups must adapt themselves to a milieu in which another ethnic viewpoint and language have taken hold.

Within a changing context, teachers often are faced with a divided classroom. The antagonisms between the new and the established orders are more painful when expressed in children. Only a thorough understanding and concern for the cultures of *both* groups of students can help the urban teacher in a situation such as this. These antagonisms can be found in northern public schools with racially-mixed populations and on college campuses with minority student populations.

What are some of the educational problems facing the urban teacher? Forced to use tests and methods based on the norms and experiences of middle class urban whites, the urban teacher may face a classroom of children who are racially separated, economically and educationally disadvantaged, and victims of one or more forms of prejudice. These factors are all related to school achievement.

Also important to educational progress is the extraschool environment of the child: the neighborhood and especially the home. It is there that the past orientations of both parent and child take their toll on the present. Deutsch (1962; 1963) and Bloom (1964) have taken a long look at the effects of preschool environment on the poor urban child. Deutsch feels that home or environmental disadvantage is maximized "when the child belongs to a minority group that until quite recently was not only excluded from the mainstream but was not even allowed to bathe in the tributaries."[1]

However, Deutsch finds the *least* disadvantage in the early grades. The suggestion is either that background characteristics do not become important until the higher grades or that the negative effects of earlier experiences become more observable as children grow older. Successive years of adverse educational experiences, particularly in the primary grades, will be reflected in cumulative disadvantagement in later years.

Many investigators have assessed the role of environment as pertinent to intellectual development. Most contemporary psychologists believe that a large portion of intellectual development is directly related to environmental factors. In fact, there is growing support for the argument that selected environmental factors may be more crucial to intellectual growth than the genetic factor. Hunt (1961) suggests that the development of central organizations for the processing of information that is required to solve problems depends upon experience. Thus, heredity may provide the basis for the molding influence of environment, which emerges as a powerful factor in the development of intelligence (Green, 1968).

To support the crucial importance of environment, several researchers have found that measured IQ tends to decrease with age in disadvantaged children. The author found an IQ drop of 23 points (95 to 72) for groups of southern rural black children between the ages of five and eighteen who had received limited education during the period when their county public schools were closed (Green, et al., 1964). Five other studies testing intelligence at varying age levels found that the IQ's of black children in less than optimal school surroundings decrease with age (Arlitt, 1922; Higgins and Sivers, 1958; Kennedy, et al., 1961; Tomlinson, 1944; Young and Bright, 1954). Higgins and Sivers also found that the IQ's of white children in depressed areas decrease with age. Tomlinson found the biggest drop between the ages of four and five. In all cases, measured intelligence of whites and blacks in depressed areas was comparable from ages four to six. The decrease in intelligence test performance among disadvantaged children is certainly contrary to what is expected normally in the growth process of children, who are continually exposed to educational experiences even though these experiences are less than optimal. It must be noted, however, that test items which depart from the disadvantaged child's background probably account for most of these differences (Green, 1969).

Nevertheless, a child's home is a powerful force in shaping his behavior and self-concept (Kvaraceus, et al., 1965; Riessman, 1962). In economically disadvantaged homes, there tends to be a scarcity of objects of all types, especially books, pencils, and paper which are necessary for the child's habituation to the tools used in school.

Deutsch (1962) focuses on other factors that he feels add significantly to a child's frustration in school: learned inattention (the result of being ignored at home since both parents often work) and lack of orientation due to frequent transfers to different schools. Lack of effective communication at home and mobility both complicate the learning atmosphere.

However, the recent interest that urban parents have expressed in the education of their children has led to conscious improvement in the home environment. The Ocean Hill-Brownsville Parent Teachers Association in New York is an example of how parents can assist the school positively in the attainment of educational objectives. Both parents and teachers can play an important role in assisting urban youth to acquire appropriate learning strategies.

Characteristics of the Urban Child

As mentioned in the preceding section, the urban teacher is sometimes faced with the task of educating children with both behavioral and learning problems. These behavioral and learning problems reflect both the urban and the rural context.

In rural Prince Edward County, over one thousand black families found their children without any educational facilities for four years because the county schools had been closed to avoid integration (Green, *et al.*, 1964). Over the years, quite a few families migrated to northern urban areas, thus becoming a part of the urban class under discussion. Nearly half of the 1,700 young people tested, aged five to twenty-two, received no schooling whatsoever for four years. Several hundred of the children attended urban schools in other counties and returned later. This unfortunate and extreme case of educational deprivation presented an opportunity to unearth the subtle disadvantages that rural children bring with them to the urban classroom.

One result of the deprivation of schooling was the overwhelming selection of the parents as admired models by all age groups. Contrary to expectation, the educationally disadvantaged child may be *closer* to home and parental influence than his better educated classmate. This could be a great asset to the urban teacher's educational efforts as poor urban parents become more academically oriented.

As expected, the group receiving no education scored significantly lower on achievement subtests and intelligence tests (both group and individual) than the educated group and other normative groups. In the younger children, achievement deficits were greatest in spelling and language, while the older children suffered a greater disadvantage in arithmetic skills. Children of all ages suffered on the paragraph meaning and comprehension tests. IQ differences between the group receiving some education and the group receiving none at all were not significantly different for children eight years and under. Beyond this age, a significant measured intellectual deficit averaging fifteen points appeared! Measured IQ tended to decrease with age as already noted.

The early grades contain more *potentially* disadvantaged children than *obviously* disadvantaged children. Since this trend reverses itself in later grades, teachers of the primary grades find more subtle signs of disadvantage than teachers of the higher grades, but they have a greater responsibility since the effects of inferior educational background can be reversed more easily at the earlier age levels. Bloom (1964) hypothesizes that measured IQ at age eight is directly related to adult measured IQ.

When disadvantage is not reversed, and perhaps is maximized, a socially dangerous process of natural selection takes place as the upper grades of the urban school lose the "problem youth" of the middle grades. That process, under the names of failure, expulsion and dropping-out, represents a negative quantitative measure of the success of the urban school. These youngsters, especially males from eighteen to twenty-one, may become the "riot youth" discussed in the *Report of the National Advisory Commission on Civil Disorders* (1968). Thus, the higher grades are composed of those who have survived the weeding-out process. Perhaps as a teacher's training and abilities increase, the grade level she teaches should be decreased.

Gottlieb (1964), Hogan (Chapter 7), and Haubrich (Chapter 6) point out the need for careful selection of personnel for the instruction of disadvantaged children. Gottlieb also observes that, at least for the crucial early grades, school may mean much *more* subjectively to the culturally-alienated child than the child of the middle class. An example is this response to an announcement that school would be closed for a teachers' meeting:

> The middle class children meet the announcement with cheers of approval— this is a holiday since this will give them an opportunity to play at home, go shopping with their mother, go on a trip, or go skating. The culturally-alienated child is not so pleased with this news for a day away from school holds little that can be considered pleasant or enjoyable.[2]

Passow (1963) points out that one of every six elementary and secondary school children attends school in the nation's sixteen largest cities. The majority of these urban areas are inhabited by lower income groups and are often labeled slum areas. The urban school most often serves economically disadvantaged students, both newcomers and established residents. Passow characterizes slum area students as often having "poor health, inadequate school motivation, malnutrition, and absence of certain learning skills" resulting in greater than normal "scholastic failure, truancy, disciplinary problems, dropouts, pupil transiency, and teacher turnover."[3]

However, Passow does not support these descriptions with data. Here we have the common stereotype of urban poor children which must be overcome if positive teacher attitudes and effective teaching are to be accomplished.

In further contrast to Passow's grim picture, the urban teacher can expect more independence in children of low income families. Unfortunately, independent behavior such as crossing streets and taking care of younger siblings is not immediately transferable to the demands of the school (Deutsch, 1962).

Nevertheless, if greater comprehension of the attitudes, values, and desires of the children in depressed areas can be meaningfully related to the classroom, the urban teacher will gain a better-than-average class in terms of attention, imagination, rapport, morale, and perhaps performance. The children in the urban classroom are eager to learn material that is compatible with their present surroundings and past experiences. However, urban children, like their suburban counterparts, are antagonistic or inattentive when confronted with alien surroundings and irrelevant applications. Their orientation to the learning environment is influenced by their past. Only by building on their experience can the urban teacher raise the sights of disadvantaged urban children to a better future.

Children who are deprived and discriminated against often bring a history of educational deficit to the classroom. Since a common practice of urban schools is to base class composition on performance, a form of de facto segregation occurs. Poor youth are clustered in remedial classes, and middle and upper class children, more familiar with the urban education scene, are grouped in average or advanced level classes. This adds to the friction of ethnic divisions, and more serious problems emerge.

When grouping on the basis of standardized achievement tests brings about intraschool de facto segregation in schools with multiracial populations, white students regard minority students as being "different" and minority students perceive themselves as being "different" since they are in special classes. The notion of "difference" centers around feelings of inferiority on the part of the disadvantaged youth and feelings of superiority on the part of their middle class peers. In other words, not only is the minority group considered different, it is often considered intellectually inferior.

Intraschool de facto segregation on the academic level leads to other forms of segregation. That is, students who attend classes together are more likely to become friends, and these friendships are apt to be carried over to cafeteria and library situations, athletic events, and school assemblies (Green, 1966). Thus, black children in integrated schools are affected negatively by any practice of de facto segregation.

Another adverse effect of intraschool de facto segregation is the reinforcement of negative self-perception in disadvantaged students. A considerable body of research indicates that good self-concepts are associated with desirable characteristics such as low anxiety (Lipsitt, 1958) and generally good adjustment, popularity, and effectiveness in group relations (Mussen and Porter, 1959). Furthermore, poor self-concepts are associated with academic underachievement. Recent research also indicates that black and Puerto Rican students develop negative self-images as a result of their experiences with the dominant society (Kvaraceus, 1965). They perceive themselves as being worthless, ineffectual and, in general, not wanted by society.

When minority students are placed in a school system that emphasizes their educational deficits, this reinforces their low self-esteem. Since teachers are aware of the fact that these students are in special classes, they may reinforce the false notion that these students are inferior intellectually. This notion may become the rationale or the excuse for classroom teachers to provide inadequate instruction for such youngsters; i.e., "they cannot profit from quality instruction." Furthermore, teachers who regard certain students as incapable of benefiting from quality instruction do not encourage them to become involved in academic programs.

Nevertheless, disadvantaged children have something in common with other children:

> The youngster who comes from a background of poverty is no less eager to learn and to discover than are other children regardless of their origin. The desire to know and to experience is a universal characteristic of all children. What happens to encourage or discourage this desire is explained by what occurs in our schools and our homes. A rigid teacher who fails to stimulate children—who fails to challenge them and to cultivate this desire for learning—will be equally effective in crushing the intellectual curiosity of both middle class and poverty-class children.[4]

Personal Values of the Urban Child

A single generalization can be made here: Urban students want meaningful material presented in the classroom. The aspirations, motivations, and self-concepts of the individual are relatively unique, but communalities are clustered about groupings of sex, age, race, ethnic group, socioeconomic status, and other points of orientation. Pressures on students of a minority race, for example, may bring about the paradox of their expressing motivation for high achievement and experiencing low performance. Green and Farquhar (1965) found this to be the case for a sizeable sample of black high school students in Detroit, but not for a comparable sample of white children.

Black children often suffer problems rare to their white colleagues. Karon (1958) points out that one-third of black families are without a male head of the family.

> Since the discipline and authority of a father are missing in the lives of the children, the process, usual in our culture, of little boys learning to grow into men by identifying with their fathers as strong figures is forestalled. Even the mother, who heads the family, is forced to neglect the children since she must earn their living.[5]

However, recent data indicate that black males are more involved in family roles today than in the past (Billingsley, 1968).

If the child's background is educationally disadvantaged, then the parent's role as the model to be admired and imitated is enhanced. Thus, the mother and father take on a powerful role in the lives of many urban black students.

What do students in the urban school want? They want training which will allow them to compete successfully in school; they want interested teachers who emphasize and reward success. For this type of child, education is meaningless without success, for ambition may be along nonacademic lines.

As already mentioned, children entering the urban school with some educational disadvantage may have low academic self-concepts. The unschooled children of Prince Edward County, however, did *not* have a significantly lower self-concept than children in a neighboring county or in a northern urban sample (Green, *et al.,* 1964). This may have been a function of the great deal of publicity and interest showered on them in the course of their difficulties. If disadvantaged children are given positive attention in urban areas, comparable results may be achieved.

On the other hand, positive occupational and educational aspirations were depressed for the unschooled children from Prince Edward County. This orientation probably was rooted in reality since employment for minorities remains a serious problem. Since chances for employment are slightly better in northern urban areas, it may be expected that the educational and occupational aspirations of urban children are higher than their rural counterparts. The author found this to be the case.

Here is one more personal value then: The student in the urban school wants a good job. Education must somehow be related to a good job before the student will regard school with sufficient seriousness.

Research Findings—Values of the Urban Child

There has been a wealth of data in the past decade or so on factors influencing the wants and values of the urban child. Taking occupational and educational aspirations as a focal value, let us expand the available facts somewhat by going directly to the data.

The thesis that social values are related to levels of aspiration and levels of achievement is supported and documented in several research studies. Hyman (1966), for example, has demonstrated that because the lower classes do not readily accept success goals nor believe in their accessibility, their social aspirations and consequent achievements are lower than those of the other classes.

These findings are corroborated by the research of Rosen (1956), who also reports a significant relationship between value orientations and educational aspirations. Rosen studied a sample of 120 white subjects ranging in age from fourteen through sixteen and selected at random from five social class strata. The sample was drawn from the male sophomores in two large public high schools in the New Haven, Connecticut, area. Achievement motivation was measured by a projective test (TAT Variant), and value orientation was determined by a direct questionnaire.

The author's hypothesis that members of various social strata differ from one another in the degree to which the achievement motive is characteristic of their members was supported by the data. Rosen found that members of the middle class tend to have considerably higher need-achievement scores than individuals in the lower social strata; that cultural factors, or values, are related to mobility; and that these values do differ from culture to culture. In this study, the sample of middle class sophomores was more achievement-oriented than the lower class sample. The differential in educational aspiration was partially a function of differences in value orientation.

Bloom, Whiteman, and Deutsch (1963) studied 292 children and their parents, including blacks and whites, who represented the lower, upper lower, and middle social classes. The children ranged from grades 1 through 5. Racial and social class were evaluated as separate factors determining social environment. The authors found that blacks had higher occupational and educational aspirations for their children than did whites and that black children themselves had significantly higher occupational aspirations than did white children among the test group.

The relationship between social status and levels of aspiration has been studied by Kahl (1953) and Sewell, Haller, and Straus (1957). The findings of these research studies support the thesis that there is a significant relationship between levels of social aspiration and social status. Kahl investigated the social influences which might explain the choices of twenty-four boys from working-class parents who had the intelligence necessary to attend college but one-half of whom chose not to do so. The latter group planned little or no education beyond high school graduation and were content with the prospect of lesser occupations that might be open to them. The sample of twenty-four boys was drawn from a larger population of 3,971 sophomore and junior boys in metropolitan Boston public schools.

The sample was studied using interview analysis in an effort to determine what social factors influenced their choices. The interviews disclosed that although there was a general way of life belonging to the common man's social class, some members were content with this style and others were not. Discontented parents tended to train their children from the earliest years to take education seriously as a means of social mobility. Only the children who had internalized these parental values were sufficiently motivated to achieve a higher goal. Almost all of the twenty-four boys tended to view the occupational system from their parents' perspective; the boy who occasionally differed had obtained his ideas from a friend, never from abstract media such as books or movies.

Sewell, Haller, and Straus tested the general hypothesis that levels of educational and occupational aspiration among young people, both male and female, are associated with the social status of their families. The authors selected data from samples of all nonrural high school seniors in public and private schools in Wisconsin during the school year 1947-48. Data on educational aspirations were taken from the responses to a series of questions on education plans after graduation. Data for occupational aspirations were taken from a questionnaire concerning their planned vocations. Social status, as measured by prestige of parental occupation, was the dependent variable, and these responses were assigned North-Hatt occupational prestige values. The students were then ranked by parental occupation in five equal categories. The control variable, measured intelligence, was treated in a similar manner, with scores taken from the Henmon-Nelson Test of Mental Ability.

They found that among females there is a significant positive relationship between level of educational aspirations and parental social status, and this relationship is independent of any correlation between intelligence and either of the other variables studied. Females from high status families chose high level occupations more frequently than did those from lower status families, but the relationship was not as consistent as the relationship between status and aspiration to attend college. Among males, high educational aspiration was characteristic of those from high status families and also those of high intelligence.

It can be seen from these studies that research has supported the thesis that there is a significant relationship between levels of social aspiration and social status.

It is believed that the manner in which a child evaluates himself and his capabilities exercises some influence on his occupational aspirations. Trent (1957) studied 202 black children, aged nine to eighteen, in Brooklyn and Manhattan. His findings indicate that social pressures, unfairness, and hostility from the larger community make it more difficult for a black youth to evaluate himself and others realistically. Self-acceptance was measured by a sentence completion test originally designed by Cruikshank. Trent found that the children who were most self-accepting expressed more positive attitudes toward both whites and blacks than did the group that was least self-accepting.

Although the data of this study do not indicate whether perception of self determines perception of others or whether the reverse holds, clinical experience indicates that a child develops an awareness of "I" before an awareness of "we" or "they." Accordingly, the data suggest that if a child does not accept himself as a person of worth or value, he may tend to perceive groups, including his own, in a derogatory and hostile fashion.[6]

The child who does not accept himself probably will not be a high achiever, nor will he aspire realistically to high level occupations because he does not perceive himself as worthwhile or deserving.

Before members of any community are able to take advantage of educational opportunities and raise their own aspirations, both educationally and occupationally, these opportunities first must be present and, second, the aspirant must be aware of their availability. Anderson (1955) studied inequalities in schooling for blacks in the South, utilizing U.S. census data for 1940 and 1950 on school grades completed, region of residence, and race. The author found that inequalities existed between different areas, between rural and urban residents, and between whites and blacks. The alleviation of such inequalities is being effected unevenly, but educational inequalities are declining on the whole. Anderson noted that more blacks than whites and more rural than urban young people do not complete the fifth grade; also, the elimination of illiteracy is progressing more rapidly in urban areas.

Amos (1960) was concerned with awareness of opportunities. He studied 64 ninth-grade girls and boys in a black high school in Virginia. He administered a questionnaire listing 75 occupations and asking three questions regarding each occupation: (1) Do you feel that a Negro, if qualified, would have an opportunity for employment in this occupation in Washington, D.C.? (2) In the United States? (3) In what quantity, few or many, do you feel that Negroes are employed in this occupation in the United States?

Amos found that girls are more aware of the occupational situation as it exists for blacks than are boys; that both sexes are more conscious of the opportunities for their race on a nationwide scale than on a local level; that both boys and girls have an unrealistic idea of the number of blacks employed within a particular occupation.

Amos' study did not attempt to present conclusions that would be applicable to the black population as a whole. However, his results indicate that if members of a community are unaware of existing occupational opportunities, their choice of vocation may be unrealistic or limited in scope. Lack of awareness within the school system of all vocational opportunities limits the choice of vocations to those accepted by members of the community. Or the school system may promote unrealistic choices for lack of knowledge regarding prerequisites.

The attitudes of the urban child toward schooling, himself, and other races and the attitudes of other people toward him are important in assessing the factors that are operative within a particular social situation.

A study of Amos (1952) sampled an equal number of blacks and whites and 75 teachers in three Flint, Michigan, schools. He studied 150 ninth-grade pupils with parents of mixed professions and occupations to determine the accuracy of the children's predictions of their teachers' attitudes toward black students. The data revealed that the white pupils predicted the attitudes of their teachers more accurately, while black students viewed the teachers' attitudes as being more prejudiced. Black students evidenced a strong feeling of rejection, and they estimated a wider distance between their own self-perceptions and what they believed their teachers thought of them.

Amos then collected data from the children of factory workers in two equated groups of blacks and whites. He found no significant differences between blacks and whites in their estimates of their teachers' attitudes. These findings indicate that at times social class can be as important as race in determining the attitudes of pupils toward teachers. Nevertheless, it is the thesis of this chapter that the urban teacher's attitude toward his student, rather than the reverse, is the more crucial factor. Rosenthal's data (1968), discussed more fully in Chapter 3, supports this point of view.

"First Aid" in the Classroom

Many school systems have professional help on call (such as school-community agents and guidance personnel), but such aid is typically reserved for the most extreme cases of disruptive behavior. Even then, help may be long in coming. Thus the urban teacher needs sound "first aid" methods for members of the class demanding immediate attention. Furthermore, the urban teacher must develop techniques for coping with disadvantaged students who often need economic as well as educational support. To do this, a teacher must develop an understanding of the members of the class and an understanding of environmental factors that produce nonacademic behavior.

First, the teacher should have a working knowledge of the background of his students. What are their points of orientation? For example, the teacher in a newly integrated urban school may be faced with hostility between racial groups based on prejudice overheard and absorbed in the home. Most important, how can their backgound be tied into the classwork? Can positive self-concepts be built and reinforced?

Next, the urban teacher must know his students. He should be familiar with their performance and their capabilities. Within the context of standardized tests of achievement and intelligence, he must keep in mind that these measures may be limited in predictive validity when used with educationally disadvantaged children (Green, 1969). He might add more noncognitive affective measures: self-concept tests, personality inventories, sociograms, and so forth.

Attention should be given to every phase of the urban child's self-expression. Each child will have some talent within which competent performance can take place. Encouragement is important. Somehow, the child must become personally involved in the classroom if any lasting success is to be realized. Encouraging discussion and continuous relating of course material to the child's own surroundings will facilitate this.

The urban teacher must also know what his students want. What are their values? As we have seen, they want their classroom time to be of some demonstrable value. The urban teacher should have at least an elementary knowledge of the psychology of personality. In the absence of a formal course, reading in this area might include A. S. Neill's *Summerhill* on the motivation of a child in the school situation and an insight into the most immediate and critical problems that urban children and their parents face.

Among the best sources of detailed information on coping with urban students are programs such as the Higher Horizons and Great Cities that have remedial projects in operation. The federal government, particularly the Department of Health, Education, and Welfare, has much important information available.

Finally, in this age of racial crisis, it is important for all teachers, both black and white, to assess their attitudes toward poor urban youth. Class and racial antagonism must be removed from the public school system if our children are to be educated effectively. The urban school is faced with the problem of educating urban youth to cope with a complex environment. The teacher in the urban community cannot avoid this challenge.

Notes

1. M. Deutsch, "The Disadvantaged Child and the Learning Process," in A. H. Passow (ed.), *Education in Depressed Areas.* (New York: Columbia University Press, 1963), p. 165.
2. D. Gottlieb, "Who Am I? Who Cares? The Challenge of Culturally Alienated Youth," p. 4.
3. A. H. Passow, *Education in Depressed Areas* (New York: Columbia University Press, 1963), p. 2.
4. Gottlieb, *op. cit.,* p. 4.
5. B. P. Karon, *The Negro Personality* (New York: Springer Publishing Co., 1958), p. 33. Reproduced by permission.
6. R. D. Trent, "The Relation Between Expressed Self-Acceptance and Expressed Attitudes Toward Negroes and Whites Among Children," *Journal of Genetic Psychology* (1957), 91, p. 30.

References

Amos, R. T. "The Accuracy of Negro and White Children's Predictions of Teachers' Attitudes Toward Negro Students," *Journal of Negro Education,* 1952, 21: 125-135.

Amos, W. E. "A Study of the Occupational Awareness of a Selected Group of Ninth Grade Negro Students," *Journal of Negro Education,* 1960, 29: 500-503.

Anderson, Charles A. "Inequalities in Schooling in the South," *American Journal of Sociology,* 1955, 60: 547-61.

Arlitt, Ada H. "The Relation of Intelligence to Age in Negro Children," *Journal of Applied Psychology,* 1922, 6: 378-384.

Billingsley, Andrew. *Black Families in White America.* Englewood Cliffs, N.J.: Prentice-Hall, 1968.

Bloom, Benjamin S. *Stability and Change in Human Characteristics.* New York: John Wiley and Sons, 1964.

Bloom, R., Whiteman, M., and Deutsch, Martin. "Race and Social Class as Separate Factors Related to Social Environment." Institute for Developmental Studies, New York Medical College, 1963.

Deutsch, Martin. "The Disadvantaged Child and the Learning Process," in A. H. Passow (ed.), *Education in Depressed Areas.* New York: Columbia University Press, 1963.

Deutsch, Martin. "The Disadvantaged Child and the Learning Process: Some Social, Psychological and Developmental Considerations." Paper presented at Ford Foundation Conference, Columbia University, July, 1962.

Deutsch, Martin. "Minority Group and Class Status as Related to Social and Personality Factors in Scholastic Achievement," *Society for Applied Anthropology, Monograph No. 2,* 1960.

Ellis, Albert and Harper, Robert A. *A Guide to Rational Living.* Englewood Cliffs, N.J.: Prentice-Hall, 1961.

Gottlieb, David. "Who Am I? Who Cares? The Challenge of Culturally Alienated Youth." Unpublished paper, Bureau of Educational Research, Michigan State University, 1964.

Green, Robert L. "After School Integration—What? Problems in Social Learning," *Personnel and Guidance Journal,* 1966, 45: 704-710.

Green, Robert L. "The Black Quest for Higher Education: An Admissions Dilemma," *Personnel and Guidance Journal,* 1969, 47:905-911.

Green, Robert L. "Intellectual Development Among Disadvantaged Youth," in H. C. Rudman and R. L. Featherstone (eds.), *Urban Schooling.* New York: Harcourt, Brace and World, 1968.

Green, Robert L., and Farquhar, William W. "Negro Academic Motivation and Scholastic Achievement," *Journal of Educational Psychology,* 1965, 56: 241-243.

Green, Robert L., Hofmann, L. J., Morse, R. J., Hayes, M. E., and Morgan, R. F. *The Educational Status of Children in a District Without Public Schools.* U.S. Office of Education Cooperative Research Project No. 2321. Washington, D.C.: U.S. Government Printing Office, 1964.

Higgins, C. and Sivers, Cathryne. "A Comparison of Stanford-Binet and Colored Raven Progressive Matrices IQ's for Children with Low Socio-Economic Status," *Journal of Consulting Psychology,* 1958, 20: 465-468.

Hunt, Joseph M. *Intelligence and Experience.* New York: Ronald Press, 1961.

Hyman, H. H. "The Value Systems of Different Classes: A Social Psychological Contribution to the Analysis of Stratification," in R. Bendix and S. M. Lipset (eds.), *Class, Status, and Power: A Reader in Social Stratification.* Glencoe, Ill.: Free Press, 1966.

Kahl, J. A. "Educational and Occupational Aspirations of 'Common Man' Boys," *Harvard Educational Review,* 1953, 23: 186-203.

Karon, Bertram P. *The Negro Personality.* New York: Springer Publishing Co., 1958.

Kennedy, W., Van De Riet, V., and White, J. *The Standardization of the 1960 Revision of the Stanford-Binet Intelligence Scale on Negro Elementary School Children in the Southeastern United States.* U.S. Office of Education Cooperative Research Project No. 954. Washington, D.C.: U.S. Government Printing Office, 1961.

Kvaraceus, W. C., Gibson, J. S., Patterson, F., Seasholes, B., and Grambs, J.D. Negro Self-Concept. New York: McGraw-Hill, 1965.

Lipsitt, L. P. "A Self-Concept Scale for Children and Its Relationship to the Children's Form of Manifest Anxiety Scale," *Child Development,* 1958, 29: 463-472.

Mussen, P. H. and Porter, L. W. "Personal Motivations and Self-Conceptions Associated with Effectiveness and Ineffectiveness in Emergent Groups," *Journal of Abnormal and Social Psychology,* 1959, 59: 23-27.

Neill, A. S. Summerhill. New York: Hart Publishing Co., 1960.

Passow, A. Harry. Education in Depressed Areas. New York: Columbia University Press, 1963.

Pittman, Joseph A. "A Study of the Occupational Awareness of a Selected Group of Ninth Grade Negro Students," *Journal of Negro Education,* 1960, 29: 500-503.

Ravitz, M. "The Role of the School in the Urban Setting," in A. H. Passow (ed.), *Education in Depressed Areas.* New York: Columbia University Press, 1963.

Report of the National Advisory Commission on Civil Disorders. U.S. Riot Commission Report; also called the Kerner Report. Washington, D.C.: U.S. Government Printing Office, 1968.

Riessman, Frank. The Culturally Deprived Child. New York: Harper and Row, 1962.

Rosen, B. C. "The Achievement Syndrome: A Psycho-Cultural Dimension of Social Stratification," *American Sociological Review,* 1956, 21: 203-211.

Rosenthal, Robert and Jacobson, Lenore. Pygmalion in the Classroom. New York: Holt, Rinehart and Winston, 1968.

Sewell, W., Haller, A., and Straus, M. A. "Social Status and Educational and Occupational Aspiration," *American Sociological Review,* 1957, 22: 67-73.

Tomlinson, Helen. "Differences Between Pre-School Negro Children and Their Older Siblings on the Stanford-Binet Scales," *Journal of Negro Education,* 1944, 12: 474-479.

Trent, R. D. "The Relation Between Expressed Self-Acceptance and Expressed Attitudes Toward Negroes and Whites Among Negro Children," *Journal of Genetic Psychology,* 1957, 91: 25-31.

Wayland, Sloan R. "Old Problems, New Faces, and New Standards," in A. H. Passow (ed.), *Education in Depressed Areas.* New York: Columbia University Press, 1963.

Young, F. and Bright, H. "Results of Testing 81 Negro Rural Juveniles with the Wechsler Intelligence Scale for Children," *Journal of Social Psychology,* 1954, 39: 219-226.

5 | INTERACTION AND TEACHING ALTERNATIVES IN DESEGREGATED CLASSROOMS

Mark A. Chesler

Dr. Mark Chesler is Project Director of the Center for Research on Utilization of Scientific Knowledge at the University of Michigan. He is also a consultant to the Ford Foundation and is involved in ongoing research on teaching methods in response to the racial crisis in the public schools.

Dr. Chesler takes a searching look at the actual and potential character of social relations among students and teachers in interracial classrooms. He notes the evidence that black students perform differently in classrooms with a majority of blacks and a majority of whites. He believes it is important to delineate the implications of interracial education on school achievement, on the development of egalitarian attitudes, on future ability to work in interracial associations, and on a more democratic way of life.

Dr. Chesler submits that school desegregation holds great potential for our society. There is a paramount need to ascertain the specific realities of desegregated classrooms and then to present these realities to people whose roles affect the situation—teachers, administrators, parents, and students.

A major framework of Dr. Chesler's chapter is provided by the criteria he proposes for success in interracial classrooms. He also discusses the problems of utilizing scientific and scholarly knowledge about racial interaction at the classroom level and retraining teachers to be more competent in interracial settings.

One of the most critical challenges facing American education in this generation is the public demand for racially integrated schooling. The United States Supreme Court's decisions of the mid-1950's declared that legal segregation of school systems on the basis of racial characteristics was unconstitutional. In the Deep South, formal and legal segregation of the schools is largely a reality, although contested by judicial and civic action. In the North, segregation of schools is as much a reality, although established and maintained more by civil custom than by legal or administrative decree. Recent studies by the

U.S. Office of Education and the U.S. Commission on Civil Rights indicate quite clearly that racial separation not only is a predominant characteristic of metropolitan school systems in the North and West, but it has been increasing over the past decade (Coleman, 1966; *Racial Isolation in the Public Schools,* 1967). Particularly in the past five years in the northern and western states, a great deal of political controversy and social activism has centered upon issues of de facto segregation, i.e., the lack of interracial school experiences for most youngsters as a function of residence, social class, or achievement.

In this chapter we seek to understand a portion of the total dilemma of quality and equality in educational experiences—the professional management of racially desegregated classrooms. Fundamentally we look beyond the debate over racial mixing or desegregation in the schools. Our major concern is to inquire into the next step: What does happen and what can happen in the classroom after desegregation occurs?

In recent years, a great deal of scholarly and public attention has been focused upon the problems of teaching and learning for "deprived" or "disadvantaged" youngsters. Until recently, most northern urban attention had been captured by Conant's proposition (1961) that we should attend primarily to raising the quality of Negro education and that this should be a greater social priority than planning for racial desegregation or integration of the schools. Thus a number of scholars have concerned themselves with education for the "deprived" of either race, and they have marshaled theoretical statements and discussed the pragmatic implications for school and classroom behavior.[1]

The report prepared by Coleman and his colleagues (1966) also indicates that the differences between largely black and largely white schools are such that we must add the category of "disadvantaged schools" to the lexicon of our urban ills. Schools with largely Negro populations seem inferior in many respects to schools with largely white populations. The age and structure of buildings, the availability of library and laboratory facilities, the curriculum alternatives, and the size of classrooms all mark the negative comparison between these schools. But the Coleman Report also points out that not all of these facilities appear to be especially relevant to academic performance; they do not explain performance differences by themselves. Of course, the potency of this finding must be diminished by the total range of available facilities studied. For instance, the fact that classroom size variations as they now exist do not correlate significantly with achievement does not mean that new and radically different classroom designs might not make quite a difference.

If facilities are not especially relevant to academic performance, then some other base must be generated for arguing that inherent educational inequality exists and for promoting school desegregation. Teacher quality does seem to be an important variable, and one that bears a stronger relationship to achievement for Negro students than for whites. The fact that Negro schools consistently are staffed by teachers with inadequate credentials and less experience is another indicator of the disadvantaged situation of these schools.

But it is even more important that the U.S. Commission on Civil Rights uses other reasons in suggesting that a national priority should be placed upon ending racial separation in schools (*Racial Isolation,* 1967). Essentially, their argument is that academic performance and social maturity suffer from the often narrow and constraining social interactions fostered by schools with homogeneous populations. This priority cuts across the delineation of social class and geography. It implies that emphasis on separate educational designs and concerns for the deprived may be quite inappropriate and that desegregated schooling should be created and intensively planned for. And it means that white youngsters are also seen as disadvantaged by the effects of school homogeneity and that they, too, stand to gain greatly from desegregation and integration.[2]

Despite recent emphases, the prior focus has meant that little attention has been concentrated upon explicitly interracial situations and that there is relatively little evidence regarding the reality of life in desegregated classrooms. Scientists and educators alike are unfamiliar with desegregated classrooms, and little help is available for the practicing teacher or principal who wishes to foster positive learning in an interracial setting. Moreover, for the politician or educator facing a potential change in the racial character of a school system, there are few studies that document whether the introduction of black students into predominantly white classrooms, or vice versa, changes the attitude of youngsters toward one another in any significant way. There are several studies documenting changes in academic performance, but few focus directly on the character or effects of social interaction. In this chapter it is my concern to review and project findings that are particularly relevant to understanding the actual and potential character of social relations among students and teachers in an interracial classroom.

Research Relevant to Interracial Classrooms

Although conclusive research on interracial classrooms and schools is limited, most of the evidence indicates that Negro youngsters do improve their achievement scores when they attend predominantly white schools. The research does not indicate clearly, however, whether this growth is due to changes in an entire school system, exposure to better teaching, contact with generally improved educational facilities and materials, or the effects of new definitions of self and others. The Coleman Report, for example, stresses the effects of social interaction and new reference associations as follows:

> The higher achievement of all racial and ethnic groups in schools with greater proportions of white students is largely, perhaps wholly, related to effects associated with the student body's educational background and aspirations. This means that the apparent beneficial effect of a student body with a high proportion of white students comes not from racial composition per se, but from the better educational background and higher educational aspirations that are, on the average, found among white students.[3]

The position expressed here stresses the social class level and collective aspirations of the student body as an important variable that sets peer system norms. But in addition to environmental norms or standards, school systems that have promoted programs of racial desegregation sometimes have combined them with massive efforts of across-the-board improvement in school facilities, curriculum, teaching, and classroom size. Thus it becomes quite difficult to pinpoint the causal factors.

But whatever the clarity of research on causal factors, the evidence seems clear that Negro students perform differently in largely Negro and largely white classrooms. Several studies examine longitudinally the effects of Negro students changing from largely Negro to largely white schools. Hansen (1960), Stallings (1959), and Lockwood (1966) report from such widely divergent areas as Washington, Louisville, and Syracuse that Negro students' performance and achievement scores rose in desegregated situations. But other research suggests that merely placing black students in contact with whites in northern classrooms may not be the best way to improve performance. Many intraclassroom variables must be considered in understanding or manipulating the learning environment in interracial situations.

Katzenmeyer, for instance, suggests that a Negro student's class performance depends upon "a communality of experience with white pupils, the adequacy of his performance having increased as the degree of social interaction increased."[4] Lockwood points out, in fact, that there is a period of a year or more in which there may be no increase or even a decrease in achievement before performance levels rise. The initial drop may be explained partly by the emotional impact of a new interracial situation on Negroes; it is probable that the initial requirement of dealing with white peers and authority figures is quite threatening. Katz's studies (1964) also demonstrate that the heightened level of threat inherent in a new interracial situation is likely to affect the intellectual performance of students.

A number of studies document empirically the important effects of classroom peer group relations on a student's self-esteem, his attitudes toward school, and the utilization of his academic potential (Schmuck, et al., 1963; Schmuck, 1963). Pupils who perceive that their peers reject them and that their peers have different attitudes utilize their potentials less effectively in class. The fear of peer rejection may constrain some students from expressing themselves in class or from confronting or competing effectively with classmates. Where social interaction is so fraught with danger or constraint that students cannot support one another's learning efforts, everyone in class may be deprived of key educational resources. The influence of such peer-related variables is likely to be quite relevant in interracial classrooms and can be expected to have effects upon performance. A more difficult and varied curriculum, different school and peer group norms, and the strangeness of a new environment in a new part of town may be part of the interracial situation. But fears of rejection, isolation, hostility, or competition from white students and teachers must also enter the picture. In the face of such fears, many Negro students will avoid or deliberately fail to compete. Similarly, fears and anxieties about Negroes and unresolved personal feelings may cripple the reactions of white youngsters.

School achievement is not the only concern of educators, however, and it cannot be the only concern of parents, scholars, or citizens. They must be concerned with the implications of interracial education for a democratic way of life, for the development of egalitarian attitudes, and for the students' future ability to work in interracial associations. Segregated learning situations, or negative experiences in desegregated situations, do not contribute to the development of interracial associations of a positive and lasting character. Several studies reported by the U.S. Commission on Civil Rights indicate the importance of desegregated schooling in interracial friendships, in decisions by white and Negro parents to send their youngsters to desegregated schools, and in the Negro's trust in whites (*Racial Isolation*, 1967). In this context, and if these outcomes are indeed among the prized products of our educational process, there is substantial support for our speculation that white students may be as deprived as black students by growing up in a uniracial, uniclass educational system. The Coleman Report, for instance, indicates that "White students who first attended integrated schools early in their school career are (most) likely to value their association with Negro students."[5] Moreover:

> Whites who attended desegregated schools expressed greater willingness to reside in an interracial neighborhood, to have their children attend desegregated schools, and to have Negro friends. They consistently were more favorable toward the elimination of discrimination in employment against Negroes.[6]

The positive effects of desegregated schooling happen neither automatically nor universally. Although it is clear from recent reports that racial mixing does not necessarily create chaos and poor learning, neither does it necessarily create brotherhood, good learning, or long term racial harmony. Some data relevant to this issue has been collected from Negro students who desegregated previously all-white schools in the Deep South (Chesler and Segal, 1968). Several hundred interviews with Negro high school students indicate that almost half the group encountered considerable resentment and hostility from their new white peers when they entered new schools. These reactions ranged from general unfriendliness and teasing to name-calling and physical violence. Another third of the desegregators experienced both positive and negative reactions or relatively neutral behavior such as indifference and avoidance. Only 15 percent of the desegregators felt they were met by peer reactions of welcome, friendship, or courteous concern. With these initial reactions as a baseline, it is easy to understand how prolonged social interaction in such an environment would fail to improve the quality of relationships between white and Negro students.

After a year of attendance at a desegregated southern school, many of these Negro students reported that they had not gained any considerable amount of faith and rapport with their white classmates. In one series of questions the desegregators were asked whether their attitudes toward their white peers had changed and, essentially, whether they trusted them more or less. Some exemplary quotations describe their responses:

> I trust them more because while we were in school they wouldn't tell the teacher what I did.

> I trust them more, because I know them better, most of the time they talk behind your back they don't mean it, they're only trying to scare you.

> It makes me feel bad because you can work side by side with them but when you come to school they act as if they didn't know you. I trust them less, I feel that they don't mean what they say. They think Negroes are easily fooled, so they always try to play you for a fool.

> Trust less, whatever you say, they try to get information from you to take back to the other white people.[7]

Overall, 30 percent of the Negro desegregators stated that their ideas about white people had changed as a result of the past year's experience. Some youngsters became more trusting but as many developed less trust in whites. Moreover, over 60 percent of the students, most of whom entered with a distrustful attitude, did not feel they had changed in either direction. Many of the youngsters who did not change may not have had enough prolonged interaction to really affect their views. The number of Negroes in the southern white classrooms was often so small that they could easily be completely rejected or ignored.[8]

Since many Americans might expect such conditions to exist in the Deep South, it is perhaps more disturbing to examine the feelings of northern youngsters. Lombardi (1963) reports one study in which classroom contact with Negroes did not change the attitudes of white high school students toward Negroes. Webster (1961) presents a more dismal picture, reporting from his research that unguided contact resulted in some white students being less friendly and accepting toward Negroes than before desegregation. Some indications of the negative lessons that have been learned from such interaction are reflected in these remarks made by white junior high school girls regarding the Negroes who recently desegregated their school.

> The colored boys don't think the colored girls are good enough for them so they get after the white girls, and this makes the colored girls mad.

> The reason why they hang around white girls is they just wanta. . . it makes them feel big. You can tell it's not because they like you.

> If you get one of them alone they're scared. I tried to act mean to her because she was alone. If they're in groups they'll kill you, they really will.

> They could be accepted if they act nice.

> I think they're trying to get on an equal level with us but I think they'd succeed if they'd just be nice. They're being so mean everyone hates them. They're always starting riots and everything like that.

> I feel sorry for them because they want to be accepted and they're doing it by force, the wrong way. . . . There are two I know who aren't so mean, and they are accepted.

> I mean we've tried to be nice. . . . I should've known better than to be nice.[9]

Some of the incidents and feelings noted in these youngsters' reports are common among all adolescents. Painful fears of rejection, awkward explorations of boy-girl relations, clique formations and rivalry, and tentative expressions of aggression represent typical high school and junior high school concerns. But clearly, other reactions are racially motivated, and even typical adolescent concerns can take on a new and dangerous meaning when they occur between youngsters of different races. This may result from the youngsters' inexperience in interracial situations and from society's ambivalence about the promises and dangers of such situations.

Centuries of cultural rejection and isolation prepare most young Negroes to be fearful and hostile of interaction with whites. Centuries of isolation and a sense of cultural superiority prepare most young whites to be both cautious and arrogant about interaction with Negroes. Contemporary cultural commitments and feelings of attraction and concern, of fear and guilt, work together to produce tremendous ambivalence and hesitance about personal or societal relationships that are interracial. This societal ambivalence is reflected in the relative inability of youngsters to accept differences as legitimate, in the fear of interracial chaos and conflict inflamed by the press, in their inability to understand our society's racial history and contemporary confusion, in the pressure of parents to protect and segregate their children, and in the students' inability to probe surely into the roots and symptoms of their own feelings about race.

These reactions are by no means idiosyncratic or unusual; apparently they lie beneath the surface in most schools that have been desegregated recently. Sometimes they are expressed openly; more often they are suppressed in ways that stifle classroom interaction, corrode individual growth and openness, and occasionally burst forth in bizarre confrontations or incidents. It seems reasonable to assume that schools and communities that have been desegregated for a long time have made adjustments and adaptations that at least permit people to work together. This does not mean that relations are necessarily positive and productive, but they are not as explosive or tense as in newly desegregated schools. But even barely satisfactory circumstances do not exist in most of our urban and suburban communities. We have just begun to desegregate large numbers of schools and school systems, and thus we must be prepared to face reactions and problems such as the ones described here.

All these forces and phenomena affect teachers and students and predispose white and Negro interactions in the classroom to negative feelings and a sense of failure. It is not our position that such negativism and failure is inevitable. On the contrary, we believe there is great promise for the youngsters, the educational profession, and our society in the potential for successful integration that exists in the schools. But to attain positive outcomes in the face of personal and cultural barriers will require great skill and energy on the part of the teacher or educator.

One of the major barriers to the exertion of positive energy is that many American educators are unwilling to accept the real difficulties along with the very real potentials. Others are willing to accept general research propositions, but they cannot specify the necessary interventions clearly enough to establish creative and effective policy. How does one go about implementing or operationalizing changes in educational systems that can take account of what is reported here? There is a paramount need to ascertain the specific reality of desegregated classrooms and then to present this reality to those embedded in roles affecting the situation—teachers, administrators, parents, and students. A confrontation with reality alone will not create change in people or institutions, but it is an important prerequisite for understanding the issues and the goals toward which they may direct their behavior.

Educators and parents often operate separately and without clear goals about educating youngsters. For some, the principal goal—although unspoken—may be to keep youngsters in school and to keep order in the classroom. For others, the contemporary curriculum establishes procedures for action that substitute gimmickry and busywork for clear thinking about goals. But the most common situation is for well-intentioned professionals to establish private goals for the conduct of their own autonomous work that are not shared with colleagues and citizens. One result is that different elements of concerned populations may work against one another, denying everyone the benefit of meaningful confrontation and collaboration. These patterns are especially dangerous in areas of instruction and learning where educators must deal explicitly with attitudes, values, and social mores. Attitudes and values regarding racial relations usually are considered to be sensitive and private matters and thus particularly difficult areas in which to generate professional sharing and interinstitutional cooperation. If teachers are without clear educational goals, without plans for school-community collaboration, and without freedom from the customs and values of a racially separate culture, they are hard put to help the students in their classrooms deal positively with interracial contact.

These data and experiences demonstrate why skilled teachers and agents for educational change must alter the classroom and the school so that white and black youngsters are able to collaborate effectively. The failure of students to relate successfully in interracial school situations reinforces the gloomy predictions regarding race relations made by many persons in our society. It is imperative that desegregated classrooms become successful learning situations; then they may provide a base of experience from which youngsters and adults can confront the racial ignorance and myths developed in our culture.

Criteria for Success in an Interracial Classroom

What would a successful interracial learning situation consist of? What criteria can be suggested as signs of positive student interaction and successful teacher management? The literature is sparse in this area, and we have no firm notion of definite criteria. However, it is important to share and test ideas in this area as a step toward clarity and planning for change.

In a number of ways, the interracial classroom is like any other classroom: youngsters relate with one another and with the teacher; youngsters are either positively or negatively motivated to perform academic tasks with vigor and delight; youngsters define their work and school relations partly in terms of their self-image and sense of esteem. Although these typical dimensions of learners and the learning environment may be helpful as a starting point, it is well to ask what dimensions may be highlighted or distorted in an interracial setting. For instance, student-peer relations and student-teacher interaction probably become crucial where extraclassroom norms do not support or encourage friendly association. By the same token, there are probably greater and more sensitive barriers to successful interaction when the parties are of different racial groups. Given the orientations and concerns expressed earlier, it is possible to describe tentative criteria for success which need to be tested in the classroom:

1. The academic performance of all students increases without relevance to their race.
2. Negro and white students are utilizing their abilities effectively and in relatively equivalent degrees.

$$\frac{\text{performance}}{\text{potential}} \text{ or } \frac{\text{achievement}}{\text{ability}} = \text{utilization}$$

3. Negro and white students alike see differences between students as legitimate and valued.
4. Students understand, as much as is possible at each developmental level, the causes of some of these differences.
5. There is a substantial number of friendship choices extending across racial lines in the class.

6. Negro and white students interact positively with one another outside of the classroom—in the lunchroom, halls, schoolyard, or neighborhood.
7. When subgroup norms occur in the classroom, they are not associated with racial groupings but with other student characteristics.
8. Negro and white students do not fear each other any more than they fear members of their own race.
9. Negro and white students trust one another as much as they trust members of their own race.
10. Negro and white students can take the role of a student of the other race accurately and have perceptions of each other that are congruent with reality.
11. Negro and white students like and respect the teachers in equivalent degrees.
12. Negro and white students feel the teacher is fair to students of both races.

The first two criteria focus directly upon patterns of academic achievement and performance. If student-student relations, student-teacher relations, and the character of the curriculum are sufficiently compatible, the performance of black or white youngsters should not be inhibited by the racial composition of the classroom itself. As students attempt to improve their academic skills and performance through the year, there should be relatively equivalent growth for Negro and white students. Where individual differences exist, they of course will be reflected in performance, but it is the creation and maintenance of group and subgroup differences that is at stake here. Groups of Negroes and groups of whites per se should not show significant differences in growth if racial barriers are overcome in the classroom.

The full utilization of a student's abilities involves the notion that he lives up to, or actualizes, his potential.[10] This concept can be operationalized in many ways, but essentially it requires that someone rate the abilities or potentials of the students and their achievement or performance. When rankings on these two dimensions are compared, the low ability-high achievers will be the greatest utilizers and the high ability-low achievers will be the lowest utilizers. For our purposes, it does not matter what particular measures of potential or performance are used; it is the pattern of utilization that is critical. We know that many reasons may account for high or low utilization, but a pattern of racial difference on this dimension would indicate the operation of forces in the classroom that maintain or promote invidious racial distinctions and inequalities.

One outstanding characteristic of our contemporary educational system is a general lack of attention to the phenomena of individual differences in the classroom. Some educators have expressed concern that teachers be cognizant of this situation and tailor curricula and teaching methods to varied student needs. But teaching individual differences as curriculum content—with student identification and understanding of these differences—is an almost neglected possibility. One positive outcome of an interracial situation should be greater student recognition of the multiple differences among peers. This means going far beyond racial differences. Further, these differences in style, personality, talent, bearing, and character should be prized, not depreciated or merely tolerated. Part of the process of recognizing and cherishing individual and group differences requires an understanding of the meanings, causes, and consequences of these differences for everyone involved. Such a mature and creative perspective on plural differences among peers should be a prized characteristic or outcome of a successful interracial learning situation.

Social interaction among students in an interracial classroom is a major concern that has received little concerted attention. The Coleman Report examined cross-racial friendship choices as one dimension of social interaction; sociometric studies can be made relative to the formal environs of the school or including extraschool situations as well. Playground and neighborhood play patterns, family or home visits, and church and other socially organized meetings represent examples of the wider context of school-related friendship networks that can be examined and encouraged. It is important to recognize that the fifth and sixth criteria are concerned with more than mere association or contact; it is the quality of such relations that help distinguish a desegregated school or class from one characterized as integrated.

Youngsters often organize themselves into overt or covert groupings based not only upon liking patterns but also based on attitudes toward school, toward peers or the teacher, or toward the material being taught. Such subgroup organization can be vital and fruitful, and the social norms developed in such groups can provide meaningful perspectives on the nature of the classroom. In a classroom where substantial open communication and interaction occurs among black and white students, we can expect that members of both races would be found among various subgroups. If the major basis for different group memberships or normative postures is racial, then the racial cleavages are evidently too great to be bridged by the typical and more generic concerns of all youngsters in American classrooms. To the extent that groups with different norms are made up of members of different races, we know that racial membership does not dominate normative posture in the classroom. The situation of overlapping or interlocking group membership is more likely to reflect an integrated classroom with substantial racial interaction.[11]

If the character of racial interaction in the classroom is generally positive, youngsters of different races should not be particularly fearful of one another and should be developing mutual trust. The existence of some degree of fear and distrust is a common human situation, one that is not limited to adolescence or to racial feelings. Since some interpersonal distrust or anxiety is present in almost any classroom, our criteria aim at reducing fear to its natural interpersonal state, not to some idyllic condition. Of course, we would hope that students can reduce general *intraracial* fear as well, but such goals are beyond our particular interest here in *interracial* peer relations. When the levels of a student's fear and trust in people of another race are generally equivalent to those levels of comfort and trust he has in persons of his own race, we have approached success in interracial schooling. No doubt we may still be dissatisfied with the general levels of fear and trust that exist for any single student or that pervade relations among youngsters or adults of any race.

One of the major problems reported in Negro-white relations is the way that Negroes are invisible to whites (Ellison, 1952). Seldom reported, but probably just as common, is the invisibility of whites to Negroes. In a culture where most of the rules are made and observed by white middle class majorities, any minority quickly learns to understand and adjust to the norms of the larger group; but the majority seldom makes such adjustments to a minority's subcultural norms. When majority whites are unable to "see" Negroes, it means they cannot get beyond group stereotypes to understand and relate effectively and intimately to the unique qualities of individual persons. Further it means that they are reluctant to recognize and admit to the cultural and economic conditions of life pervasive among American Negroes and the effects of these conditions upon personality and social role behavior (Harrington, 1962). One way of assessing the success of inter-racial classrooms is to gauge the extent to which students of both races are able to overcome the problems of mutual invisibility. An ability to take the role of the other person, in general and in particu-lar, is seen by many scholars as an indication of the degree and inten-sity of social interaction that they experience with one another (Mead, 1934; Chesler and Fox, 1966). The more black and white students can take the role of the other—in acting, as alter egos in role playing sessions, or through other means of demonstrative empathy—the more intimate and successful we can judge their social interaction to be.

The final criteria for assessing racial interaction in the classroom involve the student's view of the teacher. Of course we would like to improve American education so that more teachers are likeable, re-spectable, and fair and so that they are seen as such by their students. Certainly many teachers do not possess these qualities, and others who do may not be seen in that way by their students. Within the partic-ular context of interracial relations, however, we are concerned that no one group of youngsters should feel especially mistreated or de-valued by the teacher. Different students will feel differently about their teachers, but we would hope that these differences are not identical with racial lines.

These are certainly not the only criteria for creating a successful interracial learning situation. But together with the research on de-segregated classrooms, they do provide a starting point. From here we shall proceed to the role of the teacher as the manager of desegre-gated classroom situations and as a potential facilitator or creator of positive interracial interaction and learning.

Teacher Behavior in the Interracial Classroom

The research and related literature reviewed here clearly implies that the teacher has major responsibility for managing and affecting the character of racial interaction in his class. However, it is not clear what kinds of educational strategies and tactics are most effective in improving the quality of learning in desegregated classrooms. This is a very complex need, and as yet the vast body of scientific and educa-tional resources has not been directly applied to it.

The relative lack of scientific expertise in this area does not mean that desegregated classrooms are not being taught and that creative efforts are not being made. Teachers are constantly developing new procedures for dealing with classroom problems and are revising these procedures to make them more effective. If classroom teachers did not vary and attempt to improve their techniques constantly, they could not adapt effectively to the changing needs and behavior of their students. Experience in the study of classroom innovations indicates that many excellent new teaching designs come from creative teachers as well as from educational researchers and social scientists (Chesler and Barakat, 1967; Fox and Lippitt, 1967). Moreover, practitioner-initiated teaching designs may be more applicable to the classroom and more acceptable to peers than designs initiated by administrative hierarchies or external consultants. Scientists and educational practitioners interested in improving classroom instruction might begin by retrieving the accomplishments of creative teachers and then submitting these experimental methods to rigorous peer and scholarly inquiry.

From this perspective of potential resources existing within scientific and school settings, let us examine what educational researchers or practitioners report about the management of racial relations in the classroom.

As we have suggested earlier, many of the problems and potential strategies of interracial instruction are similar to problems of high quality educational management in any learning situation. Some particular dynamics are reflected and generated by the interracial population itself, but in many ways this uniqueness merely overlays more generic self, peer, and authority relations present in any classroom. This is not to say the interracial classroom is not different; it is different if only because it has been so rare in our society. However, one of the key management differences lies not in the youngsters and the classroom; it lies in the mind of the teacher who experiences this classroom through eyes and ears tuned by his own life in a racially separate and fearful culture.

In our attempt to understand the implications of scientific knowledge for interracial instruction, we will draw generalizations from other studies on teaching styles and strategies that may not have focused explicitly on interracial environments. While doing this we will try to be attentive to the particular nuances and modifications relevant to an interracial focus.

A number of recent reports make it quite clear that some classroom teachers are dealing positively with desegregated situations and
many more want to manage their classrooms in more successful and
effective ways. However, even teachers who are trying to deal with
the situation constructively may or may not be contributing to positive outcomes, depending upon what they are doing, how they are doing it, and how students are responding to it. The fact that teachers
are trying out new ideas, that they are moving in a direction that
seems impressive, does not mean that we can accept the quality or effects of these practices as positive. Many teachers are using new ideas
that in no way contribute to positive growth in the classroom. It is
precisely this potential for negative outcome with positive intent—as
well as the obvious dangers of stagnant or laissez-faire thinking—that
precipitates my concern for intensive training of teachers and careful
evaluation of instructional designs for interracial classrooms.

But there are also classroom teachers who are inhibited or even
paralyzed by the prospect of black and white youngsters being together, by the potential for cultural conflict, by the threat of chaos in
the classroom. Furthermore, some teachers are so resistant to the
whole idea of interracial education that they are preventing white and
Negro youngsters from learning together and subverting the attempt to
make desegregated classroom experiences successful.

The few teachers who are openly resistant to school desegregation may deliberately contribute to a negative experience in interpersonal and intergroup relations in the classroom. Teachers who are
inhibited or paralyzed by their own fears and ambivalence also may
contribute to negative student experience by ignoring or suppressing
vital issues in the classroom or by managing them ineffectively. In a
recent study of the responses of southern teachers to school desegregation, most white teachers indicated that they were quite nervous on
the first day of desegregated classes (Chesler and Segal, 1967). For
some, this anxiety was a function of their own inexperience with
Negroes; it was also connected to their concern that no major incident should erupt in their classroom. For others, it was ambivalence and confusion as to whether they should pay any special
attention to the new students or to the facts of racial mixture. When
teachers suffer from resistance, confusion, or hesitancy, the youngsters perceive these cues and are likely to become more tense and
cautious as well.

Some examples of pupil perceptions of teacher behavior reflect these issues quite openly. We have already noted the fear and anxiety many southern Negro students feel when entering white schools; under such conditions hesitant teachers are often seen as uncommitted or antagonistic.

They treated us just like we were special. . .nice. . .but it didn't last long.

[When] you want to ask or talk to a white teacher like a friend, you are afraid because you don't think she will understand.

My history teacher doesn't seem to know how to pronounce the word Negro.

The children would tease me and she would get up and go out to let them carry on.

Our history teacher, in class, she would never call on Negroes, she would give us our assignments last.[12]

Other examples are provided by the comments of northern white girls in junior high school:

The teachers are scared to do anything.

These teachers don't do a thing, they walk right past fights.

We should have colored teachers and they should have all the colored kids . . .that way they could handle them.[13]

When students have such perceptions of their teachers, they are less likely to make positive overtures and to create friendships across racial lines. The teacher who can neither model nor manipulate effective interracial relations, whether due to his own attitudes or skill deficiencies, cannot provide leadership for students who are similarly resistant or unskilled. In this regard it is clear how teachers' reactions, as expressed in classroom behavior, may help shape the quality of peer relationships.

In addition to managing classroom social relations, the teacher engages in direct interpersonal relations with his students. As role model, curriculum organizer, academic presentor, representative of the larger culture and powerful adult, the teacher carries on an important interaction with all his students. This interaction is especially crucial when it occurs between a white teacher and a Negro student. For just as Negro youngsters in a desegregated classroom have to learn to deal with white peers, they also must adjust to the intimate presence of a white authority.

In all of these relations and roles a teacher's values, attitudes, perceptions and assumptions about students of either race influence his behavior. Recent research suggests that some teachers fail in interracial situations precisely because of their attitudes. Niemeyer, for instance, argues that "the chief cause of the low achievement of the children of alienated groups is the fact that too many teachers and principals honestly believe that these children are educable only to an extremely limited extent."[14] The Haryou Report, too, concludes that teachers in Harlem schools have a "low opinion of the children's learning ability."[15] Clearly, these expectations partially determine the behavior of teachers and the way they treat their students.

Recent research points out the degree to which a teacher's expectations of student performance are present in his behavior and thus affect his eventual achievement. There are two major channels for this confirmation. In one pattern the teacher may establish expectations and never waver in their prosecution, regardless of any evidence the student may produce. A second pattern occurs when youngsters interpret the teacher's low estimate of their ability from various cues and thus are not motivated to exceed these expectations in their performance. When a teacher responds to a youngster in a way that implies the student has little ability, the student is likely to accept that evaluation and thus decrease his motivation for achievement. Low achievement then reinforces the teacher's initial presumption, encouraging similar behavior on the student's part. Thus student and teacher may collude in establishing a self-fulfilling cycle of low expectation, failure, and rejection.

Some researchers note that teachers may behave differently toward white and black children in class (Bloom, *et al.*, 1965). In their own social behavior, in their limits on peer activity, and in their use of authority, teachers may consciously or unconsciously single out Negro youngsters in negative or disapproving ways. Usually differential behavior is not hidden from youngsters in the classroom. The result is not only damage to a child's ego, or reconfirmation of an already negative self-view, but indirect license to the peer group. Thus informal peer norms of distance and rejection may arise in part because of the teacher's own discomfort or ineffectiveness in the interracial classroom.

Ideological Alternatives in the Classroom

There are a variety of ways in which these perspectives can be realized in the goals and methods of classroom teachers. Here I propose to review some of the ideological or strategic alternatives that are practiced in desegregated schools. Teachers who are concerned about race relations and education may have two essentially different goals. Although these goals are distinct and separate, they are by no means mutually exclusive. One goal is the creation of harmonious and constructive racial relations in the classroom. Examples of programs or strategies designed to accomplish this goal directly might include a course in social problems, a unit on individual and group differences, several sessions on the examination of students' own racial views, or a unit on race relations. A second possible goal focuses on better student learning in a classroom that just happens to be racially mixed. Here no special attention is paid to the interracial composition of the class, and personal and interpersonal problems are treated as they would be in any classroom. Information about racial relations and racial dynamics is utilized not to promote student learning about racial matters directly, but rather to foster a climate that would more adequately support academic learning.

In both contexts, it is critical to determine what special problems arise in the teaching of any particular subject in a desegregated classroom. In English, does one have to read Langston Hughes and LeRoi Jones as well as Walt Whitman, Arthur Miller and Edgar Allen Poe? In Social Studies, how much attention needs to be paid to the cultural history of the Negro, to the Negro's role in American history, or to the historic relationship between white and black Americans? In Economics, how much emphasis must be placed upon the racial aspects of poverty and ghetto life? What special curriculum presentation or organizational efforts are necessary and useful in promoting effective learning in an interracial classroom? At this time in our nation's life, we do not have sufficient experience or evaluation with which to answer such questions with any degree of confidence.

Almost regardless of these goals, there seem to be four basic ways that teachers handle differences among youngsters in the classroom. Perhaps the most common is what we might call the *naturalistic* approach. In this case the teacher feels differences will take care of themselves, and what he essentially has to do is to treat all children alike and ignore any differences. We have heard this orientation expressed by teachers who feel that they do not need to pay any special attention to a minority group of black youngsters in a white classroom: "I treat them just as I treat everyone else." But the history of our country is very clear in its demonstration that white people and Negro people do not treat each other alike. What is "natural" in our culture is racial separation; it would seem unreal and irresponsible to deny the fear and hostility that cultural "naturalness" has provided. To let nature take its course is to give free rein to existing patterns of separatism and racial distance. Youngsters bring these predispositions and patterns into the classroom and, if permitted, will seek to validate and maintain such teachings. Both Negro and white youngsters are wary about being in interracial classes, and some are openly resistant. This is the great cultural tide that a creative teacher or committed parent must teach children to swim against. Under these circumstances, it makes little sense to treat the interracial class as if it had no special problems.

A second posture towards the interracial classroom is the *moralistic* approach: in this case the teacher goes out of her way to preach and teach tolerance as a positive virtue. In a classroom committed to this approach everybody reads the Declaration of Independence, the Emancipation Proclamation, and the American Constitution. When every student has thoroughly memorized or understood these basic and lofty principles, then all agree that it is important to be tolerant and patient with people who are different from ourselves. It is my view that in practice this style often teaches the majority paternalism and sympathy more than it teaches true tolerance. Moreover, what tolerance is learned is acquired at the level of verbal ideology or conformity. Students are not required to test specific applications of such broad value positions; thus they can continue to seek the safety of abstract generalizations. This approach does not require the exploration of value conflicts or the resolution of dilemmas; i.e., whether there are limits to the differences a person can and should tolerate if his basic values are threatened. Moreover, it does not require the examination or exploration of behavioral change, and thus it does not permit or encourage students to actually deal with differences. Often the inquiry is considered complete when students and teachers announce that they do think that differences are permissible and can be tolerated.

The third approach is a more direct but equally abstract treatment in which we actually *teach about differences*. Students may read books or other materials about Eskimos and Africans, about poor people and rich people, about old people and young people, about political heroes and dissenters, or about groups with contrasting styles of life and cultural expression. Teachers who follow this approach suggest that youngsters of different ethnic background bring into the class some of their characteristic food, clothing, songs, and stories. Another strategy is to have students read books that show people in a variety of interracial and intercultural associations. The teacher's hope is to teach social, scientific, and biological facts of life so that students will understand and appreciate how people are different. The logical presupposition here is that when students understand the reasons differences exist, they will accept and appreciate them.

But if mere exposure to differences is not followed by an explanation of their import or origins, varied customs, dress or foods are seen as odd and they are not truly valued or integrated into a conceptual framework of cultural pluralism. In this vein, there is no evidence that greater exposure or even understanding of such differences necessarily leads to positive appreciation. Students may know a lot of facts about the genetic and moral similarity between themselves and people who are racially or economically different, but it is questionable whether such knowledge is very useful in helping people overcome the cultural isolation that characterizes our lives. People have attitudes and values that condition how they interpret facts or events and that lead to specific behaviors or life choices. Knowing such facts does not necessarily force the student to confront the interpretations made from them and the real reasons why various interpretations and feelings occur.

Finally, there is the *direct and realistic* approach: in this case the teacher attempts to highlight or recreate in the classroom portions of the reality that exists in the outside world. If racial separateness and fear exist in American society, then they must also exist in some form in the classroom. The direct exploration of this reality, painful as it may be, seems to be one very persuasive way to examine differences truthfully and effectively. Bringing community leaders of different stripes into the classroom, holding memorial services in school for Malcolm X or Martin Luther King, Jr., and inspecting black or white ghettos or riot sites are examples of this approach. Other examples may utilize classroom simulations of reality, such as the role playing of interracial threat and anxiety, exclusion and rejection, guilt and despair. It is hoped that with such direct experience, and with concrete practice in generating and testing alternatives, students can achieve new understandings and skills in living with people different from themselves.

Examples of Teaching Strategies

Thus far, this discussion of the alternatives open to classroom teachers has been fairly abstract. To illustrate more fully some of the variables and procedures suggested here, we include several brief but concrete examples of provocative classroom practices. A series of direct interracial confrontations, using student-generated materials, has been attempted by the author in his own college classroom. Students were asked to write as honestly as they could about their attitudes and feelings regarding persons of another race. University of Michigan white students and Tuskegee Institute Negro students explored and reported their feelings, and these reports were compiled and shared with others (Chesler, 1966). Students then used these essays as jumping-off places from which they could engage in discussion of their own personal and interpersonal reactions. Here are excerpts from a few of the essays written by white students:

> Today I try to compensate for others' discrimination by going out of my way to be nice to them. I actually don't label them as "Negroes" or "them" but I have to in this report. Sometimes I overcompensate and make it obvious that I am putting myself out to be *too* friendly and it appears *fake.*

> I am not an active antagonist of the race, nor do I support it. To me, deserving is a prerequisite of receiving. I will give no one my approval or regard without some basis. I see no reason for respecting a race that thinks deserving is desiring. If they want equal rights and privileges, they should be willing to contribute equally to our society—scientifically, socially, economically, politically, and individually.

This tolerance falls short of being absolute. I will not date nor would I ever consider marrying a Negro. I don't like to admit this and I do have friends who do believe in interracial dating and marriage or do it themselves and as far as they are concerned, I approve. I also find myself being nice to some Negroes just because they are Negroes. I hate myself for doing this but I can't stop myself. This whole "other" side of my attitude in most cases would seem to rise out of my middle class, northeastern, segregated upbringing.

I think the right things and my commitment is strong. I make an effort to understand and be aware of the problems. I have a desire to see a world where all men are equal. My sympathetic reactions are honest and sincere. Of this I have no doubt and for this I feel at least a twinge of virtue. But these aspects of myself make it all the more difficult to face another, and quite inconsistent, side. This is the side that says Negroes are different from me. They are janitors and maids and often stupid. They are a persecuted race and therefore I must treat them with extra patience and kindness.

The black students expressed some of their feelings and views:

Today, even when I know the reason why I never had an ice cream soda at the drugstore, I am not prejudiced, and haven't formed any stereotype. How could I have when I have never experienced Jim Crow even in the heart of Dixie. I was brought up thinking that I didn't do certain things simply for the reason that I didn't want to. My parents were conformists. They conformed, not because they had the slightest inkling that they were inferior, but because it was the easy way out. Plus they went to extreme lengths to see to it that their children never thought they were inferior.

I don't hate. I have no reason to. I have only sympathy and understanding and sometimes disgust. How can one help but to think that he is superior and that another is inferior if that is all that he has heard or seen in his entire life. For this I blame the parents. What disgusts me is this action of the parents, plus the fact that once a person is able to think intelligently for himself and intelligent he is supposed to be, why can't he realize their fallacy and detach himself from them. I feel sorry for the person who is weak and has so little confidence in himself that the only way he can feel important is to belittle someone else.

I recall a middle age white woman who worked in the office. I think she really hated me, not because I was black, but because I represented a threat. I could read, write, calculate menus, and do everything she couldn't. To compensate for this, she would always have something sarcastic to say. If that did not work, she would then praise the Negro as a whole. Example: "I am so proud of 'you' people," or "Sarah Vaughn sure sings well," or "I like Nat Cole." These remarks were cited daily.

The white man has been able to change his laws but has been unable to change the most important thing, his heart. I pity the white liberal who is so controlled by his history that he cannot help his condescending attitude toward the Negro. Most of all, I pity the white man because he will be forever placed on the defensive by some Negroes who are using and will use him as a crutch for all of their misfortunes.[16]

Evident in these self-reports are the fundamental ambivalence and guilt reported by white youngsters and the deep resentment expressed by Negroes. In the discussions, one of our major concerns was to recognize and to accept the legitimacy of such feelings and to inquire into the behavioral effects of these views, as well as their personal, familial, and cultural roots. Blame and recrimination, or the threat thereof, consistently seemed to drive honest expression underground, to be harbored deeply and supplanted superficially by expressions of tolerance and virtue. Acceptance of their views permitted the students to share them with peers and then to discuss, work with, and perhaps change them in the light of new evidence or interaction. Students reported that their understanding of how other collegians of both races felt about intimate racial matters was a source of major personal insight and intellectual growth.

There have been occasional reports by public school teachers of interesting innovations in their elementary or secondary school classes. Several examples are included here as illustrations of a more direct and open approach to learning about and managing interracial issues in the classroom.

1. TEACHING ABOUT THE FORMATION OF FEELINGS OF PREJUDICE

General Description: I was interested in helping children in a desegregated ninth grade classroom understand the basis, emotional meaning, and universality of prejudice. I wanted the children to recognize that all people are prejudiced to a certain extent. Further, it is helpful for children to appreciate the personal bases of prejudice and to be able to analyze their feelings from this viewpoint.

The class had been discussing the behavior of people who feel inferior or superior to others. They had read about prejudice before, but had not discussed it as it related to themselves. I focused the discussion on feelings of superiority and rivalry. The class found examples of rivalries between homeroom sections, high school athletic teams, colleges and universities in Michigan, and competition in boy-girl relationships. The feeling that one group or person was naturally better than another, from the point of view of a person in that group, was found to be an example of prejudice. The class felt that one important dimension of, and possibly the basis of, prejudice was pride in self and/or group.

A discussion of racial prejudice followed. Current television programs on this topic were used as a resource. One program, "East Side-West Side," prompted a discussion on the question, "Why do some people dislike Negroes?"

Preparation. Miscellaneous reading on the subject of prejudice was essential in the development of my own thinking.

Practice developed spontaneously during a classroom discussion of a social studies textbook reading on feelings of inferiority and superiority. Previous class discussions had taken place concerning prejudice. The easiest definition for them to understand was that prejudice means "prejudging a person or group before you even get to know him or them".

The development and acceptance of open and honest discussion was a necessity for any future opinion-sharing between teacher and pupils or among peers. The only diagnostic tool used was self-examination and the evocation and examination of common stereotypes of nationality groups.

Practice: The class was organized in two concentric circles, as this helped them become more involved. Class discussion first centered on group rivalries and competition, such as exists between various classes and schools. Feelings of one group toward other groups resulting from these rivalries were examined. The feeling that one group was naturally better than another was illustrated as an important dimension of prejudice. This led to discussions of racial and national prejudice. Students were then asked to hand in a short written evaluation of their thoughts and ideas during the discussion, what they had learned, what they disagreed with, and what still confused them. One student began drawing a vicious picture entitled "The Jap." I took the picture, using it to explain and illustrate the meaning of stereotypes.

Possible Barriers. Teachers need to have considerable background in their own understanding of the nature of prejudice, its characteristics, origins, etc., and to have had experiences which help them to be aware of their own prejudices and deal with them thoughtfully. Many pupils may have difficulty discussing their personal feelings at first.

Some students may begin making wisecracks. Other students may be fearful of expressing their feelings. Discussion and understanding was limited because it was only a one hour class discussion. The teacher sometimes has to rely on chance for good examples of stereotypes.

Suggestions for Overcoming Barriers. It would have been helpful to administer to the students an attitude scale on feelings of prejudice early in the year (Bogardus Social Distance Scale). Then, discussions could have begun with the feelings of prejudice of the group and would not have necessitated immediate self-examination. It would have helped illustrate that we often fear and distrust people who are different from us. This Social Distance Scale includes descriptions of "Wallonians" and other fictitious minority groups. People generally respond to these group names in a similar way irrespective of whether they are real or fictitious groups.

The students may be threatened by the nature of the discussion or may not understand portions of it. The teacher needs to help the children become comfortable in discussing these feelings. The children should understand that prejudice is something which everyone experiences. Racial prejudice should not be discussed until many other examples of prejudice have been discussed.

This could be expanded into a larger, more comprehensive unit. Students can be asked to draw pictures of nationality groups familiar to them. They could also describe in writing their stereotype of a communist ninth grade student.

2. TEACHING AN UNDERSTANDING OF INTERGROUP RELATIONS

General Description. Along with teaching the history of the Civil War period, I was interested in developing interpersonal and intergroup understanding among my students. I hoped to accomplish this by providing opportunities for my students: (1) to observe other people's behavior in unique circumstances; (2) to appreciate the circumstances which lead to misunderstandings among people; and (3) to promote insight into their own interpersonal behavior.

Classroom discussions on prejudice, supplementary lectures, and role playing were techniques used to further these goals. The students' reactions to these experiences were favorable. They seemed to develop more objective viewpoints in their attempts to understand bigotry and prejudice. They gained new respect for each other as individuals and in the process developed skills in the art of constructive thinking. The students were also more highly motivated in learning the history of the Civil War period.

Preparation. The class discussed the nature of prejudice, providing a basis for studying the Civil War period. Several forms of group work had been used over a period of time so the student would learn how to function in a framework of cooperation and compromise. The class intensively studied the Civil War period of American history.

Practice. The students supplemented their study of the textbook by using school libraries. Emphasis was placed on individual research beyond the basic facts provided by lecture and texts. A role-playing technique was used to vitalize the learning experience. Members of the class portrayed typical citizens of the North and the South during this period. They enacted skits portraying the growing differences between the North and South and the conflict of northern and southern ideology over slavery. A mock Senate debate was held on the question of secession from the Union. Any arguments offered had to be of sensible quality, although irrational impulses were not entirely excluded.

The problems of this time period were then projected to the present day. It became clear that the problems of the present day have their roots in the past, roots which have not been removed. Academic outcomes were evaluated by written interpretations of events in the past and present. Furthermore, the performance of students involved in role playing was also evaluated by peers and the teacher.

Possible Barriers. At first students may be lukewarm to this area of study. Some students may not be prepared to do individual research, and others may not be seriously prepared for the debate. The teacher has to be clear in telling students that their personal attitudes will not be reflected in their grades.

Suggestions for Overcoming Barriers. When the students become involved in role playing, interest increases. The teacher can act as a consultant in helping pupils locate materials, organize their reading, etc. Another class was present to witness the debate. The students performed well, and this proved to be the highlight of the study.[17]

In another example, a teacher who was faced with a substantial amount of apathy and hostility in an interracial classroom decided to spend class time specifically examining the existence and meaning of these phenomena. She did not want to approach the topic directly, for fear that this would result in either embarrassed silence or complete chaos. Instead she planned to come to the issue indirectly, through the use of externally generated stimulus materials. She obtained several tape recordings of white and Negro youngsters' reactions to school desegregation and played them for her sixth grade class. The students were asked whether they could identify similar feelings or reactions in themselves. When such identifications were made, the class explored the truth or error of their expectations, and they considered alternate ways of responding to each others' fears and concerns. The teacher felt that the discussion provided some legitimate support for the youngsters who desired to make new friends and helped to establish some minimal ground rules of courtesy and constraint for the others.

These brief examples only begin to illustrate the new efforts that must be tried in our classrooms. But most teachers, like most Americans, are not prepared for interracial living. By and large, they do not know how to improve racial relations in the classroom. Before large numbers of teachers can make progress on this front, we will have to provide them with helpful ideas, skills, and encouragement.

Creating New Teaching Patterns

It is clear that much more inquiry needs to be directed at unanswered questions in the area of racial interaction, but the needs of educators and citizens will not be met by more research, not even by more relevant research. It is also necessary for concerned scientists and practitioners to consider the problem of transmitting relevant aspects of theory and research literature, as well as creative educational ideas and practices, to classroom teachers and administrators.

One of the traditional ways in which such information has been communicated is through a variety of written materials such as journals, magazines, and pamphlets. It is questionable to what extent scientific reports, scholarly textbooks, or course work materials are truly helpful for teachers. In most publications and courses, there are suggestions for actual classroom usage, and even when general practices such as role playing are presented, few specific examples are given. The Beck and Saxe (1965) and Giles (1959) volumes are noteworthy exceptions to the literature in their helpful, although minimal, focus upon the classroom. Noar (1966) more successfully attempts the same task. Noar not only focuses upon the classroom, but includes a number of "do's" and "don'ts" for teachers.

It is not my position that teachers need a step-by-step manual for use in the classroom, but some concrete suggestions for new and relevant teaching procedures would be quite helpful. There is a clear need to translate theoretical generalizations or research findings into language relevant to the practitioner. In such form, scientific knowledge about education and race relations would be more useful to classroom teachers. But it is a highly developed skill to move from research data to the behavioral implications of these findings and then to operational alternatives for educators. Such skills obviously are not found in most teachers; neither do most scientists have sufficient classroom experience to generate feasible instructional strategies. The separate training patterns and professional experiences of these two groups create gaps and distance where there needs to be an integration of complementary skills. Some new patterns of collaboration between scientists and practitioners are required to fulfill this broad range of knowledge utilization functions.

The problem of creating change is made more complex by the relevancy of personal ideologies and values for instructional performance. Unlike other areas of social practice where performance may not be strongly dependent upon values, changes in teaching require the modification of a complex pattern of views and orientations as well as specific behavior. Given the pluralism and diffusion of educational goals, many teachers can resist change merely by arguing that their classroom goals are not the same as those of their critics. Moreover, since it is difficult to tie a specific teaching practice to a particular student outcome, many requests for instructional change may rest upon the quicksand of unproven ideology.

Undoubtedly, teachers must examine their own feelings and opinions about racially potent matters. Whites or Negroes who teach in racially desegregated classrooms are as much a part and product of the American society as the college students who wrote the essays excerpted in this chapter. They share many of the same feelings about racial relations with those students, and with most Americans. In some teachers, these views are held consciously and are close to the surface; in others they are submerged deeply and seldom recognized. Whether recognized or not, these views affect the alternatives teachers are able to experiment with and utilize in the classroom. It is crucial for teachers to understand their own racial views, the potential relation between such attitudes and instructional behavior, and the probable commonness of such phenomena in our culture. Once recognized and legitimated as cultural and not merely personal characteristics, such views may be more honestly shared, compared, and analyzed. In the proper setting, and amidst appropriately honest interracial discussions with peers, perhaps some of these views can be altered; at least their effects on classroom interaction may be controlled.

Reports by Coles (1967) and Chesler and Segal (1967) document southern teachers' attempts to wrestle with the inconsistencies between their personal racial views and their definitions of professional integrity and responsibility. A number of teachers in the Deep South seem to have altered or suppressed their racial ideologies in favor of offering fair and equal treatment to white and Negro youngsters.

Recent research demonstrates some other difficulties involved in changing teaching practices. One difficulty is the teacher's inadequate knowledge of new scientific developments and findings and their meaning for his classroom situation. Conditions for maximum teacher invention must include the development of opportunities for professional exchange, feelings of involvement and influence in school policy-making and respect and support from the peer group and principal (Chesler and Barakat, 1967). Without these support systems, the ideas individual teachers develop are not shared with colleagues, and teachers who learn about new practices are not likely to actually adapt them for use in their own classrooms.

None of the barriers to change that have been noted above can be readily engendered by reading a new textbook, watching a new film, or hearing a distinguished scholar lecture about the psychological or sociological backgrounds of the "disadvantaged." Few schools of education seriously attend to the special problems of interracial education, to the roles of teachers as change agents, or to the nature of the school as a peer social system. As a result, even the most willing and best-intentioned practitioner may face a variety of personal and organizational difficulties in translating desires into action. Moreover, for many teachers the major barriers to new efforts are deficiencies in skill, motivation, or orientation. All of these problems necessitate the creation of a resource support system that provides emotional and professional advice, encouragement, and skill in on-the-job problem-solving. Often the most adequate support cannot be provided by external consultants; however, it may come from the sharing of concerns and strategies among professionals experiencing similar problems.

Principals and superintendents of schools may be able to play key roles in facilitating and supporting teachers' efforts to change the way they manage race relations in class. Administrators can help directly by freeing teachers from some daily assignments and allocating funds for training programs. Moreover, they can help establish a professional atmosphere that encourages teachers to get extra training, that supports their later efforts to try out new ideas with their youngsters, and that encourages sharing of these ideas with peers in informal discussions. If the principal sets a positive and firm tone, much resistance to desegregation from teachers, students, and even the community is likely to be stifled. It is imperative for administrators to meet with teachers of newly desegregated classrooms to help prepare them, and perhaps to prepare their classes, for this new educational experience.

Another critical component of any effort to plan for teacher change is the nature of the extraschool community. We have noted above that it is important for teachers to understand how their racial views may be conditioned or influenced by the culture in which they live. Teachers need to see classroom behavior as a partial function of the same cultural background. The programmatic implications of this emphasis are twofold: first, any intraclassroom program designed for youngsters must consider how the new experience may change relations with their social surroundings; second, teachers who attempt classroom changes may have to deal with resistance and find support from their own family and social community.

Any attempt to infuse teachers with new ideas and strategies must consider the problem of teacher reentry into his own social system and must provide internal and external support for the teacher's efforts toward change (Chesler and Fox, 1967). The day-to-day pressures of home and family, of peers and principals, of records and reports strongly mitigate against the possibility that insights and plans from special training sessions will ever be realized in new classroom behavior. Many newly trained individuals are never able to utilize their skills because their new knowledge may increase their alienation from their colleagues or vice versa. Helpful elements of any training program, then, might include the sharing of findings about problems of school change and conceptualization of the teacher's role as change agent or peer helper. Some relevant skills that might help teachers fulfill these helping roles may include: (1) how to create change or offer help to a peer without offending or alienating him; (2) how to help a peer identify a classroom problem; (3) how to diagnose the classroom; (4) how to diagnose and interpret colleague and principal support for change; (5) how to derive and test alternatives from diagnostic data on insights; and (6) how to help peers understand the importance of evaluating their efforts at change.

This chapter has discussed some of the essential problems in the utilization of knowledge in the area of desegregated education; that is, how scientists and scholars can communicate what they think is reliable and valid knowledge in ways that are truly useful and helpful to practitioners. In general, and particularly in the area of racial relations, various schools and communities are desperately in need of such help and assistance. The development of sound knowledge about the dynamics and potentials of racial interaction in the classroom, the development and evaluation of successful models for the teaching of interracial classes, and the development of successful designs for retraining teachers to be more competent in interracial settings would be enormously useful to many very pained school systems.

Notes

1. Some illustrative sources of this trend include volumes by Passow, 1963; Sexton, 1961; Riessman, 1962; Beck and Saxe, 1965.
2. For an elaborated discussion of this problem, see Miel, 1967.
3. J.S. Coleman, et al., Equality of Educational Opportunity, p. 307.
4. W. Katzenmeyer, "Social Interaction and Differences in Intelligence Test Performance of Negro and White Elementary School Pupils," Dissertation Abstracts (1963), 24, p. 1905.
5. Coleman, op. cit., p. 333.
6. Racial Isolation in the Public Schools, p. 112.
7. M. Chesler and P. Segal, "Southern Negroes' Initial Experiences and Reactions in School Desegregation," Integrated Education (1968), 6, pp. 27-28.
8. At the time of this study only .40 percent of the Negro students in the state attended public schools with whites.
9. M. Chesler and L. Schaible (ed.), "Reflections on School Desegregation: IV." Unpublished paper, Institute for Social Research, Ann Arbor, 1967.

10. For a full explanation of the concept of utilization of academic abilities, see Schmuck, 1963.
11. The theory explaining the relevance of cross-group membership for the management of hostility is explored in Coser, 1956; Likert, 1967.
12. M. Chesler and P. Segal, "Characteristics of Negro Students Attending Previously All-white Schools in the Deep South," p. 43-44, 47.
13. Chesler and Schaible, *op. cit.*
14. J. Niemeyer, "Some Guidelines to Desirable Elementary School Reorganization," p. 81.
15. *Youth in the Ghetto*, p. 203.
16. M. Chesler (ed.), *How Do You Negroes Feel About Whites and How Do You Whites Feel About Negroes?* (Ann Arbor: Institute for Social Research, 1966), I, pp. 1, 2, 5; II, pp. 1, 4, 10. Reproduced by permission.
17. R. Fox and R. Lippitt, *The Innovation and Sharing of Teaching Practices, II,* (Ann Arbor: Institute for Social Research, 1967), abridged from *Appendix C,* pp. 1-12. Reproduced by permission.

References

Beck, John M. and Saxe, R.W. (eds.) *Teaching the Culturally Deprived Pupil.* Springfield, Ill.: Charles C. Thomas, 1965.

Bloom, Benjamin S., Davis, A., and Hess, R. *Compensatory Education for Cultural Deprivation.* New York: Holt, Rinehart and Winston, 1965.

Chesler, Mark A. (ed.) *How Do You Negroes Feel About Whites and How Do You Whites Feel About Negroes?* Ann Arbor: Institute for Social Research, 1966.

Chesler, Mark A. and Barakat, H. *The Innovation and Sharing of Teaching Practices I: A Study of Professional Roles and Social Structures in Schools.* U.S. Office of Education Cooperative Research Project. Ann Arbor: Institute for Social Research, 1967.

Chesler, Mark A. and Fox, R. *Role Playing in the Classroom.* Chicago: Science Research Associates, 1966.

Chesler, Mark A. and Fox, R. "Teacher Peer Relations and Educational Change," *NEA Journal,* 1967, 56: 25-26.

Chesler, Mark A. and Segal, P. *Characteristics of Negro Students Attending Previously All-white Schools in the Deep South.* Report of U.S. Office of Education contract. Ann Arbor: Institute for Social Research, 1967.

Chesler, Mark A. and Segal, P. "Southern Negroes' Initial Experiences and Reactions in School Desegregation," *Integrated Education,* 1968, 6:20-28.

Coleman, James S., et al. *Equality of Educational Opportunity.* U.S. Office of Education. Washington, D.C.: U.S. Government Printing Office, 1966.

Coles, R. *Children in Crisis.* New York: Atlantic-Little Brown, 1967.

Conant, James B. *Slums and Suburbs.* New York: McGraw-Hill, 1961.

Coser, Lewis. *The Functions of Social Conflict.* Glencoe, Ill.: Free Press, 1956.

Education and the Disadvantaged American. Washington, D.C.: National Education Association, 1962.

Ellison, Ralph. *The Invisible Man.* New York: Random House, 1952.

Fox, R. and Lippitt, R. *The Innovation and Sharing of Teaching Practices, II: Stimulating Adoption and Adaptation of Selected Teaching Practices.* Report of U.S. Office of Education research project. Ann Arbor: Institute for Social Research, 1967.

Giles, H. *The Integrated Classroom.* New York: Basic Books, 1959.

Hansen, C. "The Scholastic Performance of Negro and White Pupils in the Integrated Public Schools of the District of Columbia," *Harvard Educational Review,* 1960, 30: 216-236.

Harrington, Michael. *The Other America.* New York: Macmillan, 1962.

Katz, I. "Review of Evidence Relating to Effects of Desegregation on the Intellectual Performance of Negroes," *American Psychologist,* 1964, 19: 381-399.

Likert, Rensis. *The Human Organization.* New York: McGraw-Hill, 1967.

Lockwood, J. "An Examination of School Factors Among Negro Students in Balanced and Imbalanced Schools." Doctoral dissertation, University of Michigan, 1966.

Lombardi, D. "Factors Affecting Change in Attitude Toward Negroes Among High School Students," *Journal of Negro Education,* Spring, 1963, 32: 129-136.

Mead, George H. *Mind, Self and Society.* Chicago: University of Chicago Press, 1934.

Miel, A. *The Shortchanged Children of Suburbia.* New York: Institute of Human Relations Press, 1967.

Niemeyer, J. "Some Guidelines to Desirable Elementary School Reorganization," in *Programs for the Educationally Disadvantaged.* Washington, D.C.: U.S. Government Printing Office, 1962.

Noar, Gertrude. *The Teacher and Integration.* Washington, D.C.: National Education Association, 1966.

Passow, A. Harry (ed.) *Education in Depressed Areas.* New York: Columbia University Press, 1963.

Programs for the Educationally Disadvantaged. Washington, D.C.: U.S. Government Printing Office, 1963.

Racial Isolation in the Public Schools. U.S. Commission on Civil Rights. Washington, D.C.: U.S. Government Printing Office, 1967.

Riessman, Frank. *The Culturally Deprived Child.* New York: Harper and Row, 1962.

Schmuck, R. "Socio-emotional Characteristics of Classroom Peer Groups." Doctoral dissertation, University of Michigan, 1963.

Schmuck, R., Luszki, M., and Epperson, D. "Interpersonal Relations and Mental Health in the Classroom," *Mental Hygiene,* 1963, 47: 289-297.

Sexton, Patricia. *Education and Income.* New York: Viking Press, 1961.

Stallings, F. "A Study of the Immediate Effects of Integration on Scholastic Achievement in the Louisville Public Schools," *Journal of Negro Education,* 1959, 28: 439-444.

Webster, S. "The Influence of Interracial Contact on Social Acceptance in a Newly Integrated School," *Journal of Educational Psychology,* 1961, 52: 292-296.

Youth in the Ghetto. Also called the Haryou Report. New York: Harlem Youth Opportunities Unlimited, 1964.

6 PREPARING TEACHERS FOR DISADVANTAGED YOUTH

Vernon F. Haubrich

Dr. Haubrich suggests that we cannot determine the characteristics of the disadvantaged because the spread of differences is too great. Instead he analyzes seven interrelated conditions that induce disadvantagement among urban youth. Among these conditions are the schools. There is a lack of dialogue with the poor, the disadvantaged, and the lower class student because the typical teacher's orientation strongly reflects the values of the dominant society. The educational bureautracy also puts a lock on some children with its impersonal methods and procedures. Too often it seems that "nothing can be done."

The author reviews education programs for teachers of the disadvantaged—at the university level for prospective teachers and through in-service programs to reeducate experienced teachers. He notes positive attempts to prepare teachers by giving them direct experience with the disadvantaged early in their training. Dr. Haubrich also discusses directions and priorities for teacher education and considers several social-psychological aspects of teaching the disadvantaged.

Dr. Haubrich is Professor of Policy Studies and Senior Researcher, Institute for Research on Poverty, at the University of Wisconsin. He is currently editing an ASCD Yearbook on Bureaucracy and Schooling and is principal investigator on a five-year study of desegregation.

One of the critical issues facing educators is the education of disadvantaged youth. Whether these youth are found in urban ghettos, rural slums, migrant camps or Indian reservations, the problems of educating these youth will be a challenge for many years to come. A review of the current and historical literature concerning the disadvantaged yields several findings which must be taken into account when considering the issue of the poor today and the teachers who will serve them.

First, it is apparent that disadvantaged youth—whether economically, socially, or educationally disadvantaged—have been with us for many years and that efforts to educate them have been made since colonial days (Butts and Cremin, 1953). Second, disadvantaged youth and their families have made heroic efforts to avail themselves of schools, learning, and patterns of upward mobility. The problems of educating the disadvantaged are intertwined with related issues in housing, slums, unemployment, school costs, race, and segregation. In the face of incredible handicaps, the historic disadvantaged groups have sought a better life for themselves and their children and have consistently supported the idea of learning and schooling as a means for self-improvement and a necessary precondition for upward mobility. Third, it is apparent that the critical role which the teacher plays in all students' lives is even more central to the potential success of disadvantaged youth.[1] While not a radically new idea—for the president of Middlebury College recognized the same issue as early as 1849—it remains one of the more perplexing, yet engrossing notions in the thrust of public education toward equal educational opportunity. John Stuart Mill once remarked that the task of "fashioning the teachers" was critical to his educational scheme, and so it is when one attempts a review of the programs, policies, and patterns of curriculum and schooling today.

What this chapter proposes to do is: (1) To examine, in rather brief form, the various points of view regarding the disadvantaged and the definitional problems surrounding this cloudy and slippery arena. (2) To review some of the potentially significant experiments and findings which have grown out of society's concern for disadvantaged children and youth. (3) To indicate the common and unique strands which seem to swirl about the programs for the disadvantaged. (4) To examine the question of directionality with respect to the questions about teachers for disadvantaged youth.

Conditions Inducing Disadvantagement

The rabbit warrens of definition lead one into seemingly endless arguments about social disadvantagement, cultural deprivation, and issues which cut across terms such as poverty, race, and ethnic groups. What has happened is that we have attempted to solve the problems of school dropouts, the lack of relevance in curricular content, and the organizational structure of schooling by lumping all problems together and diagnosing them with terminology rather than by an examination of etiology. To complicate the matter there has been an unfortunate tendency to equate correlation with causation (with a resulting flurry of hyperactivity) which reveals little except that two variables may be correlated in a statistical manner.

At least one author has indicated that the spread of differences among the disadvantaged is the same as for the so-called middle class (Lipton, 1962). What seems to be emerging from mountains of literature is that one cannot, with any degree of assurance, write about the characteristics of the disadvantaged. Instead it is necessary to look at the factors which seem to cause learning problems for children in individual situations. Monolithic definitions of disadvantagement are as helpful as monolithic definitions of what all teachers must be or become. There are always exceptions. There is always uniqueness and variety in specific cases. Consequently, it is necessary to examine the kinds of problems that exist in learning, schooling, and teaching and to see what these may mean for individual children in particular contexts.

One of the central conditions which seems to affect many children who are disadvantaged, and therefore their teachers, is an underlying lack of money. It has been demonstrated in many studies that lack of funds has important effects on a student's participation in many school activities (Hand, 1955; Lynd and Lynd, 1959). Studies indicate that the cost of schooling (dues, trips, out of pocket expenses, collections for various causes) places an undue hardship on the child whose family is poor. If school is an expensive place to be and if some children cannot afford the cost of schooling, the only route is to avoid the costs by not participating or to accept the offer of some schools to pay these costs. Either route seems to be unacceptable—either the child does not participate, or the child regards himself as a second-class citizen in accepting the charity of the school. In any event, the fact of poverty generates school experiences which can be unrewarding.

A second condition encountered when one examines the etiology of disadvantagement is a lack of response to traditional methods of schooling and the present school curriculum pattern. Again, this can cut two ways. One can conclude that the children have environmental deficits and cannot adjust to schoolwork, or one can conclude that the school cannot adapt its curriculum, teachers, and organization to the uniquenesses which disadvantaged children exhibit. Whether one calls these problems verbal deficits, lack of intellective functioning, or a bias in the assessment procedures depends on what viewpoint one has. One can blame the child or one can fault the school, but the fact of nonfunctioning remains. The disadvantaged child seems to fall progressively farther behind in his achievement, in his adjustment to the demands of schooling, and in his relationship to teachers. The cause of this is what the debate in education is all about.

A third area of disadvantagement is the effect of malnutrition. The impact that malnutrition has on the child cannot be glossed over nor underestimated. Limited amounts of energy in school, depression, apathy, and lethargy are but some of the effects of poor nutrition. In a sense, a recognition of the impact of poor nutrition on the functioning of the child in school as well as out indicates the close and interrelated nature of the aspects of disadvantagement. The life conditions which a child carries to school may influence his performance in school, his view of schooling, and the teacher's opinion of the child.

A fourth condition which can affect the child is family instability, including employment difficulties among adults in the home, parents who are separated or divorced, and dependency on public welfare (Burgess, 1964). Some evidence has been accumulated on the close connection between the degree of family stability and the consequent ability to profit from schooling (Povenstedt, 1965). As with the other conditions that induce disadvantagement in the child, this factor operates with and around other factors, thereby causing a series of problems which affect the child and his adjustment to school. One way of looking at the effects of family instability and economic insecurity is drawn from the work of S.M. Miller, who postulates two basic ingredients that cause a differentiation among members of the lower class. Diagrammatically, the model looks like this:

	Family Stability +	Family Instability -
Economic Security +	The Stable Poor + + (1)	The Strained + - (2)
Economic Insecurity -	The Copers - + (3)	The Unstable - - (4)

The four groups are on a continuum from those that are relatively secure economically with a stable family pattern to those who are economically insecure with an unstable family pattern.

A fifth condition which affects many children is race. The massive and compelling evidence that documents the plight and condition of being black in our society records only too well the attitudes of many whites. Recently, adding more weight to years of scholarly findings, *Racial Isolation in the Public Schools* (1967), the Coleman Report (1966), and the Kerner Report (1968) have indicated the immense impact of segregation on many black children in our society. In short, segregation in combination with limited aspirations has worked to create in the minds of many black children a sense of inferiority, a lack of positive self-image, and the stigma of being black in a racist society.

The words of President Kennedy provide a concise statement on the conditions of disadvantagement:

> The Negro baby born in America today, regardless of the section of the nation, has about one-half as much chance of completing high school as a white baby, one-third as much chance of completing college, one-third as much chance of becoming a professional man, twice as much chance of becoming unemployed, about one-seventh as much chance of earning $10,000 a year, a life expectancy seven years shorter, and the prospect of earning only half as much.[2]

Sixth, one of the features which induces a sense of futility and low aspiration among the disadvantaged is the failure of the service professions to perform their tasks adequately in and among the poor, the blacks, the Indians, and the migrants. There is an extreme shortage of legal services. The record of police discrimination is one of the salient features of the recent Kerner Report. Medical services have been in short supply among the disadvantaged, causing some groups to give up as much as a quarter of a century of their lives for the privilege of their identity. The failure of medicine to respond to the needs of the poor is due, in part, to the desire for compensation. But it is a critical commentary on the nature of our social priorities that profit seems to play a greater part than service when the poor and disadvantaged are involved. We need look at only one more example to document the failure of the service professions to meet their responsibilities in this area, and this is the lack of response of psychiatrists and psychologists to the needs of the poor and the disadvantaged (Kardiner and Ovesey, 1964). The failure of these and other human services indicates the bias of professionals that is built into the social system (Kerner Report, 1968).

The seventh area which contributes to disadvantagement is the school system itself and those who teach and administer its program. While recent evidence from the disadvantaged themselves indicates

that the school system is not high on the list of complaints, we would
be foolish to ignore the evidence of high dropout rates, comparative
scores on tests, turnover of teachers in poor and ghetto areas, and
other measures indicating the pattern of discrimination and disadvantagement which the school may cause, wittingly or unwittingly.
There is a critical interlock between the conditions that cause disadvantagement and the seemingly endless cycle of poverty. While we
must recognize that the school cannot do everything, to say only
this and not say more is clearly immoral. This kind of analytical cop-
out may be used by physicians, dentists, lawyers, social workers,
housing authorities, and others who are supposed to serve human
beings. But what is needed is a close analysis within each of the helping professions to recognize the part each plays in causing and perpetuating disadvantagement. This I propose to do for teachers and
schools.

How the Schools Induce Disadvantagement

When we attempt to look at the process of schooling, which includes
teaching, learning, classrooms, administrators, textbooks, holidays,
and a system of rewards and punishments, what we see is a social
system. This system includes personnel, participants, roles, duties,
expectations, and a method of organization. Three aspects of this
system will illustrate the conceptual lock which is placed on many
children. Teachers, bureaucratic structures, and the dynamics between
them and the communities (which are either served or not served by
the schools) will be examined in this analysis. Let us begin with the
teachers.

The Teacher's Orientation

In the reports of the National Advisory Council on the Education
of Disadvantaged Children to the President of the United States,
stress has been laid on the critical importance of teacher attitude in
the education of disadvantaged youth. In a revealing statement,
which looks to the genesis of school problems and the disadvantaged,
the 1967 report notes that:

> Typically, the attitudes of teachers reflect the attitudes of society. It
> is society, not its corps of teachers alone, which readily applies value

judgments of "good" and "bad" to such common aspects of child behavior as use of language, cleanliness, orderliness, management of time,
diligence in lessons, and homework.[3]

Consequently, if we review what it is that the teacher values and ex-
pects, we may be able to see some of the problems that arise when
teachers and students face each other.

In the first place, teachers are committed to the competitive
ethic in American society. The structure of classrooms, the systems
of reward and punishment, the grades which are assigned, the pass-
fail system, and the grade level system itself have molded the teacher
and are used, in turn, by the teacher to mold the students.

Secondly, the teacher is probably oriented to future expectations and gratifications. The meaning of this for the students revolves
about two dimensions: time and gratification. In a real sense, schools
and teachers are always stressing future rewards, future payoffs,
future gratifications. Saving money for the future, postponing marriage until one is situated properly, conserving resources for future
generations—these ideas are built into the literature, the expectations,
and the orientation of the teacher. Then one adds the notions that
time is also money, that we must hurry and finish our work, that a
test requires a timed work period, that we plan today for tomorrow's
work. What emerges is an orientation to work, gratification, and time
that is directed to the future rather than to the present or past.

In addition to competition, future orientation, and the postponement of gratification, there is an implicit assumption that work,
in and of itself, is a positive good which enriches the life of man.
Status, prestige, and reward are related to the concept of hard work,
and some schools go so far as to grade children on the relative effort
they make in learning compared to their ability to do the work. For
example, an excellent piece of work from a very able student may
receive less than a top grade if the teacher thinks he is not working to
capacity—whatever that means. Conversely, students who do a poor
piece of work but seem to put forward extraordinary effort to finish
the job are rewarded for their effort. In effect, the students are slowly being taught the value and ethic of effort and work.

The teacher, as an agent of the social system, transmits these
explicit and implicit values to all children in the classroom, for the
basic assumption is that these values are prized by the people at large.
Indeed, a technologically oriented industrial society requires precise-

ly those habits of punctuality, order, precision, postponement of gratification, devotion to work, and maximization of effort that are required in the classroom.[4]

The Educational Bureaucracy

The second aspect of schooling which puts a lock on some children and aids in causing their disadvantagement is the structure of schooling itself. The classic analysis of bureaucratic structures was made by Max Weber in 1922. In this analysis, Weber indicated that efficiency and rationality of operation are the goals of large scale organizations, and these goals are incorporated into the structure of bureaucracies by emphasizing a division of duties, equalitarian procedures, impersonal methods of selection and promotion, and regulations and duties which adhere to the office rather than the person in that office.

When one examines the procedures of school systems today, one finds that they follow the general pattern that has developed in bureaucratic history. Duties are divided meticulously (they are referred to as job descriptions or role analyses), and each position in the school is filled by a person who carries out the duties or tasks assigned to that position. Impersonality is the order of the day, and the method of licensure and examination for positions insures that personality will not enter into the picture.

When one sees how these rules, duties, and regulations affect children, the picture gets cloudy. A position is set up for a first grade teacher, and one of the duties assigned to that role is to teach the children to read a book that enables them to pass a test which will then admit them to the next level of competition. The child takes the test and does not complete the reader successfully so he is failed and repeats the grade. The sanctions in this entire procedure are impersonal and it always seems that nothing can be done. There is the test (whatever its applicability or validity), there is the rule (whatever its logic or workability), and there is the child who has not passed. There is nothing to be done. While this example may be overstated and while the issues are never as simple as they seem on paper, the general thrust of bureaucratic organizations is to inculcate in the child and in the functionaries a sense that fairness has prevailed and that no one in the bureaucracy is at fault.

A classic problem is developing in the schools today that is rooted in historic conceptions of who the schools belong to and what they are for. They seem to be run by technical functionaries carrying out their duties, similar to those who work for insurance companies, government agencies, or water departments. But the critical questions are: who or what determines their duties and how are they to be carried out?

For answers to these questions, one must explore the history and inner workings of large scale organizations. The American school system has drawn its general philosophy from the enlightened liberal who speaks of freedom, individuality, pluralism, rooting the control of the school in popular hands. But in actual practice there is substantial evidence that the architects of testing, classification, middle class morality, and white supremacy have written the texts, taught the leaders, and established the system that has proved to be a haven for the beneficiaries of Social Darwinism (Karier, 1967). The crises of today's schools stem, at least in part, from a lack of dialogue on educational policies, practices, and philosophy—especially as they concern the poor, the disadvantaged, and the lower class.

The third aspect of schooling which discriminates against some children is the dynamic interplay that occurs when those who teach and administer develop a mythology regarding schooling, children, and who should be educated for what purpose. This mythology is necessary, it seems, to protect teachers and administrators from any realistic examination of the causes of failure. The insularity of the education system results in great reluctance to change any aspect of the system, for to admit that a change is necessary seemingly indicts past practices. Myths concerning local control of schools, class size and learning, classroom organization, and the nature of disadvantaged youth permeate education and provide teachers and administrators with protection that many need and few recognize. Efforts to change the organization of the schools, the education of teachers, the manner and means of administration, or the nature of school control will face enormous resistance because of the dynamic interplay of teachers, administrators, bureaucratic organization, and the support of ancillary structures (Karier, 1967).

The results of this interplay, or reinforcement, are the hallmarks of the educational system: the testing movement and its graded manner of classifying children; the track system which relegates most disadvantaged youth to the lower or, at best, the middle track and uses the testing system for its support; the functionaries in the school, including counselors, who observe the results of the system and begin to make the self-fulfilling prophecies of failure for the disadvantaged; the curriculum which places great stress on a white, stereotyped view of the world; and the turnover of teachers which reaches almost one hundred percent in some areas of big cities.

What these procedures, materials, methods, and policies create is the sense of hopelessness of another bureaucratic agency. This is what sociologists call a "dysfunctionality" between those who teach and those who learn. The teaching process is no longer effective nor efficient nor meaningful nor relevant. The truly unfortunate part is that everyone plays such a small part in the scenario, but how important each of these parts is to the whole scene.

John Holt suggests that children learn, in a sense, to desire failure when the expectation of teachers or adults is failure. He writes:

> Subject peoples both appease their rulers and satisfy some part of their desire for human dignity by putting on a mask, by acting much more stupid than they really are, by denying their rulers the full use of their intelligence and ability. . . . Does not something very close to this happen often in school? Children are subject peoples. School for them is a kind of jail. . . . Under pressure . . . some children may quite deliberately *go stupid*.[5]

Adults in depressed areas exhibit similar kinds of behavior and relate it to keeping children in a state of dependency. A recent study in Harlem indicated that the mothers of the addicts, while deploring the addiction, gave their sons money to buy the heroin under the pretense of giving them an allowance. Thomas Huxley once indicated that a sense of uselessness is as severe a shock as the human being can endure. Many disadvantaged youth exhibit this sense of uselessness which is, at least in part, caused and reinforced by the school.

A Review of Teacher Education Programs

Teacher education programs of necessity are tied to the concept of continuity. The teacher teaches as he has been taught and teaches material which he understands. Students whom he judges to be successful are passed on, and some of these individuals, quite naturally, become teachers. It is wishful thinking to expect that the teaching corps of this country, the prospective teachers in training, or those who are thinking about the career of teaching will radically change their beliefs, attitudes, or outlook. Consequently, "new programs for the disadvantaged" or "curriculum developments for the poor" in the organization of the schools will fall quickly into the huge bin of forgotten experiments if the education of teachers is not taken into account *first*.

If anything is to be learned from the failure of educational innovation (Miles, 1964), it is that changes by schools and innovators must be effected systematically, carefully, slowly, and with great attention to the changes that teachers are expected to make in their normal day-to-day operations. The factors which mitigate against radical change in schooling are the teacher's personality (which is more conservative than one would like to think), the abnormally high turnover of staff, courses, materials, and curriculum. Consequently, when one speaks of team teaching, early stimulation in reading, or revised methods of reading, what one must think of is the education and the reeducation of teachers who will carry out the job.

A point must be made about the nature of college programs today. The college and university that educate future teachers are dominated by a series of concerns, probably the least of which is the disadvantaged population (except when it is part of a research effort). The structure of higher education is governed by the concerns of the graduate school with its emphasis on research. The model is the German university (Rudolph, 1962). The education of teachers takes place in this context of higher education. Teachers' views and attitudes are shaped by higher education, and they enter the teaching profession as agents of the system of higher education. The social-psychological characteristics of this training include manipulation of words and symbols, the development of the critical or detached state of mind, and the development of intellectual understandings about problems, people, and places. A majority of one's time and effort in teacher education is spent at the college or university, in classrooms or laboratories or libraries, developing the attitudes, values, and appreciations of those who control the courses, write the syllabi, and give the lectures. Actual training for teaching, either in direct or indirect fashion, is minimal unless one thinks that courses alone make one a teacher.

Consequently, the connections between the reality of schools and classrooms and teacher education in colleges or universities depend on the correspondence of one situation with the other. The closer the goals, outlooks, values, behaviors, and ideals of teacher education are to those of the classroom, the less problem there will be for the teacher to adjust to the teaching situation. The more divergent the teaching situation is from the university context, the more difficult the adjustment will be. At the extreme, there are the difficulties of teachers and the disadvantaged youth—a genuine problem of two cultures attempting to speak to one another.

There are some college-centered programs for preparing teachers of disadvantaged youth, and they follow patterns that are relatively similar throughout the country (Klopf and Bowman, 1966).

First, some colleges are attempting to institute new courses on the sociology, psychology, and anthropology of the disadvantaged. These revisions or additions may be in various departments, or they may be in the department of education exclusively. This approach is as far as some colleges go (Frazier, 1968), and the haste with which the material often is presented makes this approach somewhat superficial.

Second, there are attempts to provide the prospective teacher with an orientation and realistic view of the disadvantaged by a series of firsthand experiences with community agencies serving disadvantaged youth. These contacts, designed to promote a better understanding of the culture of the disadvantaged, are usually supplemented by seminars at which the issues and problems of the youth are explored. Resource personnel may include social workers, settlement house employees, and other individuals serving disadvantaged youth.

Third, an effort is being made to bring the prospective teacher into contact with disadvantaged youth in both classroom and neighborhood settings. One of the more common methods employed by these programs is for education students to tutor the disadvantaged well before student teaching or internship is undertaken. Again, these programs attempt to incorporate the experiences of the education students into seminars which are usually held on a weekly basis (Frazier, 1968). The major advantage of direct experience programs is that they provide a strong dose of reality training for the prospective teacher, and while answers are not always available, the students usually react favorably to realistic experiences.

In addition to courses, neighborhood experiences, and internship practice for prospective teachers, some staffing and program changes have been effected by colleges and universities to prepare teachers for placement in disadvantaged areas. The utilization of outside resource personnel—as guest lecturers or to supervise prospective teachers—has been one of the innovations adopted by some colleges. These auxiliary staff are usually selected because of the degree of success they have had in school or community programs that serve disadvantaged youth. Through these and other related services to the college, efforts have been made to effect a partnership between public schools and colleges. To date, the only systematic evidence we have of the effectiveness of these newer developments are descriptive comments on the programs (Frazier, 1968) and a limited sample of student response to the effectiveness of the preparation.

At the heart of all these developments is the assumption that new knowledge *about* the disadvantaged must be supplemented by actual experience *with* the disadvantaged. This assumption follows a long and time-honored concept in teacher education that practice in the actual teaching role must supplement college studies. The practical difficulties of implementing this assumption in colleges throughout this land are attested to by the relative slowness with which extended internships have developed, especially in disadvantaged areas. The reasons for this are complicated. However, the gulf between higher education and the schools has helped to prevent genuine dialogue on the issue.

In-Service Programs

When one ventures beyond preparation of prospective teachers into the vast territory of in-service work, one is immediately confronted by the problem of the "two million." There are two million teachers in the public schools of this land, and the problem of their reeducation is so vast, so terribly complicated, and so compellingly important that one is tempted to dismiss the matter by ignoring it. But the central issues in this arena are the attitudes of teachers toward the disadvantaged and a willingness to get on with the job.

The most systematic program which exists to reeducate teachers for the disadvantaged is the NDEA Institute for Teachers of Disadvantaged Youth. A survey of this program indicates that, as in college and university programs preparing prospective teachers, heavy stress is put on understanding the problem of disadvantaged youth and relatively little emphasis is placed on instructional materials, content, and procedures which could be applied in the classroom.

Because of the variance among the disadvantaged and the range of their abilities, any attempt to categorize content, materials, or procedures as appropriate *only* for the disadvantaged probably will fail because of the inaccuracy in stating the problem. The tendency on the part of all of us is to seek the single answer, the infallible method, the right procedure, or the magic solution to teaching the disadvantaged. But what is absolutely necessary are some beginning attempts to systematically record and evaluate practices that are built on both theory and solid evidence and practices that have gained the acceptance of some teachers of the disadvantaged. Such prototypes are in short supply.

A large, as yet uncharted, area of in-service training is the re-training of teachers of the disadvantaged under Title I of ESEA. Some of these programs have been rather systematic in their research component and offer some promising leads for changing the attitudes of teachers. However, some disquieting results indicate that any changes that develop in the summer retraining programs tend to disappear when the regular year begins (Wilson, 1967). A systematic review of the kinds of approaches that may be used in retraining experienced teachers, in training prospective teachers, and in coordinating the role of higher education with the school system is yet to be accomplished on the teacher education scene.

Probably one of the most promising of new programs to prepare personnel for teaching the disadvantaged is the Teacher Corps. It draws its candidates from college graduates with a variety of educational histories who have had little or no formal preparation in teaching. Utilizing the drive and enthusiasm of dedicated young people, the Teacher Corps puts them through a two-year program which, again, places heavy emphasis on experience with the disadvantaged. An important feature of this program is the close cooperation that is required between public school systems and colleges undertaking the program. The idea of a paid internship, which is an integral part of the Teacher Corps, may be an added inducement, but it is clear that the Teacher Corps is utilizing some of the talent and energy of today's young people in the education of disadvantaged youth. Clearly, more time is needed to evaluate and refine the Teacher Corps; however, as a major thrust in the education of disadvantaged youth and as a major innovation which has caught the young and dedicated college graduate, it remains one of the more fruitful approaches to training teachers for disadvantaged youth.

The preparation of teacher aides has received wide attention in recent years (Riessman and Pearl, 1965). This program offers immense possibilities as a means for reaching, teaching, and helping youth in school programs and as a means of recruiting disadvantaged adults who wish to become aides or teachers. It seems clear that many disadvantaged groups feel left out of school policy and procedures. One of the unfortunate results of the gap between disadvantaged groups and the school has been the school personnel's lack of understanding of the hopes, aspirations, and problems which the disadvantaged face. If the teacher does not know about these problems, or is reluctant or incapable of finding out what the community is about or what its problems are, the gap between teacher and child, teacher and parent, or teacher and community can cause immense problems in the day-to-day operation of the classroom.

The teacher aide, when trained to act in tutoring, helping, interpreting, and actual teaching, can be a "translator" between the community and the school—especially if the aide is drawn from the disadvantaged community. Two programs for the preparation of aides—one operating in a bussing situation in Hartford and Farmington, Conn., the other on a Pima Indian reservation in Arizona—indicate the critical importance of aides. While classroom help for the teacher may appear to be the primary outcome of these programs, an additional dividend is the availability of the aide to talk to parents about the school program and to tell teachers about the home situation. The presence in the classroom of a person with whom the child can readily identify helps to bridge the chasm that separates some schools from those they serve.

The programmatic aspects of teacher education for the disadvantaged must center on the concept of experience with the disadvantaged and the importance of the apprenticeship theory of teacher education. We have assumed that, if the teacher had more information and experience with the disadvantaged, all would be right with the problem of educating urban youth. But if one were to review the extent of the problem, it would vary from city to city, college to college, and state to state depending on the critical press of events at each place. Clearly, there exists a close relationship between the demands of parents, the crises in classrooms, the supply of teachers that is drying up because of conditions, and the leadership personnel who fail to act in the face of crisis.

What seems to characterize the events of crisis is a plugging of holes, a patching of wounds, a lack of systematic thought on the problem. Emergency follows emergency, educational personnel are recruited and rushed into the classroom, and the education of youngsters resembles an arena for battle rather than a place where reading, thinking, and learning may proceed. I am very much afraid that the training of teachers and program development in the schools resemble this kind of crisis thinking. The note of despondency in the results of Title I programs and many special summer programs designed to prepare teachers leads me to conclude that we should take a fresh look at the problem to see if some new directions are indicated.

Directions and Priorities for Teacher Education

At the outset, let me indicate that my biases are inclined toward a social-psychological view of the situation, that the preparation of teachers for the disadvantaged is one and the same with the training of teachers who choose to teach elsewhere, and that the problems of teaching disadvantaged youth are problems which all the helping professions must attend to—and quickly.

The first general notion that is critical to an understanding of directions in teacher education is that participation and involvement are crucial to the success of any educational program in a democratic society. This includes those who live in a community, those who serve the area, and the political figures who are the decision-makers. One of the effects of involvement is that school programs and training programs consider the people who are disadvantaged—especially the parents. Schools serving many disadvantaged groups have not served them well for many reasons, as we previously noted, but one of the failings has been an almost universal lack of consideration for the desires, expectations, and feelings of parents.[6]

The second general idea is that learning on the part of children and learning on the part of teachers is supremely human centered. The kinds of connections which we expect teachers to make with children must be made first with teachers if any progress is to be made. One of the most perceptive writers on the question of reading and reading problems has written the following on the failure of special remedial programs in reading:

> The failure of our present methods of reading and language instruction derives essentially from a failure in understanding the psychology of language. The teaching machines that loom in the future are only the absurd extensions of a pedagogy that is urged on by a lunatic science to the last frontier. The educator who understands the meaning of language learning will know that it is human centered from the start and that when it is deprived of its human connections it loses its own vital substance.[7]

Consequently, the human connections which are so desperately needed by the children are also needed by teachers, who often feel that the task is hopeless.

The third position I should like to suggest regarding the social-psychological aspects of teacher education for disadvantaged youth is related to recognition and reward for teachers. It is absolutely imperative that those who are in charge of special programs to prepare educational personnel for disadvantaged youth understand that the major rewards today in our public schools belong to students who are intellectual, bright, conforming, and like their teachers in outlook and demeanor. For prospective teachers and experienced teachers to undertake tutoring, teaching, aiding, and working with disadvantaged youth is to engage in risks which not all can take. The kind of support for teachers which is woven into programs for the gifted or for those in the upper track is implicit, related to parental approval, and permeated with the rewards which schools can give. But the teachers of disadvantaged youth need and deserve all the recognition that other teachers receive and then some (Haubrich, 1964).

A fourth social-psychological aspect is that of focus. One of the easiest ways to end a program for teachers of disadvantaged youth is to expect that all of the social problems in ghettos, slums, or poverty areas will be solved by excellence of teaching. When the interconnections between the various problems in disadvantaged areas become clear, all too often the task of teaching appears hopeless. What is essential is that the teacher of the disadvantaged must have a limited focus of operation and be trained to handle that focus as well as possible. It may be that one of the first tasks in depressed areas is to end the enormous teacher-administrator turnover which characterizes some of these schools. That kind of limited goal—namely, to increase the stability of the staff—can lead to a series of other possibilities related to planning, execution of programs and a stable situation for the children (Haubrich, 1963).

In addition to involvement, participation, human-centered teaching, and a focused program, a fifth consideration in a review of programs for teachers of disadvantaged youth is that of feedback of information to leaders working in a program. In a sense, feedback to teachers should be considered a necessary reward inherent in the programs. If teachers, parents, and school administrators conceive of a program for more effectively teaching disadvantaged youth, then one of the key ingredients of the program must be the communication of the explicit and implicit results to all parties. It is most crucial to teachers who are working with children who have unusual problems in achievement and where success in the usual academic sense is not prevalent. A consistent pattern of feedback and review of programs would be one of the key items to expect in successful programs to prepare teachers of disadvantaged youth (Haubrich, 1968).

A last consideration which I should like to suggest concerns the nature of the leadership in programs for minority youth. Over and over in the literature, one sees the critical importance of the teacher who faces and works with disadvantaged youth. The kind of person who decides to work in disadvantaged areas will respond to and also create conditions which make for success. To enable this kind of person to function successfully, every effort should be made to create an environment conducive to excellence of performance; but in another sense, every effort also should be made to select those who will give the program something extra, who will give the extra effort, and who will center their teaching on the possibilities, not the limitations, of disadvantaged youth.

Evidence of the characteristics of this kind of teacher has been accumulating over the years (Freedman, 1968), but in one perceptive study, it was rather strongly stated that teachers who have a degree of success with disadvantaged youth are less authoritarian, less dogmatic, and less rigid than the norm among teachers. There is a curious paradox implied by Freedman's study of these teachers:

> In regard to personal history and trait characteristics, the pattern of volunteer responses indicated a background characterized by strivings for autonomy, for the early acceptance of childhood challenges, and by a relative freedom from symptomatic signs of diffidence and fearfulness. . . .[8]

The paradox is that middle class home-school environments tend to produce rather rigid persons, and because of the upward mobility patterns and social origins of teachers, we cannot expect to find unusually large numbers of open, nonauthoritarian persons among prospective teachers.

It seems from this that one of the prime organizational prerequisites is that teachers who wish to work with disadvantaged youth and who bring qualities of openness and flexibility to their professional tasks should be placed in positions of school leadership as rapidly as possible. It is paradoxical that this often means that teachers must leave the classroom. But as principals, supervisors, and middle management personnel, they can contribute greatly to a climate of openness in the schools which will allow other teachers to alter patterns of instruction and organization in the classroom.

In summary, the evidence indicates that the social-psychological underpinnings of programs to prepare teachers for teaching disadvantaged youth are as important to eventual success as any gimmick, technique, or lesson plan which seems to be momentarily fruitful. In addition, to speak as if teachers of migrants, blacks, or Puerto Ricans should utilize major variations of the basic principles of education is, again, to miss the point that teaching is centered on the human possibilities inherent when one person inducts another with skills, tasks, procedures, and ways of thinking. In conclusion, the following considerations seem to come through the haze and dust of journals, papers, and books:

1. The involvement of all relevant parties in a program is an absolute prerequisite to a program's success. This includes parents, teachers, administrators and, where feasible, students and community leaders.
2. A commitment to the human-centered aspect of teaching is crucial if the teacher is to reach the child.
3. Support and reward must be provided to those teachers who carry the program forward.
4. The focus of teaching must be directed to goals which are more proximate than not and more clearly related to the function of teaching. All social problems cannot be solved in the classroom, but those things which are clearly centered on teaching, learning, reading, computation, and other topics of essential concern to success in schooling must be the center of activity.

5. Feedback to teachers concerning the results of programs, new procedures, community concerns, and other matters relating to the school in a disadvantaged area is critical if programs are to receive the support of the teaching staff.

6. The kind of person—open, flexible and willing to change—who is able to carry forward the program of teaching and administration must be actively recruited and given leadership roles in disadvantaged schools.

Notes

1. As an example, see *Report of the National Advisory Council on the Education of Disadvantaged Children*, Washington, D.C., June, 1967, p. 25.
2. L. A. Cremin, *The Transformation of the School* (New York: Alfred A. Knopf, 1961), p. 66.
3. O.M. Wilson, *Report of the National Advisory Council on the Education of Disadvantaged Children*, Washington, D.C., June, 1967, p. 5-6.
4. *Remaking the World of the Career Teacher*, 1966.
5. J. Holt, *How Children Fail* (New York: Pitman, 1964), p. 156.
6. The best account of this is the record of frustration faced by parents in Jonathan Kozol's work, *Death at an Early Age* (Boston: Houghton Mifflin, 1967).
7. S. Fraiberg, "The Great American Reading Problem," *Commentary* (1965), 39:56. Reprinted by permission from *Commentary*; copyright 1965 by the American Jewish Committee.
8. P. Freedman, "Racial Attitudes as a Factor in Teaching Education for the Deprived Child," in V.F. Haubrich (ed.), *Studies in Deprivation* (Washington, D.C.: American Association of Colleges for Teacher Education, 1968), p. 10.

References

Burgess, Elaine M. "Some Implications of Social Change for Dependency Among Lower Class Families," *American Journal of Orthopsychiatry*, 1964, 34: 895-906.

Butts, R. Freeman and Cremin, Lawrence A. *A History of Education in the American Culture.* New York: Holt, Rinehart and Winston, 1953.

Coleman, James S., et al. *Equality of Educational Opportunity.* U.S. Office of Education. Washington, D.C.: U.S. Government Printing Office, 1966.

Frazier, Alexander (ed.). *Educating the Children of the Poor.* Washington, D.C.: National Education Association, 1968.

Freedman, Phillip. "Racial Attitudes as a Factor in Teaching Education for the Deprived Child," in V.F. Haubrich (ed.), *Studies in Deprivation.* Washington, D.C.: American Association of Colleges for Teacher Education, 1968.

Hand, Harold E. *Hidden Cost Studies.* Springfield, Ill.: Illinois Curriculum Development Program, 1955.

Haubrich, Vernon F. "The Culturally Different: New Context for Teacher Education," *Journal of Teacher Education*, 1963, 14: 163-167.

Haubrich, Vernon F. "Successful Programs for the Disadvantaged: Basic Considerations," in H. Rudman (ed.), *Urban Schooling*. New York: Harcourt, Brace and World, 1968.

Haubrich, Vernon F. "Teachers for Big City Schools," in A.H. Passow (ed.), *Education in Depressed Areas*. New York: Columbia University Press, 1964.

Kardiner, Abram and Ovesey, Lionel. *The Mark of Oppression*. Cleveland: World Publishing Co., 1964.

Karier, Clarence J. "Elite Views on American Education," *Journal of Contemporary History*, 1967, 2: 150.

The Kerner Report. *See Report of the National Advisory Commission on Civil Disorders.*

Klopf, Gordon J. and Bowman, Garda W. *Teacher Education in a Social Context.* New York: Mental Health Materials Center, Inc., 1966.

Lipton, A. "Cultural Deprivation," *Journal of Educational Sociology*, 1962, 36: 17-19.

Lynd, R.S. and Lynd, H.M. *Middletown: A Study in American Culture.* New York: Harcourt, Brace and World, 1959.

Miles, Mathew B. *Innovation in Education.* New York: Columbia University Press. 1964.

Povenstedt, Eleanor. "A Comparison of the Child Rearing Environment of Upper Low and Very Low Class Families," *Journal of Orthopsychiatry*, 1965, 35: 89-98.

Racial Isolation in the Public Schools. U.S. Commission on Civil Rights. Washington, D.C.: U.S. Government Printing Office, 1967.

Remaking the World of the Career Teacher. Washington, D.C.: National Education Association, 1966.

Report of the National Advisory Commission on Civil Disorders. U.S. Riot Commission Report; also called the Kerner Report. Washington, D.C.: U.S. Government Printing Office, 1968.

Riessman, Frank and Pearl, Arthur. *New Careers for the Poor.* New York: Free Press, 1965.

Rudolph, Frederick. *The American College and University: A History.* New York: Alfred A. Knopf, 1962.

Wilson, O.M. *Report of the National Advisory Council on the Education of Disadvantaged Children*, Washington, D.C., June, 1967.

7 | RACISM IN EDUCATORS: A BARRIER TO QUALITY EDUCATION

Ermon O. Hogan

Dr. Ermon Hogan is Chief Educational Specialist of the National Urban League. She is a member of Secretary Finch's Urban Task Force and the National Education Association's External Council for Human Relations.

Dr. Hogan takes an extensive look at racism in the public school system and offers critical comments about white experts on the black community. The Moynihan Report, the Coleman Report, and *Racial Isolation in the Public Schools* have illuminated the inequities in the American social order, but they have also added to the stereotype of the black American.

The author suggests a set of conditions necessary for providing quality education. But primary among these conditions are educational personnel who are aware of the black community and aware of their own attitudes toward black students. Only after racist attitudes are neutralized will educational innovations and material improvements be effective.

Somehow, I happened to be alone in the classroom with Mr. Ostrowski, my English teacher. . . . I was one of his top students, one of the school's top students. . . . He told me, "Malcolm, you ought to be thinking about a career. Have you been giving it thought?". . .

"Well, yes, sir, I've been thinking I'd like to be a lawyer."

Mr. Ostrowski looked surprised, I remember, and leaned back in his chair and clasped his hands behind his head.

"Malcolm, one of life's first needs is for us to be realistic. Don't misunderstand me, now. We all like you, you know that. But you've got to be realistic about being a nigger. A lawyer—that's no realistic goal for a nigger. . . ."

The more I thought afterwards about what he said, the more uneasy it made me. It just kept treading around in my mind. It was then that I began to change—inside![1]

Autobiography of Malcolm X

Educators react with horror, anger, and condemnation at this incident of paternalistic racism from the *Autobiography of Malcolm X*. However, racism and social class bias are very much a part of the curriculum in schools serving poor and minority youth. This "hidden curriculum" is conveyed covertly to students in inferior schools through low expectations, assignment to tracks, vocational-oriented counseling, rigidly controlled classroom behavior and, most insidiously, in disparaging references to intellectual limitations, family background and values. The negative psychological impact resulting from this curriculum has caused students to counter with aggressive or withdrawn behavior.

Social scientists, recently awakened to the problems of poor and minority youth in America's schools, have attributed this dilemma to the pathology of the ghetto family, community, and life style and to the hypothesized chasm existing between the middle class values of the school and the lower class values of the students. Few have dared look at the pathology caused by racism in educational institutions.

In assessing criteria for quality education in urban schools, it is imperative that we examine critically the influence of racism and social class bias on educational personnel, the promulgation of racism through the socialization process, the relationship of racism to educational theory and the attitudes of school personnel, and then delineate variables critical to developing quality personnel for urban schools.

Institutionalized Racism and American Education

Maxine Green writes in *The Public School and the Private Vision:*

> When, in the early nineteenth century, campaigns for public education began in America, the men who argued for the cause of common schools linked them to the ancestral promise and to the images of the American dream. Not only would the schools, they said, promise a common experience and a common heritage for the diverse children of the nation, they would also equip the young for the responsibilities of freedom, insure universal equality and guarantee prosperity through the years to come.[2]

However, during the last decade many educators and social activists have become painfully aware that the ancestral promise and the American dream for many children in this country have been analogous to Tantalus' penance. Although our schools have provided a quasi-common heritage, they have not provided a common experience out of which youth could learn to develop the responsibilities of freedom, to respect universal equality, and to acquire the skills necessary to guarantee prosperity through the years to come. The resulting social tragedy was conceived and nurtured by means of the subjective interpretation of the concept "equality of educational opportunity." Historically, this major aim of education has reflected the values of the dominant class. Such "equality" has been interpreted and misinterpreted as a benefit for white Anglo-Saxon Protestants from distinct social classes. Rarely has this birthright included minority and poor youth.

The recent inclusion of minority and poor youth among those qualified for the benefits of equality of educational opportunity has not always evolved through an awareness of social injustice nor through increasing humanism and a new morality on the part of the great society. More often, it has been a reaction to pressures from civil rights groups, confrontations with black militants, and violence in urban communities. Most important, it is directly related to economic factors in our technological era. Brookover asserts:

> The contemporary concern with the education of the disadvantaged in American society reflects the failure to adequately educate certain sub-societies' youth for the contemporary social system. So long as the society needed large proportions of people with relatively low levels of competence and our beliefs in equality of educational opportunity were not too strongly held, the maintenance of a differentiated school program served the society adequately. . . . The schools have functioned to maintain the differences which are now identified as cultural or education disadvantages.[3]

Deutsch, too, acknowledges that the schools have not assumed a leadership role in attacking racism and social class bias in our society. He writes:

> Generally education has been satisfied to offer an inferior intellectual diet in the urban ghetto, and the demand for change has not come from educators, but from external social forces demanding equality of opportunity. . . . The changes that are taking place in education . . . are for the most part being stimulated from the outside.[4]

The 1965 Elementary and Secondary Education Act encouraged

school systems to begin educational reforms in ghetto schools. Ironically, the most ineffective districts were often rewarded for their past inefficiencies with large grants to continue to miseducate minority youth. In addition to this act was the Civil Rights bill espousing the necessity for equal educational opportunity for all children. Additional funds were made available for school districts that had separate but unequal educational facilities and wanted to remedy an undemocratic, unconstitutional situation. This legislation produced a flood of confessions by school districts and state departments of education analogous to those of sinners at a Billy Graham rally. After this act of penance and the reward of additional federal funds, all too frequently business was conducted as usual.

White Experts on the Black Community

During this period, white experts on the black community came into view. Riessman, Passow, Ausubel, Jencks, ad infinitum, categorized, classified, and stereotyped minority groups and the children of the poor so successfully that few teachers perceived these children as educable. One critic angrily stated after reviewing one of Passow's books:

> By equating negritude with a metaphysical category called the "disadvantaged" we assert that the Negro is not merely poor—but he is tainted with a stigma of racial inferiority no less virulent for its covert assumptions.[5]

Few of the theories postulated by these eminent scholars were based on empirical reseach. The early body of knowledge regarding the "disadvantaged" was based upon "experts" quoting other "experts" until speculation became fact.

Three important research studies were conducted that illuminated the inequities in the American social order and served to further stereotype the black American: (1) Moynihan's analysis (1965) of the Negro family; (2) *Equality of Educational Opportunity* (Coleman, 1966); and (3) *Racial Isolation in the Public Schools* (1967).

The Moynihan Report was the vanguard of recent national studies that focus on the plight of the black American. This report stated that the fabric of Negro society is deteriorating and at the heart of this process is the deterioration of the Negro family. The report asserted that the pathology is due to slavery and past oppression rather than the racism prevalent in American society. Whitney Young of the National Urban League wrote in answer to this report:

> The picture of prevalent pathology it presents just does not fit reality and is a gross injustice to the overwhelming majority of Negro families which are as stable as any in the nation.
>
> Further, the statistics it quotes leave out factors which put its findings in doubt. Nowhere among the many charts in the reports is there a breakdown of comparative statistics which contrast figures for Negro families with those for white families of comparable income. What appear to be racial differences in regard to family stability are more probably class differences which Negro lower-class families share with white.[6]

In response to the Moynihan Report, Andrew Billingsley, a black professor at the University of California, authored *Black Families in White America* (1968). This book discusses the 75 percent of Negro families who have stable marriages, the 50 percent of Negro families who have managed to pull themselves into the middle class, the 90 percent of Negro families who are self-supporting, and the even larger proportion of Negro families who manage to keep out of trouble, often despite the grossest kinds of discrimination and provocation.

The study *Equality of Educational Opportunity* (Coleman, 1966) was conducted in response to Section 402 of the Civil Rights Act of 1964 and sought to document: (1) the extent to which racial and ethnic groups are segregated in the public schools; (2) whether the schools offer equal educational opportunity; (3) how much students learn as measured by performance on standardized achievement tests; and (4) the possible relationship between student achievement and the kinds of schools they attend. James Coleman of Johns Hopkins University had major responsibility for the design, administration, and analysis of the survey. Ernest Campbell of Vanderbilt University shared the responsibility. The Coleman Report, like the Moynihan Report, has been the object of much controversy. It verified the assumption that the vast majority of black and white children are educated in segregated schools. However, the findings regarding the other three concerns are tenuous at best.

Levin's critique (1968) of this report asserted that it suffered from important methodological errors, inadequate descriptions of the actual data used to test hypotheses, and sweeping conclusions which are often misleading and sometimes completely unsupported by the evidence that is presented. He stated that the report was overwhelmingly weighted in a direction that understated the importance of school resources in explaining variations in achievement. This report tends to take the heat off the social system that produces ill-educated students, and it continues the pattern of censoring the cultural influences of the environment.

The third report, *Racial Isolation in the Public Schools* (1967), is a reanalysis by Thomas F. Pettigrew, *et al.*, of the Coleman Report data. Four major findings emerged from this report:

1. Racial isolation in the public schools, whatever its origin, inflicts harm upon Negro students.
2. Racial isolation in the public schools is intense and is growing worse.
3. Compensatory efforts to improve education for children within racially and socially segregated schools have been ineffective.
4. School desegregation remedies have been devised which will improve the quality of education for all children.[7]

Pettigrew contends that only through racial integration will the deficits experienced by minority and poor children be overcome. Without this panacea, there is no hope. Quality education cannot be provided for the ghetto child within the framework of the inner city school because:

> . . . the performance of Negro students is distinctly less related to differences in the quality of schools and teachers than the social class and racial composition of their school.[8]

In discussing their findings, the researchers stated:

> The major source of the harm which racial isolation inflicts upon Negro children is not difficult to discover. It lies in the attitudes which such segregation generates in children and the effect these attitudes have upon motivation to learn and achievement. Negro children believe that their schools are stigmatized and regarded as inferior by the community as a whole. Their belief is shared by their parents and by their teachers.[9]

Notice that this statement refers first to deficiencies in the children, then the parents, and finally the teachers; i.e., segregation has caused students to have negative attitudes toward learning and achievement, has caused students to believe that their schools are stigmatized and regarded as inferior, and their belief is shared by parents and teachers. Is it not possible that school boards and administrators view the schools as stigmatized and inferior, that teachers view the children as uneducable, and that these attitudes are conveyed to parents and children? And, could it not also be possible that motivation and learning are reflections of teacher expectations along with nonacademically oriented community environments?

Pettigrew obviously was aware that the root of racism is deeply entrenched in both black and white Americans. Therefore, he could perceive no means other than integration of black children into middle class white schools to overcome this barrier.

Educators, civil rights activists, and social scientists were enchanted at first with the findings of the Coleman Report and *Racial Isolation*. Integration was the panacea for the miseducation of black and poor youth. Then advocates of this theory suddenly discovered that there weren't enough middle class white children near black communities to raise the intellectual achievement of black and poor youth. And in communities where there were, little effort was made to move in this direction. Compensatory education had failed, and open occupancy legislation added little to the reality of the "ideal" of integrated education. As Edward Forte, superintendent of schools in Inkster, Michigan, wryly stated: "Integration is the brief interlude between the time the first black family moves in and the last white family moves out."

Integration as a reality was as great a hoax on black people as the melting pot myth. And most important, it gave further credence to the stigma of racial inferiority because the burden of implementing it was placed on the black American. Black children rode the bus out of their neighborhoods into white communities. Black teachers who were considered superior were placed in white schools, leaving black children with average or poor teachers, both black and white. Some black teachers were declared inferior and dismissed because there was no place for them in integrated schools. Black parents were charged with being unconcerned about their children's education. And black children who did attempt to attend integrated schools outside their neighborhoods experienced physical, social, and emotional retribution—overt hostility, segregated ability grouping within an integrated school, apartheid in extracurricular activities, and a curriculum designed to "meet the needs" of the disadvantaged migrant.

The above discussion does not mitigate integration as a viable goal for all children in a democratic, pluralistic society. However, if we establish integration as a priority, then it must be pursued on an equalitarian basis, with all groups recognizing its merit and working diligently toward its achievement.

Racism in the Socialization Process

If, as the Kerner Report states, racism is a reality in America, and if we are to combat the insidiousness of its curriculum in American schools, we must view the manner in which it is developed and nurtured in the socialization process.

Harley (1968) has carefully analyzed institutionalized racism engendered in American society and draws upon Rose's (1950) "social control" or caste structure theory to explain American race relations. He uses Berreman's definition of caste: "a hierarchy of endogamous divisions in which membership is hereditary and permanent." This statement, Harley believes, historically characterizes the composition and relations between the races in our society. The races are perceived in a hierarchy with whites in the superior role. The races are thought to be separate species, and status is defined by parentage, with crossbreeding between the races forbidden. Caste membership is seen as permanent as evidenced by the persistent effort to "keep the Negro in his place" and the tremendous resistance to all change in the system. Harley continues:

> Color bars, cries of white supremacy and purity of the races and all the other catch phrases and ideological harangues of the prejudiced are essentially statements made to announce and reinforce the sanctions of the dominant caste. When these sanctions or racial types are closely examined, they have all the primary characteristics of a caste system. Thus, the genesis of racist attitudes is seen to be part of the total process of enculturation and the attitudes themselves part of the fund of social common knowledge.
>
> The mechanism of caste distinction in America is simple and straightforward—the social perceptions are learnings and distinctly social products. And that which must be learned by the members of the society is also simple and straightforward. As Dollard indicates, "Whiteness indicates full personal dignity and full participation in American society. Blackness represents limitation and inferiority."[10]

He also refers to Davis' discussion of the mechanism for enculturation of racist attitudes:

> For learning and maintaining the appropriate caste behavior, an individual of either the black or white group is rewarded by approval and acceptance for this caste; if he violates the controls, he is punished physically, eco-

nomically, socially, or legally, depending upon the seriousness of the infraction.[11]

Black people in America have been striving constantly to free themselves from the caste system. During the late 1960's, after years of sit-ins, wade-ins, pray-ins, and other humiliating pleas to the white community for racial justice, the black people escalated their efforts. They realized that any improvement in their condition would have to be attained through other methods. Recognizing that racism is perpetuated through enculturation, they decided to inhibit this phenomenon by controlling the second major social institution that influences the minds of black children—the schools. This effort to defy the caste-class system caused the mechanism for social control to whip into motion.

In New York City, for example, the public schools were paralyzed for several months during an intense power struggle. Strange alliances were made in an effort to maintain the status quo. Physical, social, and legal punishment was inflicted upon those who attempted to change patterns of control in the New York public school system.

Racism and Teacher Attitudes

Ruth Benedict writes in *Patterns of Culture:*

> No man ever looks at the world with pristine eyes. He sees it edited by a definite set of customs and institutions and ways of thinking. Even in his philosophical probings he cannot go behind these stereotypes; his very concepts of the true and the false will still have reference to his particular traditional customs.[12]

Smith (Chapter 3) illustrates this concept when he points out that nowhere has the effect of white supremacy been more pervasive and more debilitating than in the American school. White racism has poisoned the American school, and the most deadly paralysis of all is that which renders school personnel almost totally unaware of their social sickness.

Research relevant to teacher attitudes, expectations, and behavior toward disadvantaged youth demonstrates how racism produced by the socialization process has been stronger than professional responsibility. Becker (1962) and Clark (1964) used the interview as a research tool to identify teachers' perceptions of inner city students.

Becker found that teachers believe inner city children are difficult to teach, uncontrollable, violent, and morally unacceptable on all criteria. Clark asked a group of white students to interview a sample of white teachers in the New York inner city. Fifty percent of the teachers stated that Negroes are inherently inferior in intelligence and therefore cannot be expected to learn. They believed that the humanitarian thing to do is to provide schools essentially as custodial institutions.

Groff's survey (1963) of 294 teachers in sixteen inner city schools corroborates the findings of Becker and Clark. Forty percent of those interviewed in Groff's study stated that the personalities of socially disadvantaged children are responsible for the dissatisfaction that leads to high turnover rates among teachers.

Gottlieb (1964) also assessed the views of Negro and white teachers toward students in a northern urban community. He found differential perceptions of students by their teachers. White teachers typically selected adjectives indicating that black students are talkative, lazy, high-strung, rebellious, and fun-loving. Black teachers viewed the same students as happy, cooperative, energetic, ambitious, and fun-loving. The adjectives attributed to the students by white teachers are similar to the stereotypes of Negroes held by American society. Allport (1954) relates that Negroes are traditionally stereotyped as mentally inferior, lazy, superstitious, emotionally unstable, happy-go-lucky, religious, dirty, and morally primitive.

Attitudes held by prospective teachers do not differ markedly from those of experienced teachers. Grambs (1950) found that undergraduate education students expressed good, tolerant attitudes toward children of all groups in our society but that the degree of acceptance dropped markedly if the personal lives of the future teachers were involved. A recent study conducted by the author (Hogan, 1968) shows that attitudes have not changed in the last eighteen years. Undergraduate education students were asked to react to a hypothetical situation. When they were asked to reside in the community of an inner city school, a majority of the students stated they would accept the teaching assignment, but few could accept the idea of living in the community. The modern acculturation mechanism obviously is plastic enough to permit the utterance of verbal platitudes but strong enough to prevent interaction other than at sanctioned levels.

An exploratory study also was conducted on the attitudes of

undergraduate education students at a large midwestern university toward teaching in the inner city (Hogan and Boca, 1968). Only sixteen percent of the students stated that they preferred to teach in the inner city. Fear, value conflicts, and job difficulty were given as primary reasons for not desiring such an assignment. The students said their reasons were based on personal feelings and information from the communications media. Personal feelings may be attributed to cultural conditioning of racial attitudes, which in turn have been supported by the communications media.

Findings of the Michigan Public School Racial Census conducted in 1967 for the Michigan State Department of Education showed that teacher attitudes toward pupils were negative in classes with a large proportion of black pupils. The report states:

> It appears that the greater the proportion of Negro pupils in a class, the lower the teachers' rating of their pupils' academic ability and motivation.

A seminal study conducted by Jacobson (Rosenthal and Jacobson, 1968) clearly points out the influence of racism on teachers' perceptions of their students. Jacobson asked two groups of teachers to rank a set of children's photographs by their American or Mexican appearance (American was not defined). Essentially, the teachers agreed on their rankings. They were then asked to rank photographs of Mexican children who were unknown to one group of teachers but were the students of the other group. Here there was little agreement. The teachers who knew the Mexican children saw those with higher IQ's as looking more American. The significant correlation of IQ and appearance was present only when the IQ scores were known. Apparently, teachers agreed in their perception of "Mexican-looking" until they knew how a child tested—then their perceptions showed a marked change.

The above research demonstrates that teachers, reflecting the institutionalized values of the larger society, have traditionally held negative perceptions of disadvantaged and minority youth. We shall now look at the manner in which these perceptions have caused educators to misinterpret educational and psychological theory.

Racism and Educational Theory

Racism wears many faces in the classroom. We are all too familiar with the type of teacher who told his student, "We just got a new dog at our house. As a matter of fact, he looks very much like you; he looks so much like you that we've decided to call him 'Blackie'."[13] Overt hostility such as this receives much publicity and—like the behavior of Mr. Ostrowski in the excerpt from the *Autobiography of Malcolm X*—arouses horror and indignation in most school personnel.

However, the covert and often unconscious behavior of teachers and administrative personnel who interpret psychological and educational theory to mean that poor and black children cannot learn is equally damaging. Frank Riessman first popularized the term "culturally deprived," a sophisticated synonym for inherent inferiority, and delineated the dominant characteristics of this child: slow mentally, which may give the impression of stupidity, physically-oriented, anti-intellectual, pragmatic rather than theoretical, inflexible and not open to reason about many of his beliefs, deficient in auditory attention and interpretation skills, an ineffective reader and generally deficient in the communication skills, ignorant in many areas, and often suggestible, although he may be suspicious of innovations. In later writing, Riessman described the "overlooked positives of disadvantaged groups." The "positives" were as damaging as the original stereotypes.

Armed with this ammunition—in addition to the alleged pathology of the culture of poverty and other concepts exhorted by educational, sociological, and psychological theoreticians—school personnel justified their behavior toward minority and poor children. For example, the concept of "readiness" has been the major rationalization for the miseducation of ghetto children.

E. L. Thorndike never dreamed he was creating a monster when he stated the Law of Readiness: "A learner must be ready to learn." This rather hazy concept simply meant that the desired response is available and likely to occur. However, defining readiness was tenuous at best. If an organism learned, apparently it was ready. If it did not, apparently it was not ready.

Many educators have overlooked motivation and teacher expectation as selected factors that relate to readiness. Educators, utilizing their usual eclectic approach to psychology, meshed this principle with maturation and concluded that readiness for learning tasks follows a pattern similar to physiological readiness. The process was fixed and could not be accelerated. Therefore, children who were not enchanted by the dry, sterile curriculum and rigid teaching methods obviously were not ready to learn. Such middle class children were considered underachievers, and lower class and black children were considered dull. Teachers awaiting the "teachable moment" busied the children with activities such as coloring maps, cleanliness, manneriness, resting, field trips, and so forth. In the meantime, they empathized with each other in the faculty lounge for their martyrdom and maliciously exchanged tidbits about the children's lineage and abilities.

Readiness was soon superseded by the concept "critical period"—the time in which certain tasks are most likely to be learned. If this period is passed without task attainment, then the specific task may never be fully learned. The critical period, eclectically interpreted, further absolved the schools from responsibility for the low level of learning in ghetto schools. Children who failed to achieve "readiness" certainly missed the "critical period," and so schools in the inner city became custodial rather than educational institutions.

Next, the term "motoric" was applied to the ghetto child. Miller and Swanson (1960) asserted that if the teacher enables the lower class child to express himself with the large muscles of the torso and limbs, the students may make surprising educational progress. Other theorists have written long essays about the physically-oriented child who learns best through role-playing, games, and dramatic play. However, a visit to any middle class public or private school, pre-kindergarten through graduate school, will find these students, too, involved in a variety of active learning experiences that serve to make education exciting and challenging.

The Teacher and Quality Education

The teacher is a significant person in bringing quality education to ghetto schools. Arthur Combs (1962) asserts that some improvements sought by educators can be brought about by spending more money, by building better schools, be introducing new courses of study, new standards, or new equipment. However, he believes the most important changes will occur only as teachers change, for institutions are made up of people and it is the classroom behavior of teachers that will finally determine whether our schools fail or whether they meet the challenge of our times.

Carl Rogers (1967) also stresses the importance of the teacher's attitude and behavior in the classroom. He postulates that one of the most important conditions facilitating learning is the quality of attitudes in the interpersonal relationship between teacher and learner. He emphasizes the need for teachers to be genuine instead of putting on a facade. Teachers must prize, accept, and trust their students in addition to developing an empathic understanding of them. According to Rogers, individuals who hold attitudes of genuineness and trust in their students are more effective in the classroom than those who do not. Weinberg (1967) also believes that teachers hold the key to progress in education. He believes that what counts in the classroom and *throughout the schools* is the human meaning of the interaction of professional personnel and children.

In ghetto schools, the interaction between professional personnel and children has operated in the racist frame of reference. For many years humanism has taken the form of kindly missionaries collecting cast-off clothing for the natives. Humanism has meant concern for hygiene, deportment, and nutrition with little concern for encouraging children to learn.

Rapidly replacing the missionary is the educational mercenary who has suddenly become concerned about the education of poor and black children. This individual is often employed as an instructional specialist, curriculum specialist, or communications media specialist, who has been given the responsibility of helping teachers meet the learning needs of disadvantaged children. Like the specialists in Jonathan Kozol's *Death at an Early Age,* many special school personnel neither like nor understand the black child. They continue to measure him by white middle class standards and believe there is gross pathology in the black community. With the aid of Title I funds, they have purchased books, tapes, projectors, tape recorders, and films that collect dust in the closets of the school. Few teachers know how to use these new media, and even fewer want to use them. The specialist plans numerous field trips for the children that are totally unrelated to the curriculum.

One critic of these practices cited the following incident. A field trip was planned to acquaint the "disadvantaged" children with trains (even though planes are more relevant to this age). Much time was spent insuring that the children had the correct change for the fare, had brought their lunch, and were dressed properly. No preparation was given regarding trains as a mode of transportation. The children then rode the train, ate their lunch, and talked about the same experiences they talked about on the playground. Any learning that took place was incidental.

Humanism in the classroom should mean that the teacher is a professional educator who accepts the child as an individual, believes he can learn, and provides educational experiences to insure that he does learn. This teacher respects the child and is concerned about his personal life but does not use the handicaps he brings to the classroom to obviate learning. Hunger, hygiene, and health certainly must be taken care of before the child is ready to learn, but the ultimate goal is education.

An effective teacher in an urban school recognizes the importance of involving parents in the education of the child. Numerous contacts must be made with parents. These contacts should include visits to the home to discuss the mutual responsibility to encourage learning. The teacher's role is not to educate the parent but to learn more about the child from the parent. Notes should be written and calls should be made to praise the child's efforts and to encourage improved performance.

It is extremely important that teachers exercise control over the quality of education in their colleagues' classrooms. The teacher has a responsibility to insure that students throughout the school receive the best education. It is inexcusable for a teacher, under the guise of academic freedom, to be oblivious of miseducation in other classrooms.

An effective teacher in any school must have mastery of the subject matter. One critical problem in poor schools is the large number of permanent substitutes and individuals teaching out of their field. It is indeed strange that educators concerned about providing an abundant educational environment for deprived children begin with teachers who are so ill-equipped to provide such an environment.

For example, the Chicago public schools announced in 1968 that for the first time in many years they had a waiting list of teachers for the inner city. College students who could no longer qualify for draft deferments were promised deferments if they taught in inner city schools. A two-week orientation to teaching was provided. School personnel asserted that ghetto children would have "good" male models in their classrooms and would benefit from the expertise of these scholars. However, in a Chicago newspaper article, the prospective teachers were quoted as saying they would not have accepted the positions if the war in Viet Nam were over, and only a small percentage intended to remain in the field of education.

To insure that teacher quality is maintained, in-service education should be continuous, and it should be conducted during school hours. It is unrealistic to expect teachers to be receptive to continuing education programs held after school and on Saturdays.

In-service education should include the updating of subject matter. Experts in curriculum areas should be brought in to share the most recent findings with the faculty. Instructional specialists should demonstrate the latest instructional methodology to teachers. Concepts such as individualized instruction and skill grouping should be demonstrated in a realistic setting to prove that they are possible. Social psychologists and sociologists should help teachers interpret problems in the student-teaching environment and determine strategies to resolve them. Parents should be invited to in-service sessions to inform teachers of their aspirations and concerns for their children. In planning in-service sessions, teachers should have the responsibility for determining the priorities and developing the calendar. In-service education should also include a teacher-exchange program. Teachers could gain experience in other community schools, while other teachers should welcome the opportunity to teach in a challenging inner city situation.

In-service education should be stimulating and motivating. It should include incentives for teachers, such as expense-paid trips to regional and national professional conferences, scholarships for culturally-enriching travel, and additional salary for the development of curriculum guides and materials.

Other Resources Essential for Quality Education

In addition to the teacher, we must provide other resources to insure quality education. In order to do this, expenditures for schools should be in direct proportion to the needs of the students. In schools where academic achievement is lowest, the per-pupil expenditure should be highest. At present, the reverse is true. We must have a pupil-teacher ratio that corresponds with the needs of the students and the skills of the teacher. We must utilize the services of para-professionals in order that the teacher may function as a learning and behavioral diagnostician, rather than perform many roles inadequately.

We must provide curriculum materials that are relevant to the student's background and interests. We must extend the school day and the school year in order to achieve and maintain high levels of learning. We must have, in each school, a learning center where a variety of educational hardware and software are available for individualized and group instruction. And we must make available on the school premises the necessary health services for the prevention and remediation of physical and psychological problems. Early childhood education should be provided for preschool children so they will begin school with the cognitive and affective skills essential to success.

Finally, parents must be involved in the education of their children through a range of experiences—as representatives on school governing boards and advisory committees and as room mothers and para-professionals. Parents, school personnel, and boards of education have served as a check and balance system in middle class communities to insure high levels of educational attainment. A similar system must be developed in schools for the poor.

Parents in black and poor communities often appear to be unconcerned about the education of their children. This is not true. These parents are deeply concerned and view education as a way of insuring that their children will have a better life. However, because they are able to recall bitter experiences as children enrolled in the public schools, they are hesitant about interacting with the educational establishment. Because their language is not sophisticated and their dress is often less than fashionable, they are reluctant to come to school and express their opinions. School authorities often are paternalistic and use educational jargon to talk down to parents. They put them on the defensive and make them feel guilty and uncomfortable. Hostility and confrontations are the result. Mechanisms must be developed to facilitate the involvement of low income parents in the education of their children. A climate of mutual respect must be developed if school personnel and parents are to cooperate in educating poor children.

Summary

Providing quality education in low income schools is one of the most critical problems in American education. Many have viewed this problem simplistically and assert that quality will come in poor schools through reduced class size, through educational hardware and software, and through new physical plants. Material improvements are essential to quality; however, they do not insure quality. The major barrier to improving the quality of the educational environment for black and poor children is covert and often unconscious racism in educational personnel.

In this chapter, we have seen how racism is inculcated in black and white Americans through the socialization process and how it is reflected in teacher attitudes, expectations, behavior, and interpretations of educational theory.

How can the influence of racism be eliminated? This is the question that white Americans ask, for they believe it can be obliterated as easily as removing an uncomfortable garment. Few people recognize that racism is deeply entrenched. Young black Americans recognize this and are working desperately to attack the racism that has clouded their minds and their self-images. With slogans such as "Black is Beautiful" and "Black Power," natural hair styles and dashikis, they are rejecting the norms set for them by white society and developing new values and standards of their own. White America can learn from this search for identity. They, too, should be searching for the true relationship between the races and casting off the paternalistic role they assume so readily. Rather than attempting to rationalize black America's behavior, they should be studying white America and developing strategies to combat racism. With both groups aggressively attacking this insidious phenomenon, we may look forward to a multiracial, pluralistic nation that is truly democratic.

To eradicate the influence of racism on school personnel, educational institutions must consider it a major priority. Efforts should include pre-service and in-service seminars designed to make personnel sensitive to their attitudes and able to deal with them objectively. Because racism is deeply ingrained in all individuals, it is unrealistic to assume it can be eliminated in a short period of time. Programs to attack this phenomenon must be on-going. It is also extremely important that the entire spectrum of educational personnel from superintendent to custodian be involved in this process.

When people become aware of their attitudes and learn techniques and behaviors to change them, then educational innovations will play a meaningful role. Without this first step, material improvements will be utilized in the traditional paternalistic manner that has

retarded the educational development of black children.
Once people can deal effectively with racist attitudes, perhaps
teachers like Mr. Ostrowski will respond to their students' ambitions
with remarks that will encourage them to reach for the stars. And
the dream of Dr. Martin Luther King, Jr., will be realized.

Notes

1. *Autobiography of Malcolm X* (New York: Grove Press, 1965), pp. 36-37. Reproduced by permission.
2. M. Green, *The Public School and the Private Vision* (New York: Random House Inc., 1965), p. 3.
3. W. Brookover and E. Erickson, *Sociological Foundation of Educability* (New York: Allyn and Bacon, in press). Reproduced by permission.
4. M. Deutsch, "The Principal Issue," *Harvard Educational Review* (1966) 36: 492. Reproduced by permission.
5. S. W. Itskoff, *"Book Reviews"* in *The Record*, Columbia University (November, 1967).
6. W. M. Young, "The Real Moynihan Report" in L. Rainwater and W. L. Yancey, *The Moynihan Report and the Politics of Controversy* (Cambridge: MIT Press, 1967), pp. 415-416.
7. *Racial Isolation in the Public Schools*, Summary, p. 1
8. *Ibid.*, p. 11.
9. *Ibid.*, p. 11.
10. D. Harley, "Institutionalized Racism in America," unpublished paper, Michigan State University, Lansing, Mich., 1968.
11. *Ibid.*
12. R. Benedict, *Patterns of Culture* (New York: Mentor Book Company, 1946), p. 18.
13. *Report of the Task Force on Human Rights* (Washington, D.C.: National Education Association, 1968) p. 47.

References

Allport, Gordon. *The Nature of Prejudice.* Cambridge: Addison-Wesley, 1954.

Ausubel, David P. and Ausubel, Pearl. "Ego Development Among Segregated Negro Children" in A. H. Passow (ed.), *Education in Depressed Areas.* New York: Columbia University Press, 1963.

Becker, Howard S. "Career Patterns of Public School Teachers," *Journal of Sociology,* 1962, 57: 470-477.

Billingsley, Andrew. *Black Families in White America.* Englewood Cliffs, N.J.: Prentice-Hall, 1968.

Clark, Kenneth B. "Clash of Cultures in the Classroom," in M. Weinberg (ed.), *Learning Together.* Chicago: Integrated Education Associates, 1964.

Coleman, James S., et al. *Equality of Educational Opportunity.* U.S. Office of Education. Washington, D.C.: U.S. Government Printing Office, 1966.

Combs, Arthur W. "A Perceptual View of the Adequate Personality," in *Perceiving, Behaving, Becoming.* Washington, D.C.: Association for Supervision and Curriculum Development, 1962.

Gottlieb, David. "Teaching and Students: The Views of Negro and White Teachers," *Sociology of Education,* 1964, 27: 345-353.

Grambs, Jean. "Are We Training Prejudiced Teachers?" *School and Society,* 1950, 71: 196-198.

Groff, Patrick J. "Dissatisfaction in Teaching the CD Child," *Phi Delta Kappan,* 1963, 45: 76.

Harley, David. "Institutionalized Racism in America." Unpublished paper, Michigan State University, Lansing, Mich., 1968.

Hogan, Ermon O. "Prejudice in Teacher Candidates." Unpublished paper, Michigan State University, Lansing, Mich., 1968.

Hogan, Ermon O. and Boca, Thelma. "Inner-City Versus Outer-City: Opinions of Undergraduate Education Students." *Journal of Teacher Education,* Winter, 1968, 19: 495-497.

Jencks, Christopher. "Private Schools for Black Children." *New York Times Magazine* (November 3, 1968).

Kozol, Jonathan. *Death at an Early Age.* Boston: Houghton-Mifflin, 1967.

Levin, Henry M. "What Difference Do Schools Make?" *Saturday Review,* January 20, 1968, p. 57-58.

Miller, Daniel R. and Swanson, Guy E. *Inner Conflict and Defense.* New York: Henry Holt, 1960.

Moynihan, Daniel. *The Negro Family: The Case for National Action.* Washington, D.C.: U.S. Government Printing Office, 1965.

Passow, A. Harry (ed.) *Education in Depressed Areas.* New York: Columbia University Press, 1963.

Racial Isolation in the Public Schools. U.S. Commission on Civil Rights. Washington, D.C.: U.S. Government Printing Office, 1967.

Report of the National Advisory Commission on Civil Disorders. U.S. Riot Commission Report; also called the Kerner Report. Washington, D.C.: U.S. Government Printing Office, 1968.

Rogers, Carl R. "Humanizing Education: The Person in the Process," *ASCD News Exchange,* 1967, 4: 2.

Rose, Arnold M. "The Causes of Prejudice," in F. E. Merrill (ed.), *Social Problems.* New York: Alfred A. Knopf, 1950.

Rosenthal, Robert and Jacobson, Lenore. *Pygmalion in the Classroom.* New York: Holt, Rinehart and Winston, 1968.

Weinberg, Meyer. "Techniques for Achieving Racially Desegregated Superior Quality Education in the Public Schools of Chicago, Illinois." Paper for U.S. Commission on Civil Rights Conference, Washington, D.C., 1967.

8 | THE NEED FOR POSITIVE RACIAL ATTITUDES IN TEXTBOOKS

James A. Banks

Dr. Banks focuses on the significant impact of textbooks as a tool either to perpetuate racial stereotypes or to increase understanding between blacks and whites. He believes that we need a realistic and comprehensive view of blacks in teaching materials for four basic reasons: both black children and white children must have healthy racial attitudes in our society; the school must assume the initial responsibility for fostering healthy racial attitudes and positive intergroup relations; textbooks do influence racial attitudes; and students in a democratic society should have opportunities to gain insights into racial problems and conflicts.

The author cites evidence that textbooks have ignored the role of blacks in American society. Texts have contributed to the negative evaluation of blacks held by many whites and to the negative self-image of black children.

To bring about more accurate treatment of blacks in textbooks, Dr. Banks submits that educators must admit that they are responsible for past omissions and distortions. The pivotal strategy for changing the image of blacks must be an attempt to modify the racial attitudes of professional educators.

Dr. Banks is Assistant Professor of Education at the University of Washington. He is author of *Black Americans: A History for Young People* and *Teaching the Black Experience in the Elementary School.* He is also a consultant to the U.S. Office of Education Follow Through Program.

Educators, after decades of apathy and indifference to racial problems, have begun to confront the anguished truism that the school must play a central role in mitigating racism in America. Historically, our schools, like the society of which they are a part, have lacked a commitment to the assimilation and education of Negroes and to the education of other Americans about Negroes. Belatedly, educators have realized that unless the school plays a decisive role in ameliorating social injustice, our society is destined for decades of racial cleavage and strife.

Discrimination because of race, creed, or national origin is antithetical to the democratic ideology. Since the public school is committed to the democratic ethos in principle, it has a major responsibility to foster racial attitudes which will contribute to the elimination of discrimination in American society.

Racism is reflected and perpetuated in the textbooks that children spend hours studying. As Hillel Black has written:

> Among the perversions committed in the name of education, few equal the schoolbook's treatment of the Negro and his history. For more than 150 years he was presented to millions of children, both black and white, as a subhuman, incapable of achieving culture, happy in servitude, a passive outsider in the development and struggles of the American people. Indeed, it may be said that both white and Negro youngsters have been exposed to a form of racism in America more damaging than apartheid.[1]

Green has noted the gross omission of the Negro in textbooks: ". . . the history of the Negro has been systematically excluded from our schoolbooks."[2] A study by Nancy Larrick indicates that racism is equally pervasive in trade books. After studying more than five thousand children's books published during a three-year period, she concluded that ". . . our children are brought up on gentle doses of racism."[3]

Only in recent decades have educators en masse expressed concern about the treatment of blacks in textbooks. Since 1960, many studies and articles have focused on this subject. There were earlier attempts by individuals to focus attention on this problem, but they were largely futile. Early in this century, Edward A. Johnson (1911), a leading Negro historian and teacher, decried the "sins of omission and commission" of white authors. Johnson argued that authors had studiously left out many creditable deeds of the Negro. In the 1930's and 1940's, civil rights groups also stated their concern about the image of blacks in textbooks. Walter White (1939), national director of the NAACP, published a pamphlet entitled "Anti-Negro Propaganda in School Textbooks." These men foreshadowed the critics of the 1960's.

It is important for all educators to recognize that a realistic and comprehensive depiction of the Negro and other minority groups in teaching materials is necessary for these basic reasons: (1) all children in our society must have healthy racial attitudes; (2) the school must assume the initial responsibility for developing and fostering healthy racial attitudes and positive intergroup relations; (3) textbooks can influence racial attitudes; and (4) students in a democratic society should be given opportunities to gain insights into racial problems and conflicts.

This chapter will elucidate these four premises, it will review the literature on the treatment of blacks in textbooks in order to document the extent of the problem, and finally, it will promulgate strategies for change and positive approaches to the problem.

Negative Racial Attitudes in Children

There is an urgent need for black children and white children to develop healthy racial attitudes. Within recent decades, evidence has been adduced which indicates that Negro children frequently have ambivalent racial attitudes, deflated self-images, and low educational and occupational aspirations. Clark and Clark (1950) found that a majority of black children from ages five to seven prefer white skin color to brown. They also found that by age seven black children often avoid realistic self-identification. Some showed emotional conflict when they were asked to indicate a color preference. The Clarks reported that:

> It is clear that the Negro child by age five is aware of the fact that to be colored in contemporary American society is a mark of inferior status. This apparently introduces a fundamental conflict at the very foundation of the ego structure.[4]

Morland found that both Negro and white subjects prefer white children to Negroes in pictures:

> A preference for whites was shown by a majority of subjects, including the youngest. . . This indicates that preference for whites by children of both races developed early, even before racial differences could be communicated. Such results can be interpreted to mean that learning to prefer whites comes through "indirect" rather than through "direct" verbal instruction.[5]

Other studies confirm these findings. Grossack (1965) found that black children, aged three to five, showed a preference for white dolls in a collection of white and black dolls. Goodman (1952) found that black children not yet five years old sense that they are marked.

A study by Keller (1963) indicates that black children typically have lower self-images than whites. She found that fifth grade Negro children showed more negative self-evaluations than white children and over half of the Negro children (as judged by their teachers) had little motivation, were sad or preoccupied, or were working below capacity. Further, research by Brookover and associates (1964) has established the fact that negative self-concepts are related to academic failure.

Although research suggests that black children value white skin over black, often at an early age, recent research by the author (Banks, 1967) indicates that Negro youngsters perceive whites as people who feel that they are superior and who deliberately oppress blacks. A group of Negro subjects were asked to complete the statement "Most white people . . ." A majority believed that most white people hate Negroes because of their color and that whites dislike integrated situations. However, the same subjects held many of the pervasive stereotypes of Negroes—for example, a majority felt that blacks are "lazy." These findings suggest that the racial attitudes of black youngsters are confused, bizarre, and ambivalent. They seemingly accept the superiority of whites, which is taught in the larger environment, but as they grow older, they express hate for their "superiors."

Many factors influence the black child's adjustment to school, but research indicates that negative racial attitudes and poor self-images contribute to the massive failure that many Negro youngsters experience in school (Coleman, 1966).

There is evidence that white youngsters are aware of the dominant attitude toward Negroes in American society and that they often respond negatively to Negroes. In a study by Trager and Yarrow (1952), more than two-thirds of the white subjects in kindergarten, first, and second grades verbalized hostility toward blacks. These negative racial attitudes intensify as children grow older. Radke, Trager, and Davis (1949) found an increase in the percentage of children expressing prejudice between kindergarten and second grade.

Trent (1953) found that children who are self-accepting tend to express positive racial attitudes, while those who reject themselves verbalize negative racial attitudes. It seems imperative that we help *all* children to develop positive self-concepts as well as positive racial attitudes.

The School's Role in Fostering Healthy Racial Attitudes

The public school has a responsibility to help children develop positive racial attitudes. The American Council on Education contends that the educational forces and institutions of the United States have a responsibility for direct effort toward the improvement of intergroup relations:

> Because it is a public and a social force, education cannot avoid a high degree of responsibility to the social context in which it operates.[6]

Racial tension is high in the United States, and the school has a responsibility to help reduce it because racial tension and conflict are directly adverse to the growth and development of a healthy and vigorous democracy.

Respect for others, regardless of race, creed, economic status, or national origin is a central tenet of the democratic ideology. The idea of the brotherhood of man is also central to American democracy. According to Michaelis (1968), one of the central goals of the social studies curriculum is to help children develop attitudes, appreciations, and behavior patterns which are consistent with democratic beliefs. Jarolimek (1963) states that the main objective of the social studies curriculum is the same as the main objective of the total school program—the development of citizens who adhere to democratic ideals.

If we are to inculcate democratic racial attitudes, we must perpetuate an image of the Negro that is conducive to the development of democratic citizens. The exclusive presentation of white achievements in textbooks perpetuates an ethnocentric chauvinism among white youngsters and develops in them a false and tenuous sense of racial superiority. White children may well be baffled and perplexed by the disparities and inconsistencies in our teaching democratic ideology and at the same time degrading the Negro in textbooks. Such contradictions in ideology and practice create conflict and ill feelings in all children. In addition, white children are unable to gain respect for the black American and his contributions to American life. Such respect is requisite to the development of racial harmony and understanding in a nation that is currently characterized by racial turmoil.

Teaching Insight into Racial Problems

Children in the elementary and high school grades should have ample opportunities to gain insights into racial problems and racial conflict. Krug (1960) contends that teaching which ignores racial conflict is inconsistent with democratic education and new insights into the theory of learning. Democracy grants every individual the right to explore, examine, and reach his own conclusions through reflection and discussion. To deny students opportunities to reflect on racial problems is to refute the very tenets of democracy.

With the unprecedented accumulation and proliferation of knowledge, educators have become increasingly concerned with augmenting children's abilities to reflect and to solve problems. Hunt and Metcalf (1955) contend that issues such as racial conflict, which force students to examine their values, provide the best material for stimulating reflection. They believe that doubt is the basis for reflection and that reflection is the basis for understanding.

Kvaraceus (1965) contends that curriculum experiences are irrelevant and pointless to many youngsters because there is a tremendous gap between reality and the school curriculum. He writes:

This educational lag between the outside world and the classroom has been handicapping to all categories of learners, both advantaged and disadvantaged.[7]

The Michigan Department of Public Instruction suggests that majority group children are likely to suffer from guilt feelings if there are obvious and gross discrepancies between what they are taught about democracy and what is practiced in American society.[8]

Textbooks and Racial Attitudes

It is recognized that the textbook does not constitute the whole curriculum, and children may be exposed to other materials and activities which provide them with opportunities to gain insights into racial problems. However, most evidence indicates that the textbook is the *bulk* of the curriculum for most schools.

Elkin (1965) states that textbooks are the de facto courses of study for most classrooms and also the major source of information for the teacher. The latter is especially true on the subject of the

Negro in American life. Since most college history courses omit the role of the Negro in our heritage, teachers are not well informed about the historical, sociological, and psychological aspects of the Negro's role in American society.

Black (1967) points out that a child will either commit to memory or attempt to absorb at least 32,000 textbook pages during his elementary and high school years. Textbooks impart most of the skills and knowledge which the child will learn in school. About seventy-five percent of a child's classwork and about ninety percent of his homework centers on the textbook. Thus, the textbook has tremendous opportunities to influence children's attitudes.

While the evidence is not massive, some research indicates that textbooks and other curriculum materials affect children's racial attitudes. Litcher and Johnson (in press) investigated the effects of all-white and multi-ethnic readers on the racial attitudes of white youngsters in the second grade. The children who made up the experimental group used a multi-ethnic reader which included characters from several different racial and ethnic groups; the children in the control group used a reader with all-white characters. The authors concluded that "Use of the multi-ethnic reader resulted in marked positive change in the subjects' attitudes towards Negroes. . . ."

A study by Trager and Yarrow (1952) indicates that curriculum experiences influence the racial attitudes of students. These researchers found that children who were exposed to books which emphasized cultural pluralism experienced a gain in positive racial attitudes. Those who were exposed to books stressing cultural ethnocentrism experienced a decrease in positive racial attitudes.

Johnson studied the effects of learning Negro history on the racial attitudes of Negro children (Johnson, 1966). The children studied both African and Negro history in a Freedom School each Saturday morning. Johnson used interviews "to determine changes in superego strength, in self-confidence, in attitudes toward Negroes and toward civil rights." The results indicate that studying Negro history can affect the racial attitudes of Negro children positively:

> . . . they become more confident in themselves, more convinced that Negroes and whites are equal, and more militant toward civil rights.

> The most striking effect of participation in the Freedom School is the increased conviction that all people are equal.

The findings of the study . . . can be taken as tentative evidence that programs, such as the Freedom School, which teach Negro history and culture can be effective in raising Negro boys' attitudes toward self and toward Negroes.[9]

The Treatment of the Negro in Textbooks

This section will review the most significant literature on the image of the Negro in textbooks.

The most comprehensive study conducted to date was completed in 1949 by a committee of the American Council on Education (*Intergroup Relations in Teaching Materials,* 1949). The committee found that most content about blacks was in history texts, and it dealt chiefly with the slavery and Reconstruction era. Authors usually depicted slaves as well treated, happy, and contented. The slave revolt led by Nat Turner was attributed to Turner's fanaticism and the activities of northern Abolitionists rather than to discontent born of devastating conditions. While few texts noted the Negro's positive participation in the Civil War, most gave accounts of his share in the failure and corruption of Reconstruction governments.

The committee also found that Africa was treated as a continent of strange and backward peoples possessing the simplest culture, vastly different from our own. Blacks in contemporary society were largely ignored. There was a tendency to evade problems related to discrimination in housing, voting, jurisprudence, education, and public accommodation. While the committee disclosed blatant bias in textbooks, they concluded that:

. . . the more recent the text the greater the likelihood that a full, varied and balanced treatment of the Negro will be found.[10]

Marcus (1961) studied the treatment of minorities in the most widely used junior and senior high school social studies textbooks. He found that very little progress has been made since the study conducted by the American Council on Education in 1949. The most obvious weakness was a lack of any serious discussion of the Negro's current struggles and changing status. Authors treated racial inequality and attempts at its eradication with complacent generalizations rather than hard facts. The achievements of contemporary blacks were mentioned in only a minority of the books. Blacks were portrayed primarily as simple, childlike slaves and as uneducated, bewildered freedmen. Marcus reported two other significant facts: (1) scientific knowledge and sound understanding of the basic similarity and equality of the races of mankind was absent from a majority of the books; and (2) with few exceptions, photographs and other illustrations continued to portray America as a lily white nation, not as interracial and increasingly integrated.

Golden (1964) studied the treatment of minority groups in primary social studies textbooks and found more emphasis on European immigrants than racial minorities.

> So much information is omitted on the lives of Negroes, Orientals, Jewish, and Mexican persons that pupils probably find few similarities to their own lives.[11]

She also found that all Negro adults in the textbooks had low status jobs.

A team of historians at the University of California at Berkeley, headed by Kenneth M. Stampp (1965), studied the treatment of American blacks in the most widely used American history textbooks in California. They found that textbooks virtually omitted blacks and played down or ignored the long history of violence against them ". . . suggesting in different ways that racial contacts have been distinguished by a progressive harmony."[12]

There was a tendency for authors to implicitly deny the obvious deprivations suffered by Negroes. The investigators contend that textbook authors often implied approval for the repression of Negroes or patronized them as being unqualified for life in a democratic society. The books also avoided controversial issues ". . . to purvey a sweet-and-light picture of American history that is both false and vicious in its effects."[13]

Anderson (1966) studied a sample of elementary social studies textbooks and made the following generalizations: (1) The textbooks suggested that blacks *arrived* in America and overlooked the fact that they were forced to come. (2) The slave trade and slavery as an institution were not discussed. (3) Abolitionism as a protest movement was omitted. (4) The emancipation of the slaves was related primarily as a feather in the cap of Lincoln. (5) Blacks were usually not mentioned between Reconstruction and the 1954 Supreme Court Decision. The textbooks did not attempt to discuss differences in skin color and the concept of "race" but perpetuated unscientific, nineteenth century notions.

In reviewing the study by Anderson, Sloan (1966) wrote:

> In that part of her survey dealing with the treatment of the American Negro in elementary school texts, Miss Anderson shows a far worse and therefore more deplorable situation than that in the secondary school texts. Elementary school students . . . are in their most formative years and the need for historical truth and perspective is at least as vital as it is in the upper grades . . . the grade school history texts are insipid, inadequate, and inaccurate.[14]

Sloan studied the treatment of the Negro in thirteen secondary American history textbooks and concluded that:

> In most of the texts it can be said that the Negro is considered only a slave before the Civil War and a problem since the Civil War.[15]

But Sloan did note some progress:

> One need go back only to the 1950's and compare these editions with 1966 editions of the same texts to see the startling changes and improvements.[16]

In summary, blacks are often omitted in contemporary American textbooks or are treated in stereotypic fashion. While progress has been made, much more must be done before blacks are presented in a comprehensive and realistic fashion.

Many recent attempts to portray the cultural diversity of American life in textbooks have been expedient, superficial, and ineffective gestures made by publishers responding to the demands of educators who, in turn, have been coerced to take action by enlightened community pressure groups. Often these attempts have been little more than coloring all-white faces *brown*. A study by Glancy (1964) indicated that Negroes are often "positively stereotyped" in children's trade books. Coloring white characters brown, or perpetuating a sterile middle class image of the Negro, will not meet the criteria of objective treatment of the Negro because such images are inconsistent with reality. The American child should be exposed to *all* types and classes of Negroes in American life, with illustrations depicting the diversity of Negroid racial traits. Overemphasis on one type or the creation of an ideal type will not suffice.

Trade books, like textbooks, portray a lily white world. Nancy

Larrick (1965) studied more than five thousand trade books for children published from 1962 to 1964. Only 349 included one or more blacks.

The Publisher's Role

Educators must admit that they are primarily responsible for the omissions and distortions in the treatment of the Negro in textbooks. To contend that publishers are responsible would be analogous to arguing that cigarette manufacturers are responsible for the alarming number of cancer victims in America. Textbook manufacturing, like cigarette manufacturing, is a business. Textbook publishers create and distribute materials which are *demanded* and *purchased* by their customers. Whether we condone their policy or not, most publishers are more committed to increasing sales than to ethical principles. Their interest is in producing materials that will be purchased by their customers.

Textbook publishers have no desire to usurp the responsibility for determining the content of textbooks from educators. Lyle M. Spencer, president of Science Research Associates, said to a group of publishers:

> You are the service guy behind the cafeteria counter. Your job is to supply the customer with what he wants, not the dietitian telling him what he should have for dinner.[17]

Kenneth Lund, a senior vice-president and editor-in-chief at Scott, Foresman and Company, explained why his firm publishes both all-white and integrated editions of textbooks:

> We continue to serve our existing customers who want all-white texts and those adopting customers who want new materials. Educational policy does not rest with us. It is made by the states, local school boards, administrators, and teaching staffs. We produce for them the kinds of materials they want. In our business the customer chooses.[18]

When, in rare instances, a publisher is innovative, he may suffer financially. Thus, he becomes reluctant to take further risks in the future. Follett Educational Corporation in Chicago was one of the first publishers to issue integrated textbooks. When the company issued its integrated reading series in cooperation with the Detroit Board of Education, it faced financial hazards. Robert J. R. Follett, president of the firm, recalls:

> In 1960 Follett Educational Corporation began working with the Detroit Board of Education to bring out an integrated reading series. The first book showed children of different races in an inner city environment. The black community in Detroit protested. Since non-integrated readers showed a suburban environment, they said the book implied that black families or integrated groups could only live in the inner city while all-white groups could live in the suburbs.
>
> The protest resulted in our destroying 10,000 copies of the book, and a new version was prepared showing a more suburban type of environment. This new version was well received by Detroit parents—but it was roundly denounced from a variety of sources for being unrealistic.
>
> For several years after Follett began publishing this integrated series, it was not officially adopted by any school system except Detroit. The publisher was told time and again, "Our schools are not ready for integrated textbooks. We will buy a few to put into our Negro schools, but the climate is not right to adopt them for the whole school system."

Follett was far ahead of the dominant educational policies and practices of the time. This case clearly illustrates the fact that the school has basic control over the content of textbooks.

Lip service frequently has been given to the objective and realistic treatment of blacks in textbooks. But if such verbalizations were not merely attempts to reduce guilt, massive constructive action would have been taken, beginning with the simple refusal to purchase books that distort the image of minority groups.

Major distortions of other historical and social facts are not tolerated in textbooks. If a textbook stated that the Colonists had no legal right to rebel against the British (although a good case could be made for this assertion), the book would be on the blacklist of every large school district before the ink was dry. Yet educators have continued to purchase thousands of books that present the image of the contented slave whose emancipation was forced upon him by a benevolent Lincoln.

When educators shift the responsibility for the treatment of blacks in textbooks to publishers, they are rationalizing their contentment with the stereotypic and distorted image of the Negro. Educators have accepted teaching materials that are unprofessional, but these materials have been consistent with educators' current attitudes, expectations, and perceptions. Educators have looked for a scapegoat to mitigate guilt; and textbook publishers, who rarely have been apostles in race relations, have been convenient, logical, and vulnerable targets.

Strategies for Change

The pivotal strategy for changing the image of blacks in textbooks is to modify the racial attitudes and disposition of professional educators.

Teachers, like most Americans, bring negative racial attitudes to school and later to college. There is little to suggest that the typical college experience challenges their earlier indoctrination, and their record of professional activity does not support the notion that teachers have strongly opposed our racial system (Solomon, 1968).

While research has indicated that curricular experiences can modify children's racial attitudes, it is less certain that such experiences can significantly affect the attitudes of adults. However, in spite of the limitations of our knowledge in this area, the urgent need for change makes it imperative that we attempt to modify the racial attitudes of teachers, administrators, and supervisors with appropriate curricular experiences. Courses in cultural anthropology, sociology, social psychology, and history—with emphasis on the role of minority groups in American life—may effect constructive changes. Certainly, we must help teachers and other educators who sit on textbook adoption committees to examine their own racial attitudes.

Concomitant with training teachers, school districts could commission classroom teachers to write textbooks and offer them for publication. Under the Great Cities project, the Detroit Board of Education initiated such a plan. They insisted upon final approval of the content and illustrations in the texts, and the publisher granted the school board these privileges.

School districts could cooperate by assigning writers to such projects. Each participating district would have a voice in the selection of content and would also agree to adopt the finished texts. Under such a plan, school districts would have appropriate control of content without having the responsibility for the technical aspects of book production, such as printing, artwork, sales, and distribution. This plan would also be advantageous to publishers since they would be *assured* that their books would be adopted.

Classroom teachers should be encouraged to do much more writing. They should be given time during the year or paid during the summer months to write creative and challenging materials for children. A reward system for writing, such as extra compensation or promotion, could be established. However, the "publish or perish" edict that exists in our leading colleges and universities must not be emulated. Effective teachers who do not wish to write should not be expected to write. But many teachers are potential authors. Publishers take advantage of this fact and solicit authors and editors in our public schools.

Because teachers may lack the academic background needed for writing in some disciplines, they could work with experts at local universities, or academic experts could conduct workshops so that groups of teachers would benefit from their knowledge.

School districts produce many excellent text materials inexpensively without the cooperation of textbook publishers. The Winnetka Public Schools in Illinois have produced excellent textbooks in social studies and mathematics for local use. These texts have an additional asset in that they are designed specifically to meet the unique needs of the children in the community. Classroom teachers are provided time and extra compensation for writing. The texts are printed on quality paper with black and white pictures, utilizing a relatively inexpensive printing process such as multilith.

There is little empirical evidence that the colored pictures and ostentatious paraphernalia in today's commercially-produced textbooks contribute to learning. This author suspects that many of these "aids" actually distract the students from essential learning tasks. A school district should not be reluctant to plan a text because elaborate pictures and charts cannot be included.

Another strategy for changing textbooks is for school systems to utilize boycotts to demand accurate, quality text materials. When Harper and Row produced a science series that did not include pictures of minority groups, the Newark school system attacked the publisher for using "stereotyped middle class" illustrations (Black, 1967). Within a short time, Harper and Row issued an "Intercultural Edition" that included pictures of minority groups. However, the publisher continued to sell its all-white edition to school districts that requested them.

The Detroit Board of Education, responding to pressure from

civil rights groups, initiated an effective boycott. When the NAACP complained that Laidlaw's *Our United States: Bulwark of Freedom* presented a stereotyped and inaccurate view of slavery, the Detroit Board concluded that the criticism was justified. At first the Board released a supplement which corrected the flaws, but they later withdrew the book from use at the NAACP's request (Black, 1967). The publisher revised the book with great speed. These incidents illustrate the tremendous influence and control that school systems can exercise.

Any school that wishes to initiate a comprehensive program in intergroup relations must formulate a policy for dealing with pressure groups in the community. If civil rights pressure groups had not demanded reforms in Detroit, perhaps the students would still be reading texts that are insulting to black students. Indeed, much educational reform emanates from without rather than from within educational circles. For example, the emergence of public universities to serve the masses was not initiated by educators; it was a response by educators to society's demand for large numbers of trained individuals to fill positions created by technology and industry.

The school should be sensitive to the demands of community pressure groups and consider the validity of their ideas. The community should have the right to determine the goals of education for its children; however, the school should insist on its right to determine the means to achieve those ends. Among the major goals which our society has set for the schools is the development of democratic citizens capable of making rational decisions through reflective and critical thinking and citizens who have a basic respect for the integrity of individuals of all races and creeds. Since a major goal of American education is the development of democratic citizens, the school should consider the demands of each pressure group in terms of whether such demands, if implemented, would contribute to a democratic society.

Educators themselves must formulate educational policies which are consistent with our democratic heritage. If the schools instigate policies which are a breach of our democratic ethos, community groups have a right to demand change. But as long as educators are performing their duties with the best interests of all children in mind, they have a right to determine the means to educational goals— because of their professional status and because they are the ones who are ultimately responsible for the education of the children in the community.

Thus, the schools should always consider the demands of community pressure groups and respond to them in terms of their consistency with the basic aims of public education. If the demands of pressure groups are consistent with our democratic legacy, then the school should implement changes that reflect those demands. However, if the demands are inconsistent with a democratic education, then the school must stubbornly resist them. Too often educators have been too sheep-like in dealing with pressure groups whose demands violate our democratic creed (Hogan, 1968). Educators frequently have used unreasonable demands as an excuse to relieve them of their professional responsibility, to justify their apathy and educational neglect, and to rationalize their contentment with questionable educational policies.

Every community wants the school to assume the responsibility for developing democratic and patriotic citizens. In order to accomplish this momentous and elusive goal, the school must help children develop racial attitudes that are consistent with a democratic ideology. The school must help children become aware of racial problems and sound approaches to solving them if we are to perpetuate a democratic society. Each generation must make its contribution. Democracy is not merely an inherited legacy; it is a process which must be perpetuated deliberately if it is to remain viable.

Racism in textbooks must be eliminated, and this fact must be communicated clearly to the community. Hunt and Metcalf (1955) contend that the community frequently reacts negatively when the school deals with controversial issues, such as race relations or communism, because the community is not sufficiently aware of the educational goals which educators seek by teaching such issues. The problem is largely one of communication. The school has a responsibility to inform the community of the goals that it seeks when it deals with race and other controversial topics.

With an immense challenge before them, educators cannot afford to seek scapegoats, such as textbook publishers or community pressure groups, for the racism that exists in our textbooks. They must confront the fact that the image of blacks in textbooks accurately reflects educators' perceptions and attitudes toward blacks. Seeking rationalizations will not help solve the problem. Educators must face the dilemma, attempt to clarify and modify their racial attitudes, and take constructive action to ameliorate the situation. Only then can progress be made in building positive racial attitudes that are consistent with our professed national ethos. In facing this immense challenge, educators also have a tremendous opportunity to prove their professional leadership. If they fail to act *now,* they may find themselves trying to justify their existence to the communities that they allegedly serve. Acting now is *imperative,* for time is running out.

Notes

1. H. Black, *The American Schoolbook* (New York: William Morrow, 1967), p. 106. Copyright 1967 by Hillel Black. Reproduced by permission.
2. R. L. Green, "After School Integration—What? Problems in Social Learning," *Personnel and Guidance Journal* (1966), 45: 704-710.
3. N. Larrick, "The All-White World of Children's Books," *Saturday Review* (1965), 48: 63-65.
4. K. B. Clark and M. P. Clark, "Emotional Factors in Racial Identification and Preference in Negro Children," *Journal of Negro Education* (1950), 19: 341-350.
5. J. K. Morland, "Racial Acceptance and Preference of Nursery School Children in a Southern City," *Merrill-Palmer Quarterly of Behavior and Development* (1962), 8, p. 279.
6. *Intergroup Relations in Teaching Materials* (Washington, D.C.: American Council on Education, 1949), p. 10.
7. W. C. Kvaraceus, "Negro Youth and Social Adaptation: The Role of the School as an Agent of Change," in *Negro Self-Concept* (New York: McGraw-Hill, 1965), p. 94.
8. "Treatment of Minority Groups in Textbooks," Publication 529 (Lansing, Mich.: Department of Public Instruction, 1963).
9. D. W. Johnson, "Freedom School Effectiveness: Changes in Attitudes of Negro Children," *Journal of Applied Behavioral Science* (1966), 2, pp. 325, 328, 329.
10. *Intergroup Relations in Teaching Materials,* p. 136.
11. L. Golden, "The Treatment of Minority Groups in Primary Social Studies Textbooks," doctoral dissertation, Stanford University, 1964.
12. K. M. Stampp, *et al.,* "The Negro in American History Textbooks," p. 2.
13. *Ibid.,* p. 8.
14. I. Sloan, *The Negro in Modern History Textbooks* (Chicago: American Federation of Teachers, 1966), p. 7.
15. *Ibid.,* p. 7.
16. *Ibid.,* p. 5.
17. H. Black, *op. cit.,* prologue.
18. *Ibid.,* p. 120.

References

Anderson, Astrid C. "The Treatment of Racial and Cultural Diversity in Elementary Social Studies Textbooks." Report of The Lincoln Filene Center for Citizenship and Public Affairs, Tufts University, 1966.

Banks, James A. "Disadvantaged Negro Children's Racial Attitudes and Understandings of Minority Group Problems." Unpublished report, Michigan State University, 1967.

Black, Hillel. *The American Schoolbook.* New York: William Morrow, 1967.

Brookover, Wilbur B., Paterson, Ann, and Thomas, Shailer. "Self-Concept of Ability and School Achievement," *Sociology of Education,* 1964, 37: 271-278.

Clark, Kenneth B. "Clash of Cultures in the Classroom," *Integrated Education,* 1963, 1: 7-14.

Clark, Kenneth B. and Clark, Mamie P. "Emotional Factors in Racial Identification and Preference in Negro Children," *Journal of Negro Education,* 1950, 19: 341-350.

Coleman, James S., et al. *Equality of Educational Opportunity.* U.S. Office of Education. Washington, D.C.: U.S. Government Printing Office, 1966.

Elkin, Sol M. "Minorities in Textbooks: The Latest Chapter," *Teachers College Record,* 1965, 66: 502-508.

Glancy, Barbara J. "Changing Characteristics of the American Negro in Children's Fiction of 1951 through 1963." Unpublished Master's thesis, Ohio State University, 1964.

Golden, Loretta. "The Treatment of Minority Groups in Primary Social Studies Textbooks." Unpublished Doctoral dissertation, Stanford University, 1964.

Goodman, Mary Ellen. *Race Awareness in Young Children.* Cambridge: Addison-Wesley, 1952.

Grossack, Martin M. "Psychological Considerations Essential to Effective Educational Integration," *Journal of Negro Education,* 1965, 35: 278-287.

Hogan, Ermon O. "Backtalk: Kvaraceus and the Nonbooks," *Phi Delta Kappan,* 1968, 49: 416-417.

Hunt, Maurice P. and Metcalf, Lawrence E. *Teaching High School Social Studies.* New York: Harper and Row, 1955.

Intergroup Relations in Teaching Materials. Washington, D.C.: American Council on Education, 1949.

Jarolimek, John. *Social Studies in Elementary Education.* New York: Macmillan, 1963.

Johnson, David W. "Freedom School Effectiveness: Changes in Attitudes of Negro Children," *Journal of Applied Behavioral Science,* 1966, 2: 325-330.

Johnson, Edward A. *A School History of Negro Race in America.* New York: Golfman Company, 1911.

Keller, Susan. "The Social World of the Slum Child: Some Early Findings," *American Journal of Orthopsychiatry,* 1963, 33: 823-831.

Krug, Mark M. "Safe Textbooks and Citizenship Education," *School Review,* 1960, 68: 463-480.

Kvaraceus, William C. "Negro Youth and Social Adaptation: The Role of the School as an Agent of Change," in *Negro Self-Concept.* New York: McGraw-Hill, 1965.

Larrick, Nancy. "The All-White World of Children's Books," *Saturday Review,* 1965, 48: 63-65

Litcher, John H. and Johnson, David W. "Changes in Attitudes of White Elementary School Students After Use of Multi-Ethnic Readers," *Journal of Educational Psychology* (in press).

Marcus, Lloyd. *The Treatment of Minorities in Secondary School Textbooks.* New York: Anti-Defamation League of B'nai B'rith, 1961.

Michaelis, John U. *Social Studies for Children in a Democracy.* Englewood Cliffs, N.J.: Prentice-Hall, 1968.

Radke, Marian, Trager, Helen G., and Davis, Hadassah. "Social Perceptions and Attitudes of Children," *Genetic Psychology Monographs,* 1949, 40: 327-447.

Sloan, Irving. *The Negro in Modern History Textbooks.* Chicago: American Federation of Teachers, 1966.

Solomon, Benjamin. "Educators and the Racial Issue in Education," *Illinois Schools Journal,* 1968, 48: 25-34.

Stampp, Kenneth M., et al. "The Negro in American History Textbooks." Report of the California Department of Public Instruction, Sacramento, 1965.

Trager, Helen G. and Yarrow, Marian R. *They Learn What They Live.* New York: Harper and Brothers, 1952.

Trent R. "The Correlates of Self-Acceptance Among Negro Children." Doctoral dissertation, Teachers College, Columbia University, 1953.

White, Walter. "Anti-Negro Propaganda in School Textbooks." New York: National Association for the Advancement of Colored People, 1939.

9 | COMPENSATORY EDUCATION AND EDUCATIONAL GROWTH

Robert F. Morgan

Dr. Robert Morgan is Associate Professor of Psychology at St. Bonaventure University. In 1966 he organized and directed Hawaii's first compensatory education program for inpatient emotionally disturbed children. He is on the advisory board of the Association for Children with Learning Disabilities.

Dr. Morgan begins his examination of compensatory education with a look at its origin in 1956 and its growth with the impetus of the federal government.

The author analyzes the opponents of compensatory education—those who feel that special education threatens the status quo, overly favors blacks, opposes the national virtues of free competition and survival of the fittest, or moves faster than valid scientific evaluation would justify.

A major portion of this chapter is concerned with aspects of educational growth that affect compensatory education practices. Selected learning and motivational factors such as input, response, reinforcement, and social interaction and the relevance of these factors to compensatory education are discussed. Of interest and value are references to many source books, a guide to further exploration of some of the areas examined by the author.

Dr. Morgan concludes with a promising look at the future. He believes that we have the power to change the character of compensatory education from remedial charity for the environmentally retarded to self-actualization and academic growth.

The history of compensatory education is short but lively. While an ingenious historian might well trace its elements to the Greeks, Gauls or Ghengis, modern educators place its formal beginning in the United States on or about 1956 (Gordon and Wilkerson, 1966). At that time, the Demonstration Guidance Project was initiated in New York City's Junior High School 43 to pre-select and stimulate students with high potential from disadvantaged environments. Special education projects were decades old (the Harlem Project, for example), but the Demonstration Guidance Project was the first major probe at systematic model building for compensatory programs, complete with implied responsibility for local and federal government support of such efforts. The project's initial years were declared a success (Schreiber, 1958). From it sprang such massive offspring as the Higher Horizons Program (64,000 children in 1962) plus several hundred programs across the nation, all in the fresh and hopeful field of compensatory education.

In its turn, compensatory education received tremendous impetus from the massive federal funding of poverty programs such as Project Head Start, circa 1965. Major private backing paralleled this investment with single grants as large as half a million dollars; the Ford Foundation's Great Cities Project was one of several efforts. A nonexhaustive inventory of compensatory education projects in 1965 included several hundred programs in forty major cities. However, both major urban areas and smaller communities received government or private funds in order to begin compensatory educational efforts.

Unless continued defense commitments stem the necessary financial support, compensatory programs will continue their phenomenal growth for some time. These efforts are a response to the price of squandered human resources. But as ubiquitous and varied as compensatory programs are, this brand of education lags farther and farther behind the needs of its recipients. In 1960, one child of every three attending public school in the nation's fourteen largest cities was disadvantaged enough to need compensatory education. In 1970, the ratio will be one child of every two (Shaw, 1965).

Comprehensive background sources in this field are few, but the exceptions are outstanding. There are three general source books that should suffice for any novice. Gordon and Wilkerson's *Compensatory Education for the Disadvantaged* includes a city-by-city directory of compensatory programs. Their final chapter, a critique of the field, is outstanding for its unusually high level of candor, insight, innovation, and scholarship. A second source, Bloom's *Compensatory Education for Cultural Deprivation,* is a brief work containing a clear exposition of the generally accepted concerns and recommendations of compensatory educators. The pace in this field is such that this book is largely out of date; yet it remains an excellent orientation text. The most intriguing background source of the three is the U.S. Civil Rights Commission Report, *Racial Isolation in the Public Schools.* It includes a clear discussion of compensatory objectives as well as a critique of several major programs.

To get a feel for the dilemma of urban education for the disadvantaged, Passow's *Education in Depressed Areas* and Kerber and Bommarito's *The Schools and the Urban Crisis* are helpful. Both supply a wide variety of viewpoints from front-line educators and researchers in short, readable chapters.[1]

The Information Retrieval Center of the Disadvantaged (IRCD) is a specialized unit of the Educational Research Information Center (ERIC) of the U.S. Office of Education. IRCD is probably the most comprehensive continuing source for those interested in urban compensatory education. Materials are circulated freely on request.

Research, innovations, and implementation in compensatory education generally have come from programs at the extremes of clinical, socioeconomic, and educational dimensions rather than from the middle ground. Along clinical lines, we find drug research offering hope to organically disadvantaged children, and fresh approaches to psychotherapy, particularly group techniques, seem to have been helpful to the emotionally disturbed child. These psychogenic and somatogenic approaches have begun to influence educationally-oriented compensatory programs (Hobbs, 1966; Morgan, 1966a,b). Unfortunately, the middle ground of clinical programs, state hospitals and community clinics, are only in the early stages of compensatory program development for children of school age. Clinic and hospital-based education programs too often have lagged behind their public school counterparts in applying the insights of clinical psychology to solid programs.

Along the socioeconomic continuum, the impetus for innovation also comes from the extremes: the disadvantaged and the extra-advantaged. While it was concern for the disadvantaged that initiated compensatory education, it was from the quality education techniques of schools in high income communities that techniques powerful enough to be compensatory were first drawn. Shaw (1965) has pointed out that upper class suburban schools are referred to as "lighthouse schools" by many educators. It can be conjectured that the most creative and able educators are attracted to top salaries and facilities in the extra-advantaged schools or to top educational challenge and social utility in the disadvantaged schools. Other schools are left to follow progress from above and below. Educational level is another dimension along which progress is concentrated at the extremes: college and preschool. More and more college techniques are being used in high school compensatory programs. Such practices are seminars, colloquia, cooperative campuses for several schools, inter-school achievement level competition, student counseling and guidance procedures. At the preschool level, programs such as Head Start have become more popular than other federal programs focusing on later stages of development.

Much of the fledgling theoretical structure of compensatory education along with the majority of its soundest research comes from preschool educators. For one thing, preschool and post-school are periods of rapid change for any child. Bloom's (1964) longitudinal studies of over one thousand subjects support the view that variations in the environment have their greatest effect on any human characteristic during the most rapid period of change. But there seems to be another reason why the extremes of educational level are especially significant:

> If school people were not such a decent lot, one would think that these two emphases (preschool and dropout) have been so widely accepted simply because they require the least change in the school itself. It is often easier to add extensions than to change the basic structure of institutions.[2]

Thus, extremes tend to lead the middle ground because there is less vested interest in the status quo. The middle remains more resistant to innovation and change. If greatest effect occurs during periods of rapid change, perhaps generating more rapidity in change would generate more positive effects—particularly in the more somnolent educational areas.

Definition

What, specifically, do we mean by compensatory education? Gordon and Wilkerson define it as special education for the disadvantaging effects of hostile, different, and indifferent backgrounds:

> . . . programs of special and extra services intended to compensate for a complex of social, economic, and educational handicaps suffered by disadvantaged children.[3]

Another definition of compensatory education is:

> . . . a term which, as used by educators, may embody one or more of several distinct approaches to improving the quality of education for disadvantaged children.[4]

These approaches include cultural enrichment, remedial instruction, raising of self-esteem and confidence, and preschool education. Most definitions agree on two points: compensatory education is concerned with raising the quality of education and it is focused on the disadvantaged child. Thus, a useful working definition might well be: *Compensatory education is the special application of quality education to the needs of disadvantaged children.*

This definition still begs the issue of what we mean by "disadvantaged." Gordon and Wilkerson suggest that the disadvantaged child is any pre-adult of depressed social, economic, or caste status. They quote the California Advisory Commission on Compensatory Education, whose definition of the disadvantaged child is quoted as follows:

> ... below average in school achievement as measured by standardized tests and any one of the following: economic deprivation through an absent or ineffective wage earner *or* social alienation through racial and ethnic discrimination *or* geographic isolation through transiency or rurality.[5]

These definitions focus on *assumed causes* more than *observed effects.* Perhaps this is a reaction to the behavioral inventories of the disadvantaged child or his namesakes: the culturally deprived child (Riessman, 1962), the educationally depressed child, and so forth. It is apparent that while hostile, unconventional, and sterile life experiences have disadvantaging consequences which can be reflected in poor school achievement, the specific disadvantages are as varied as the quantity and timing of the causes. More and more frequently, mental retardates are being rediagnosed as emotionally disturbed or culturally deprived. The latter, on reevaluation, frequently are recategorized as emotionally disturbed. In fact, it is a rare exception when several different dimensions of pathology do not run concurrently. This is hardly surprising since early inadequate environment has been known to induce retarded behavioral abilities. What is optimistic, however, is the realization that compensatory education techniques can be used successfully to raise intellectual functioning and other behavioral abilities of the mentally retarded (Clarke and Clarke, 1954; Kirk, 1958), the emotionally disturbed (Lathen, 1966; Morgan, 1966b) as well as the culturally disadvantaged.

It is primarily among the black victims of racial isolation and white racism that we find disadvantaged children. While theories of innate racial inferiority have been laid to rest (Klineberg, 1963; Pettigrew, 1964), the environment has been creating intellectually disadvantaged black children. In Prince Edward County, Virginia, officials opposed to school integregation succeeded in halting public education for four years. With a certain amount of justification almost two thousand children could be referred to as a "disadvantaged generation."

This particular group of children was studied for characteristics of disadvantaged behavior subsequent to the closing of the schools and subsequent to attempts at compensatory education and reschooling (Green, *et al.,* 1964, 1965). The massive disadvantage of these children included deficits in a wide variety of behavioral and cognitive areas, from reading to telling time to pencil-holding. Their average intelligence was such that most would have been classified as mentally retarded. At some age levels, the main difference between the totally unschooled and the partially schooled was as great as thirty IQ points. Thus a single event—four years of educational deprivation—produced a multiplicity of disadvantaged behaviors in the student population.

Since multiple effects and multiple causes are typical of disadvantagement, a broad working definition would be: *A disadvantaged child is one for whom more than average effort is needed to achieve average performance in an average educational context.* (More than average effort refers to the efforts of the child. More than average efforts on the part of the school or the teacher are part of compensatory education.)

In this definition it is not achievement per se but the effort needed to achieve it that is at issue. Thus, the adolescent preoccupied with sports or sex whose achievement falls below class average would not be considered disadvantaged. On the other hand, organically impaired or emotionally disturbed retardates would certainly be considered disadvantaged. Such boundaries imply the importance of compensatory education in the fields of mental health and social work as well as education. The importance of sharing techniques and resources between professionals in several fields becomes apparent.

Standard Program Elements

Children who are disadvantaged by elements of their very early environment are more in need of compensatory education than their peers, and some very specific treatments are possible for them. Besides the elements of remedial instruction, cultural enrichment, self-attitude change, and preschool education, these children may be exposed to at least a few of the following in a typical compensatory education program: extra teachers for smaller classes, team teaching, curriculum innovation, reading and language development, special counseling and guidance, extracurricular innovation, and efforts directed toward parental and community involvement and dropout prevention. Through the use of these elements, it is hoped that the child who is disadvantaged very early will start school earlier, stay in school longer, enjoy a widened range of human experience, and learn from a teacher who has extra training and specialist assistants (Wayland, 1963).

The Loyal Opposition

Opposition to establishing and funding compensatory education programs generally comes from one or more of five directions: from those who believe that special education changes the status quo, overly favors Negroes, opposes the national virtues of free competition and survival of the fittest, strains the brain and health, or moves faster than valid scientific evaluation can justify.

Supporters of the status quo are generally "fiscal conservatives" who must receive inordinate proof that any change is worthwhile before blocking it in any case. An even more effective subgroup are those with emotional, financial, or status stakes within the present educational or administrative system, those whose roles would be threatened by educational innovation and structural change.

Many who oppose compensatory education on the grounds that it overly favors Negroes are sincerely afraid that it is favoritism at the expense of non-Negro children. It should help to communicate the facts that white achievement rarely loses and usually grows with school desegregation and other compensatory education techniques (Green, et al., 1967). But even this tack makes little headway, for there is powerful white racist psychological and economic resistance to progress among blacks in any direction. Despite economic and educational sanctions against blacks, individual and highly visible survivors of American racism have become judges, athletes, intellectuals, authors and entertainers. This has led to a good deal of psychological anxiety among those who feel most responsible for the Negro's plight. Karon calls this the "horse driver" phenomenon—the higher caste white feels he could not compete as an equal:

> ... if the horse knew how strong he was, he would grab the whip out of the driver's hand and say, "You pull the wagon." So you must not let the horse know how strong he is.[6]

A major objective of adequate compensatory education must be to give the disadvantaged child knowledge of where his strengths lie.

Spokesmen of our country's radical right have long opposed compensatory procedures under the slogan "survival of the fittest through free competition." A leading National Socialist of another country expressed this philosophy:

> ... hence to preserve a certain culture the man who creates it must be preserved. This preservation is bound up with the rigid law of necessity and the right to victory of the best and stronger in this world. Those who want to live, let them fight, and those who do not want to fight in this world of eternal struggle do not deserve to live.[7]

According to this view, as adapted to American shores, disadvantaged children are held back by inherent lack of intellect or motivation. The assumption is that all of our country's children have equal opportunity and only the "stupid" or "lazy" fail to prosper. Thus, fostering compensatory education supposedly diverts the energy of the strong to supporting the weak. In 1964, the conservative senator running for the United States presidency opposed equal opportunity programs on these grounds, insisting that what has made this country great is the freedom of every individual to take his own risks and make his own mark. Before the 1968 presidential election, a prominent conservative and potential candidate emphasized this view:

> ... we offer equal opportunity at the starting line in life, but no compulsory tie for everyone at the finish line.[8]

The advocate of compensatory education, of course, is not concerned with a tie at the finish line but rather with having everyone finish the race. The position of the freedom-of-competition philosopher has shown some evolution, however. Now equal opportunity is promised "at the starting line." Reduced resistance to prenatal care and preschool programs follow from this. On the other hand, programs closer to the finish line (Job Corps, Adult Literacy, Upward Bound) are still opposed.

In fact, competition *can* be a powerful motivator for progress. In the context of compensatory education programs where competitive progress is measured toward common goals, in social and academic teamwork, it seems to be effective. However, each individual, given abundant opportunity, makes his own winning contribution somewhere along the line. This is cooperative success experience versus the overwhelming "thirst after first."

That extra education may strain the brain and health is not a particularly modern point of view. In 1883, Dr. R. V. Pierce, president of the World's Dispensary Medical Association, had this to say:

> One of the greatest mistakes which people make in the management of their children is to overtask their mental faculties . . . excessive mental exertion is liable to result in softening of the brain, and various nervous diseases, sometimes culminating in insanity, and in many instances proving fatal.[9]

Parents' fears about brain strain have dogged quality education for some time, and there is no reason to assume that compensatory education will be immune. Scientists, however, tell us that any experience which children are too young to assimilate has little or no effect at all, negative *or* positive (Hebb, 1958), and this has been demonstrated in a wide variety of interactions between learning and maturation. On the other hand, motivationally speaking, it is true that an announcement "Caution: Learning the Material in This Textbook May Be Dangerous for Your Health" might well be a compensatory education technique in its own right.

The last faction among the loyal opposition stands on the firmest ground. Indeed, concerns that the speed of compensatory education's growth is out of proportion to any valid evaluation of its projects come from the ranks of compensatory educators and social scientists themselves. Hunt (1966), in a review of the literature, suggests that the growth of publications has far outstripped the effectiveness of the programs, which are too often action projects with "crash program quality." Gordon and Wilkerson (1966) surveyed compensatory education programs in 224 institutions of higher learning, and only eight (3 percent) reported systematic evaluation, either with simple before-and-after tests or more carefully designed experiments. Systematic evaluation is vital to the effective growth of compensatory education. However, this author hopes to see evaluation catch up with the high rate of program growth that is needed rather than a slowdown of program growth to match the amount of evaluation. Administrators must be sold on the need for valid project evaluation despite fears that "the truth shall set us free—in pursuit of other jobs."[10]

Compensatory programs are in a rapid state of change. The beginning of this chapter has focused on the evolution to the present and makes no pretense of being the final word. In the balance of this chapter, I would like to explore some of the aspects of educational growth that affect compensatory education and examine selected learning and motivational factors that are relevant.

Traits versus Situations

McLoughlin (1966) has criticized civil rights research for focusing on aspects of personality traits to the exclusion of situational determinants of behavior, which are more in keeping with the activist philosophy of "change the situation and you change the man." The history of psychology as a science has followed the controversy of instinct versus environment, nature versus nurture, unearthing of past experiences versus dynamic conceptions of therapy as a present-oriented interaction between patient and therapist.

Education has not escaped this controversy. To what extent does the here and now (teaching, for example) determine the achievements of the student? There are some who feel that the student brings a rigid basic personality into the school which includes a very limited set of response patterns which are difficult to modify. This trait-oriented approach was initially tied to instinct, native ability, and the supposedly dominant influence of genetic heritage on specific behavior. Explanations based on instinct soon gave ground to opposing data. In education, the proof that IQ could be varied with situational change was devastating to the genetic approach (Clarke and Clarke, 1954; Green, *et al.*, 1967; Kirk, 1958; Klineberg, 1963).

As a result, the brain was thought of as the seat of broad personality and behavioral traits more than specific intelligence or achievement. Populations of children were categorized as being a specific type of person in any number of situations.

Today's trait theorists lean not so much on genetics as on formation of personality in infancy, prior traumatic experiences, and organic roadblocks. While all of these have significant effects on behavior, none have shown the irreversibility or resistance to situational modification once theorized by trait-oriented psychologists and educators. Brain-damaged children have been reeducated successfully and have responded to psychotherapy (Kirk, 1958; Gordon and Wilkerson, 1966; Morgan, 1966b). Today, compensatory education offers hope to those disadvantaged in any combination of basic traits, personality, and prior experiences.

Recent data suggest that combined racial and psychological isolation is such a potent force that some of the best funded compensatory education programs have folded in its context (Coleman, 1966; McPartland and York, 1967; Pettigrew, 1964; *Racial Isolation*, 1967). It has been shown that attitude and achievement are affected by segregation deficit in the context of the school more than in the home neighborhood (Wilson, 1959; Wilson, *et al.*, 1967). Within the school, racial isolation has a depressing effect on achievement in the individual classroom more than in the school as a whole. Again and again, characteristics of fellow classroom students are the most significant predictors of achievement—even more than teacher characteristics and certainly more than the student's background.

The data suggest what is termed an *interactionist* approach. Not a strict and rigid environmentalism, it recognizes that an individual brings a basic repertoire of behavior patterns, modified by prior experience, into any given situation. However, the behavior that occurs is elicited by elements in the immediate situation, an interaction between individuals and their environment. Through this interaction, behavior may be modified profoundly. As Gordon and Wilkerson say:

> Implicit to the interactionist position is the assumption that change is possible. It follows that educational intervention functions as more than a catalyst for the stimulation and release of latent potentials . . . learning experience appropriate to given characteristics of the individual can produce certain potentials.[11]

Thus, while change is limited by the potential limits of the response repertoire of the species, behavior capacity may be expanded through learning experiences to an extent that we have only begun to develop.

In clinical psychology, therapists have long realized that few men are cowards categorically, but many men have developed a pattern of behaving that way in response to specific situations, retaining the capacity for the opposite behavior in other contexts. Now educators have come to terms with the fact that the mentally retarded child or the "culturally disadvantaged" child is so only in context and can be changed with appropriate changes in that context.

Without going into parallel developments in related fields—such as philosophy (situation ethics, existentialism) or psychotherapy (situation therapy, behavior therapy, group therapy)—it might be of interest to explore areas relevant to compensatory education where trait orientation has had some influence.

Assigning children to classes on the basis of tested IQ or specific "ability groupings" is one procedure that is buttressed by basic trait or ability orientation. As in Blake's analysis of the track system (1965), the very young and the very poor are found much more often proportionately on the bottom levels. Even where the lowest levels receive proportionately better attention in terms of quality education (a rare event), the very act of assignment to lower levels is a stigma with serious consequences for learning. Interestingly enough, when one study tested ability grouping *within* the classroom, no significant achievement gains were found over the control group whereas three alternate approaches were successful (Smilansky, 1966).

In Blake's study, IQ determined the track assignment. At one time, IQ was the closest friend of trait-oriented educators. However, its lack of predictive validity for achievement in disadvantaged populations is generally well known, not to mention its situational variability (Green, *et al.*, 1967). Just how much assessment of general abilities or intelligence should tie in to educational treatments is still an open issue. It would seem that, at its best, IQ is a measure of student potential *at the time of testing* and that this potential is an important evaluation measure of past and present teacher and program effectiveness; i.e., a good IQ test measures past educational deprivation (or advantage) at the beginning of the school year while IQ change over that year measures school effectiveness.

Another seemingly reasonable concern that supports trait orientation is the recent interest in individual "learning styles" (Bloom, et al., 1966; Hunt, 1966; Strom, 1965). Supposedly, compensatory education should vary with the learning style of a specific population. While a study of learning styles is most meaningful to educational growth, it is most likely that, on closer inspection, *styles* will become *stages* of growth towards greater cognitive development. Thus, while the individual retains a unique style or approach to learning, it will vary with the situation and with his development. Self-defeating styles should change in a supportive atmosphere enriched by success experiences; slow and perseverant styles should become quick and flexible with greater self-confidence and experiential enrichment. Thus, learning styles are highly relevant to compensatory education as indicators of developmental stage or symptoms of nonadaptive prior learning—but *not* as invariant traits around which to build a program or assign a year's treatment.

Some of the attributes applied to learning style bring to mind the very trait-oriented book, *The Culturally Deprived Child* (Riessman, 1962), which gave the field of compensatory education such an admirable boost at a critical time in its growth. Riessman gave us quite a few style characteristics categorizing the culturally deprived child: he is physical and visual (not aural), content-centered (not form-centered), externally oriented (not introspective), problem-centered (not abstraction-centered), inductive (not deductive), spatial (not temporal), slow and perseverant (not quick and flexible), lacking formal language skills (not lacking informal language skills). His weaknesses include anti-intellectualism, limited creativity, alienation, political apathy, suggestibility, naivety. His strengths are cooperativeness, mutual aid in extended families, informality, humor, freedom from self-blame and parental protection.

Riessman's contribution was twofold: he gave us a good proportion of the vocabulary now used in compensatory education (see Booth, 1966) and he was among the first to emphasize that disadvantaged students bring strengths as well as weaknesses to the classroom. However, Riessman's characteristics seem to break down into descriptions of the culturally *different* (as opposed to national middle class norms) and descriptions of learning styles in specific situations which, as has been suggested, are developmental or symptomatic behaviors capable of evolution. Nor have all of Riessman's essentially sound observations held true regarding how children react to the specific context of poverty, low caste status, and inferior segregated education. For example, Gordon and Wilkerson (1966) found that differences in abstraction ability vanished when IQ was controlled.

However, even Gordon and Wilkerson most often speak of the "disadvantaged" child in terms of poor language development, poor concept formation, and other Riessman-like observations and emphasize that, despite these characteristics, "selective motivation, creativity, and proficiency are present." It is my contention that these positive attributes are present in all children, each of whom has different interests with which to develop and different strengths to offer any compensatory education class. When cultural patterns learned in the home prove nonadaptive in the schools, it is the school's responsibility as well as the child's to be flexible and develop more variability in its approach.

Perhaps the most rigid believers in basal personalities that are resistant to change are teachers who work with populations with whom they under-identify or over-identify. Gottlieb (1964) found that low income black students who were rated as "fun-loving, cooperative, energetic, and ambitious" by black teachers were rated as "fun-loving, talkative, lazy, high strung, and rebellious" by white teachers. Also, white teachers were significantly less satisfied with their jobs and more concerned with discipline problems than their Negro colleagues. Thus, we don't know if the Negro and white teachers were describing different behavior *in reality* as a result of their attitudes or if their attitudes were so strong as to *project* their trait-oriented stereotypes on the students. In an otherwise ambivalent situation, at least we may conclude that the students were universally seen as fun-loving. I've noticed that, too.

Input: Modality and Timing

Since the pioneer research of Pavlov half a century ago, it has been acknowledged generally that more successful conditioning and learning takes place through the stimulation of not one but several sensory modalities of the subject: taste, touch, smell. All of these were relevant characteristics of the meat powder that Pavlov used to condition his dogs to the sound of a bell. It was not only the sound of the bell but its sight that triggered anticipatory reactions in the conditioned animal. Further, by pairing a buzzer with the bell, conditioning occurred even more quickly. Thus it was demonstrated that the more sensory modalities are activated by the input, the greater is the probability of learning. (Kimble, 1961; Ratner and Denny, 1964).

This is also true in human learning. Educators use materials that gain attention through the use of color-coding, sound tracks, three-dimensional illustrations, and related technical innovations (Frost and Hawkes, 1966; Hechinger, 1966a,b; Webster, 1966). Growth in this area of technology far exceeds other areas of compensatory education although development and change typically outstrip any up-to-date comprehensive evaluations of their utility. However, the use of multiple modality input materials is encouraging and should be expanded whenever possible.

The timing of educational input has always been acknowledged as critical to learning, and the formative or early years are often being cited as the most critical. Three points of view illustrate the heightened significance of learning in the preschool years: (1) rate of change; (2) fractional life experience; and (3) critical period incidence.

Bloom (1964) has presented evidence that the first few years of life hold the greatest potential for environmental intervention because the developmental growth rate is highest. Gains or losses in intellect and skill development occur that are supposedly nonreversible.

The concept of fractional life experience has been expressed by Margaret Mead:

> ... the younger the child is, the more each day counts because it is a larger fraction of the child's whole life. One day in the life of a two-day-old child is half of his whole life, and if he is ill or unhappy, he has indeed been ill or unhappy for half of his lifetime.[12]

This concept has been used to explain the subjective speedup of time that is experienced with age or, conversely, the impact of a single day's experiences on the very young (Fraisse, 1963).

Both of these points of view suggest that compensatory education techniques would show significantly greater effect on very young children. But the third outlook, critical period incidence, qualified the latter conclusion. This point of view states that compensatory education techniques will show significant effects only when utilized during a *specific* age period, a brief critical period in human development. Once this brief time span has passed, learning is more difficult;

and before it has arrived, the child may not have the physiological development to learn.

The theory of critical periods gives primary significance to the preschool years, not because of the rate of overall change, but because of the concentration of certain critical periods in that time span. On the other hand, the theorists also suggest that many behaviors critical to educational growth may be most sensitive to developmental change from adolescence to senescence. The teenager, with budding primary and secondary sex characteristics, shows critical periods for socialization with the opposite sex, competitive and antagonistic behaviors with the same sex, and sensitivity to peer interaction that most certainly influence learning readiness in the classroom. Sex education classes and therapeutic group activities are typical interventions at this stage.

Initially, critical periods were seen as the crossroads of heredity and environment: heredity specified time and person and environment determined place and event. When critical periods occurred in an abundant environment, the relevant behavior was developed and assimilated. When critical periods occurred in sterile surroundings development failed to take place, perhaps irreversibly. Hebb (1958) cites the classic example of cataract patients who were blind during critical periods of visual exposure to the environment. When the removal of the cataracts gave them functional vision, the patients were able to differentiate a square from a triangle, or one person from another, only after months of painstaking education. Another example is the critical period of approximately one month when an infant younger than two years will swim reflexively and naturally. Taking advantage of this has developed some of the most outstanding swimmers of our time.

While critical periods are seen as an innately scheduled developmental sequence, it has been demonstrated again and again that environment can change that schedule. Changing light cycles, introducing cross-species parent surrogates, isolation, novel environments, and other techniques have been shown to affect the incidence and length of developmental events among higher animals (Morgan, 1964a; Ratner and Denny, 1964). Thus, for our purposes, the critical period can be regarded as a hyper-optimal age period for learning specific behaviors, regardless of whether these behaviors are initiated by heredity or environment.

A few of the critical periods important for effective compensatory education have been unearthed in areas of intelligence, achievement, and cognitive growth (Deutsch, 1963; Deutsch and Brown, 1964; Green *et al.*, 1964, 1965; Bloom, 1964), verbal skills (Jensen, 1963), art and the elements for early reading and writing (Kellogg, 1967), telling time (Green, *et al.*, 1964), and for impact of high teacher expectancy on student achievement (Rosenthal, 1967).

Timing is important for the effectiveness of educational input in more contexts than that of when it is applied in the chronological or developmental process. Certain kinds of learning are facilitated by conditions of massed or nearly continuous exposure, other kinds by spaced timing or rest intervals (Kimble, 1961). Furthermore, research suggests that the timing of presentation, particularly with automated teaching machines, slide projectors, etc., can be designed to maximize the probability of continuous attention (Berlyne, 1960). Periodicity of stimulus presentation in itself elicits a form of learning called temporal conditioning. Specific abilities may be learned best if they are consistently taught at the same time of day or the same day of the week. Certainly there is much evidence that students synchronize with periodic events, and more easily at some intervals than others, and that this synchronization can be learned and unlearned (Morgan, 1966c).

Output: Response Involvement

Many learning theorists feel that learning is facilitated to the extent that the subject responds actively to the stimulus (Kimble, 1961). At times, adherents to this point of view question whether learning takes place at all without response (Denny and Adelman, 1955). Educators have been able to test these theories in the classroom context and, generally, they seem to be valid. For example, Fowler (1962, 1967) calls for *active* physical manipulation of curriculum materials in preschool programs. He states that discrimination, sorting, construction tasks, and small group interaction all proved more valuable than the teacher's verbal corrections and exhortations. In discussing programmed instruction materials, Cronbach (1962) differentiates between "good old-fashioned workbooks" calling for little response involvement and programmed materials eliciting active, meaningful responses.

Gordon and Wilkerson (1966) have related the importance of *doing* rather than *listening* to the entire field of compensatory education. On a clinical-emotional level, behavior change (or the attitude change hoped for in many compensatory programs) is no longer expected to occur in an emotional vacuum. Rather, interpersonal change occurs in the context of highly charged emotional involvement. A release of highly charged feelings can heat rigid behavior patterns until they are sufficiently fluid for reshaping.

Response involvement on these two levels—learning and motivation—is being applied increasingly via group techniques. Fowler (1967) has used preschool peer group activities to enhance concept formation and problem-solving behavior. Moreno, the father of psychodrama, has applied his role-playing techniques to conflict resolution and concept formation in children (1946; 1964). He used role reversal on preschool infants: "Now you and your friend change places. You are he and he is you. Okay, who gets the tricycle?" Moreno was led to conclude that "the child has his memory in the *act* and not the *word.*"

Response involvement via groups has been carried to its productive extremes by Maxwell Jones (1953; 1956) in his "therapeutic communities" wherein all are actively involved with the successful functioning of the entire program through specific individually meaningful roles. Neill (1960, 1966) used the similar procedure of program administration through participatory democracy in his Summerhill schools. A strong policy-making body composed of students and staff (one vote each) has held the reins in Summerhill for its half century of history. Since democracy may be defined as "those who are affected by a policy determine the policy," such response involvement seems to prepare children for participation in a democratic society. Therapeutic community and participatory democracy approaches are potentially powerful tools for compensatory education, and they are being slowly integrated into programs for disadvantaged children.

Output: Response Repertoire

The choice of *which* responses we wish to actively elicit in an educational context is critical to effective educational growth. The closer the target behaviors conform to the responses readily accessible to the student, the more effective learning will be. Modification of behavior and learning always involves activating established behavior patterns within the limits of species capabilities (Ratner and Denny, 1964).

Educators have been stressing the application of this principle to the classroom in recent years. Cronbach (1962) states that active response elicited by effective programmed learning materials should also be a response readily available to the pupil. Loretan and Umans (1966) stress the use of concrete experience with environmental relevance when teaching the disadvantaged. Gordon and Wilkerson (1966) recommend multilevel teaching materials geared to the life situations and the spread of achievement in the heterogenous compensatory education classroom. Fowler (1967) singles out one meaningful content area of the child's reality (housing, weather, etc.) as a learning focus. Levin (1966), using what might be called the idiom method, teaches reading skills to disadvantaged children on the basis of one word of dictionary vocabulary to one word of the child's personal vocabulary. Programs using a similar technique have been established in Hawaii to teach children who speak only pidgin English. The children's personal vernacular is accepted as legitimate material for study and expression, thus supporting the child's self-concept.

Reinforcement: Delay of Reward

The more immediate the reinforcement or feedback, the more effective the learning. Research supports this principle up to a half second interval between the event to be learned and its reinforcement (Fraisse, 1963). (Intervals smaller than a half-second tend to confuse reinforcement with the stimulus event.) While this has been supported in a wide variety of human and animal contexts (Ratner and Denny, 1964; Kimble, 1961), education is only beginning to apply the potential of immediate feedback to classroom education, chiefly in the area of programmed instruction. In fact, it may be the immediate feedback aspect of teaching machines that has often made them more effective than teachers. Most professional educators acknowledge that the longer test results are withheld, the less they instruct. Imagine the power of giving a child instant feedback after every question while his curiosity is hot! Thus, in the compensatory education situation, programmed instruction has done reasonably well for itself, even at preschool ages of three to five years (Long, 1966).

It has been suggested that excessive delay of reward damages some children more than others. Le Shan (1952), in an often-cited study of children from different socioeconomic classes, found that lower income children had less tolerance for delay of reward than middle and upper class peers. However, in a more recent study by Seagull (1966), the situational context proved to be more powerful than race or class. Seagull used broken and fulfilled promises of reward to artificially vary the children's faith in the experimenter-teacher. Interestingly enough, both Negro and white children of low socioeconomic class showed the *highest* tolerance for delay of reward when promises to them were broken. Thus, tolerance of frustration may be found more often in the behavioral repertoire of socially disadvantaged children than that of their more affluent peers.

Delay of reward through interpolation of unreinforced trials has been the substance of operant approaches to learning since Skinner's first efforts a quarter of a century ago (Kimble, 1961). Skinner boxes for infants and other automated teaching machines have used these schedules of reward effectively. The massive data compiled to date have much relevance for compensatory education.

Reinforcement: Quality of Reward

Reward is a motivator of behavior, particularly learning. The way in which reward is applied in the classroom will affect not only achievement but attitudes toward the self, toward others, and toward the world. Recent substantial data suggest that these attitudes are critical to measured achievement, particularly self-concept and acceptance of caste identity (Kvaraceus, 1965; Gordon and Wilkerson, 1966). In the compensatory education situation then, reward is effective if it is meaningful to the child's life experiences and if it supports his self-respect.

Many programs of "behavior therapy" and "operant learning" have tended to overlook the significance of quality of reward. While techniques such as candy-tossing and head-patting may re-shape behavior, they are often used in so paternalistic a fashion as to communicate to the subject an image of inadequacy and inferiority. Another damaging aspect of over-simplified behaviorism is the deadening of initiative and self-determinism. What we communicate is: "I know what you should be doing and how you should do it. When you do it properly, *I* will give you a token (piece of candy) to make sure you do it next time." Most socially disadvantaged kids won't buy these methods at all.

More complex rewards, supportive but without paternalism, include the implicit social pull to join peer groups in activities they appear to enjoy. Neill (1960) refused to make school attendance compulsory at Summerhill; nevertheless, nearly all newcomers voluntarily joined their peers in the classroom. More directly, Hobbs (1966) used special after-school outings as rewards contingent on specified behaviors. One must be very careful with this approach or group activities will be denied to those who need them most, those whose behavior is so nonadaptive as to preclude reward. Unfortunately, it is true that in many compensatory education settings, activities that are "fun" are withheld as an incentive to better behavior when it is precisely the lack of fun (quality of reward) that is eliciting poor classroom behavior.

Low or nonsupportive rewards tend to breed and perpetuate self-defeating behavior and expectancy of failure that is reflected in low achievement (McCandless, 1952). By definition, a disadvantaged child is not able to meet the demands of the school situation as readily as his peers. This situation, left uncorrected, is negatively reinforced so that deficits in ability accumulate with years of exposure. This cumulative deficit has been outlined by Deutsch (1963, 1964) and is particularly noticeable in the areas of language and general intelligence (Green, *et al.,* 1967).

One very simple application of reward might be discussed. The reward I have in mind is the one most of us receive as payment for our daily labor—money. Klugman (1944) tested black children aged seven to fourteen on the Stanford-Binet test and found that those given financial incentives performed better than those motivated by the experimenter's praise. The differences in a comparative white sample were not significant. It is difficult to tell whether the praise was more convincing or the money was less convincing to whites. Of course, it was not necessary for Klugman to prove that money is meaningful to disadvantaged children.

Gordon and Wilkerson (1966) have suggested the need for financial assistance even at elementary levels. I would go beyond doling out scholarships based on achievement or charity based on need and pay a salary for the socially useful labor of being a student. Such a compensatory technique would have to be applied universally in the program or school lest it be stigmatized as charity. From kindergarten on, each additional year of education could be dignified with annual salary increments (perhaps $10 a month in kindergarten and a $10-a-month increment for each additional year). Thus, seniority in a respected division of labor would provide a wage for students as well as staff. In addition, extra salary and status incentives could be paid for performing auxiliary staff roles—as custodians at one extreme or as assistant faculty on the other. Teenagers could set aside a free hour daily to assist elementary teachers. In return for their useful aid, these adolescents would receive wages, training, built-in role reversal leading to better understanding of the teacher and the school, and, most important, self-respect through a sense of productivity and belonging. By using therapeutic community concepts in this way, educators could maintain a high quality of reward throughout the system. The child of low socioeconomic background would gain respect for himself and for his education in the eyes of his parents since he would be a wage earner. It is difficult to imagine a serious dropout problem in such an environment.

Reinforcement: Secondary Elicitation

A major theoretical contribution to the psychology of learning has been the insight that omission of a stimulus is in itself a stimulus, one with potentially strong reinforcement or motivational consequences. Denny and his colleagues (Denny and Adelman, 1955; Ratner and Denny, 1964) integrated this idea into their concept of "secondary elicitation"; that is, eliciting a response by the omission of a stimulus that was part of an established behavior sequence. Unlearning or extinction occurs when an incompatible response (a competing response) is elicited consistently in the place of what was learned originally. According to the principle of secondary elicitation, omission of expected reward elicits frustration and anxiety.

On the other hand, omission of a noxious stimulus elicits approach behavior that is incompatible with the initial responses oriented to the noxious stimulus. Thus, learning can take place in contexts previously thought difficult or impossible.

The importance of a child's expectancy of reward or punishment depends upon the perceived magnitude of that reward or punishment. The greater the expectancy of incentive, the greater is the frustration when the incentive is removed. While all of this sounds like good common sense, it cannot be stressed enough how careful compensatory education projects must be in creating expectancies. The initiation of a program implicitly creates high expectancies in the child and the community. The initial high hopes of the school staff, intensive public relations work, an adequate budget—all tend to establish effective behavior patterns in the classroom under a basically sound program.

However, with the passage of time budgets do get slashed, the future of staff jobs may be insecure with the uncertain longevity of the project, and measured gains may not come up to expected highs. When this happens, program teachers may not be *openly* hostile or unsupportive, but there may be a lowering of teacher morale, energy, and enthusiasm. The teachers may become neutral professionals rather than educational reformers—but the effects on their children may be far from neutral. Loss of the teacher's support and enthusiasm create real frustration in the disadvantaged child, and the self-defeating behavior of frustration comes to the fore. A decrease in high level teaching skills can also occur with the unexpected departure of a single trusted teacher or an unexplained switch to a new classroom. The point is that productive learning behaviors must be elicited *consistently* throughout the course of compensatory education. This is more likely to occur when the longevity of the program is guaranteed, when staff morale is high, and when the children and the community are not led to expect what the program cannot fulfill.

Perhaps one of the saddest examples of inflated expectancies was the first year of a massive compensatory education program for disadvantaged adolescents, the Job Corps. The high-powered publicity included the mass media and endorsement by political figures and celebrities. The publicity focused on a public recruitment drive with mass distribution of application blanks for interested adolescents. Thousands of presumably disadvantaged adolescents took an important step in their lives and submitted written applications. Program facilities were able to accommodate less than ten percent of the total.

Ninety percent of the applicants met with little or no response. Regardless of what happened to the ten percent enrolled in the program, the thousands of adolescents rejected by the program were likely to react with frustration and antagonism.

Secondary elicitation is a principle that is concerned with the enhancement of learning as well as its destruction. While omission of reward leads to frustration and unlearning, the omission of noxious stimuli leads to approach behaviors which may promote learning. The power of a single relevant omission may be striking. Neill (1960, 1966) provides us with one example. He omitted compulsory classroom attendance and compulsory courses. Yet, while Neill did not force his students to attend school, nearly all of them did. One force that may have led to voluntary participation was the pull of the peer group (friendship, conformity, curiosity). Contrast this to the public school setting where the rewards are days away from class (weekends, holidays, snow days) and where punishment typically includes forced attendance (staying after school). The message is clear to all children: staying in school is punishment and should be avoided.

Omitting behavior forced by adult authorities and substituting peer group example as incentive and model are two vital components of Neill's school. One is indispensable without the other. Omission of adult controls without substituting peer group controls would be anarchic; on the other hand, strong and well-organized peer groups run by adult authority would be intellectually sterile, conforming if successfully controlled, and unstable and rebellious if not. Neill says:

> My pupils at Summerhill study voluntarily and therefore they study with zest. In contrast, millions of public school pupils are obliged to study even when they hate the subject. I took seven years to learn enough Latin to enter the university. One of my boys achieved the same standard of proficiency in fifteen months . . . that boy *wanted* to know Latin; I didn't.[13]

It is possible that so simple a tactic as omitting forced feeding procedures may contribute toward making children *want* to learn. Secondary elicitation—the art of knowing what *not* to do—is fundamental to motivating self-education.

Reinforcement: Latent Learning

Within the context of experimental psychology, latent learning has long been a household phrase. It refers to learning that occurs in the absence of apparent reward. Animals allowed to wander freely in a maze are able to learn more quickly than when they are motivated to run for rewards at the end of the maze. But closer scrutiny of this experiment shows that there are more aspects to the latent learning situation than meet the eye. Exploratory drives may be invoked, but learning also may result from the frustration of running into blind alleys. Perceptually oriented psychologists have pointed to a wide variety of meaningful cues that are necessary before latent learning takes place. Latent learning has become a descriptive term for behavior acquired in the learning context which the experimenter has not formulated in his experiment.

Transferring the concept of latent learning to the classroom is easily done and quite relevant to urban compensatory education: students continually learn, but *what* they are learning is not always what the teacher anticipates. The advantage of the so-called abundant or enriched environment is that no matter where the child turns, he learns something of value; that is, something that will be to his advantage. Thus, magazines on the shelves are better than empty shelves, although *Playboy* is more likely to be read than the *Reader's Digest.*

Any compensatory education program should expose its participants to as many life situations and materials as possible in support of the planned teaching. Latent learning accumulated over the years has pulled many daydreamers through higher education.

Racial Isolation

The psychological consequences of racial isolation have a major effect on the disadvantaged child. However, it cannot be stressed enough that there is no inherent disadvantage in voluntary aggregations of students of a common racial stock. For example, many African educational institutions are all Negro and yet of excellent quality. What makes such clustering disadvantaging in our country is that it is often *involuntary* and *stigmatizing.*

The power of racial stigma is immense. The Demonstration Guidance Project, the first and very successful program of the compensatory education movement, failed years later in a highly expanded form as the Higher Horizons program (*Racial Isolation,* 1967). Two factors tied to this failure were decreased per-pupil expenditures and counselor time. But another critical aspect, often overlooked, was the negative perception of the Higher Horizons program held by its students and their parents. Whereas the smaller demonstration program was seen by many as a "talent search," the larger program was seen as a remedial effort for less intelligent blacks.

A lack of significant achievement gains was found in major programs in Syracuse, Berkeley, Seattle, Philadelphia, and fifteen other urban areas. In all cases, the program participants were racially isolated *and* their perceptions of this isolation were not conducive to high self-esteem or academic drive.

One answer to this problem has been the creation of the Follow Through program (Park, 1967; Berson, 1968), a continuation of programs similar to Head Start but carried into the first grades of the public school. Operating since 1967, it offers a unique and interesting blend of cooperation between the Office of Economic Opportunity and the Office of Education. The former provides funds and the Head Start blueprint; the latter administers the program. Thus, we have at least one translation of compensatory education into workable components of the regular education system. Minimally, the program includes parent participation, nutrition, medical and dental services, and psychological services, as in Head Start. Thus, at least on a demonstration level, the school's functions are being productively expanded to encompass the needs of its clients.

As an experimental program, Follow Through offers local programs a choice of instructional models. Some of these models are mentioned in this chapter (Bereiter, *et al.,* 1965, 1966; Klopf and Bowman, 1966). Generally they range from behaviorist to developmental to parent-centered to parent-controlled. With adequate evaluation of these modern blueprints planted in traditional educational soil, we have a chance to develop the potential of American education.

Yet, it is not only the preschool and early grades that influence educational growth. Black children in the best quality preschool and early school programs must ultimately move into higher education. The higher they go, the more limited the opportunities seem to be.

For the racially-isolated, Negro colleges have long been an oasis in a closed society. Nevertheless, Negro colleges have suffered the consequences of the stigma of involuntary caste isolation—not the least of which is the subsistence budget of most of these institutions. Despite the fire they have drawn recently as the product of racist philosophy, the fact remains that black colleges are functional institutions responsible for educating the majority of black students and into which generations of good men have poured their lives and energies.

The majority of Negro colleges are now developing survival plans that in many ways make them vanguards of educational growth through compensatory education. Upward Bound and similar pre-college programs are sound efforts to upgrade freshmen. Faculties and student bodies are being desegregated with varying success. One of the more successful desegregation procedures has been ethnic integration with students from abroad on black campuses. One index of tolerance for new ideas and general academic potential at a black college is its percentage of foreign students. By this measure, black campuses have grown more cosmopolitan in recent years than is generally known. In yet another form of compensatory education, many black colleges are moving seriously into significant areas of research and scholarship. An effort is being made to try out fresh techniques and teaching methods so potent that, should their validity be established, the impact on higher education for the disadvantaged will be felt across the country.

In one such study, for example, thirteen predominantly Negro colleges banded together to attempt an innovative curriculum for the freshman and sophomore college years, a curriculum designed to bring their students to a high level of achievement. While the student populations of these thirteen colleges remain isolated racially, the psychological climate is better than in past compensatory programs of this scope. Students are *allowed to apply* for enrollment in the new and special program; that is, they are given an opportunity, not remedial punishment. Teachers participate in writing their own curriculum in summer conferences with curriculum experts. Evaluation along the dimensions of aptitude personality, values, creativity, and achievement has been built into the program from the very beginning. The willingness to pour time, energy, and funds into program assessment is a hallmark of the new life that is apparent in many Negro colleges. In this day and age, they must produce or go under. Those that have hesitated to plunge into fresh approaches may not survive. Those who have taken the plunge may lead the way.

In many segregated primary and secondary schools in the recent past, racial isolation was deprived of its psychological sting to some extent by serious attempts to develop racial pride through the use of special Negro history materials. These documents emphasized the role of Negro historical figures who were excluded from traditional history books. There was some controversy over whether such materials should be maintained in the compensatory setting. Some students complained of feeling embarrassed by what was seen as an overemphasis on their race; they felt that the black history effort was too obvious an attempt to bolster self-pride. However, this has changed completely. Black history is now demanded by black students for inclusion in the elementary through college curriculum.

To understand the place of Negro history in education, it is helpful to review the development of the black revolution. The teaching of history always reflects the attitudes of the time.

An Outline of the Black Revolution and Parallel Textbook Developments

Stage 1	Slavery	A period of total white supremacy and control. No books are given to slaves.
Stage 2	Abolition of Slavery	Mixture of paternalism toward blacks and fear in the reactions of whites. Most blacks learn enough reading to get by, but history texts generally are not read.
Stage 3	Segregation	Separate but equal. Schools exist and history books are read. Students read that Columbus discovered America because he was the first *white man* to set foot here.
Stage 4	Desegregation	There is token integration in the schools after the Supreme Court decision, but no striking progress economically or socially. Students learn that blue jays don't mate with blackbirds. Negro history materials are made available; special editions with Dick and Jane as Negroes are published. Texts are separate but equal.
Stage 5	Black Power	Young blacks realize that racial isolation continues and they rebel. Separate but equal means unequal. Negro history books are published separately. Texts begin to picture races in familiar urban living situations.

Stage 6 Multiracial Integration	Full equality in all respects. Housing is de- segregated. Negro history books are obsolete. Basic texts contain nonwhite history. Next to the Tomb of the Unknown Soldier is the statue of the unknown Indian who discovered America. The word "Negro" passes into history.

Thus the goal in a compensatory education setting is to integrate authentic black historical figures into the history curriculum. While the black revolution is far from the idyllic multiracial stage, there are enough seeds sprouting to hope that the plant may flower. Black power prospers when white power is a meaningful reality; riots flourish when nonviolent black power fails.

New Directions: From Crutches to Wings

The disadvantaged child may look forward to many exciting and hopeful developments in his educational future. His teachers are beginning to help him discover his strengths and to accept him as a person of value. His peer group is becoming organized in a positive way and is experimenting with democracy and ideas in ways that include him at the center. He is developing an ability to understand others, to look with their eyes through experiences such as role reversal and doubling that he learned in psychodrama class. Just as important, his teacher seems to understand, accept, and respect him. He may be getting grades in the form of progress reports. He may be establishing his own goals and redirecting them from time to time. Perhaps his progress is based on his growth from a starting point and not on an absolute level. He may be helping the leaders in his school to design segments of a new educational park for high schools and elementary schools.[14]

There are new directions for compensatory education on the urban scene. At one time or another, we have heard that any child can grow up to be President. The disadvantaged child and his peers will carry our society on their backs in the future. Perhaps it is possible that a disadvantaged child will grow up to run our country. I would like to see it happen because I believe we would deserve the results, good or bad. We have the power to change the entire character of compensatory education from remedial charity for the environmentally retarded to self-actualization for the potentially gifted. The disadvantaged child is potentially gifted in unique directions. He can go from crutches to wings in any program that will give him half a chance for educational growth.

Notes

1. Source books with good sections on innovations in compensatory education are Hechinger (1966b), Frost and Hawkes (1966), and Webster (1966). Other general sources include Crow (1966) and Hunnicutt (1964).
2. E. W. Gordon and D. A. Wilkerson, *Compensatory Education for the Disadvantaged* (New York: College Entrance Examination Board, 1966), p. 59.
3. *Ibid.*, p. 11.
4. *Racial Isolation in the Public Schools* (Washington, D.C.: U.S. Government Printing Office, 1967), p. 116.
5. Gordon and Wilkerson, *op. cit.*, p. 11.
6. B. P. Karon, *The Negro Personality* (New York: Springer Publishing Co., 1958), p. 2.
7. A. Hitler, *Mein Kampf* (Boston: Houghton Mifflin, 1943), p. 289.
8. R. Reagan, speech reported in *Newsweek* (May 22, 1967), p. 36.
9. R. V. Pierce, *The People's Common Sense Medical Advisor in Plain English or Medicine Simplified* (Buffalo: World's Dispensary Printing Office, 1883), p. 280.
10. On the contrary, striking data suggest that open, obvious, and periodic evaluation from the beginning of a project can in itself greatly accelerate the educational growth of that project. Rosenthal (1967) and Rosenthal and Jacobson (1966) show that the "Hawthorne effect" holds true in educational contexts.
11. Gordon and Wilkerson, *op. cit.*, p. 26.
12. M. Mead, *A Creative Life for Your Children* (Washington, D.C.: Children's Bureau, Department of Health, Education, and Welfare, 1962).
13. A. S. Neill, *Freedom Not License* (New York: Hart Publishing Co., 1966), p. 58.
14. In *Racial Isolation in the Public Schools*, see J. H. Fischer, "The School Park"; F. Keppel, "Educational Technology and the Educational Park"; D. C. Lortie, "Towards Educational Equality: The Teacher and the Educational Park"; N. V. Sullivan, "Desegregation Techniques." Also see Jacobsen (1964).

References

Bereiter, Carl E. and Engelmann, Siegfried. *Teaching Disadvantaged Children in the Preschool.* Englewood Cliffs, N.J.: Prentice-Hall, 1966.

Bereiter, Carl E., Osborn, J., Engelmann, S., and Riedford, P. *An Academically Oriented Preschool for Culturally Deprived Children.* Institute for Research and Exceptional Children, University of Illinois, 1965.

Berlyne, D. E. *Conflict, Arousal, and Curiosity.* New York: McGraw-Hill, 1960.

Berson, M. P. "Follow Through: A Promise for School Reform," *Educational Leadership,* 1968, 25: 459-465.

Blake, E. "The Track System in Washington, D.C.," *Integrated Education,* 1965, 3: 27-34.

Bloom, Benjamin S. *Stability and Change in Human Characteristics.* New York: John Wiley and Sons, 1964.

Bloom, Benjamin S., Davis, A., and Hess, R. *Compensatory Education for Cultural Deprivation.* New York: Holt, Rinehart and Winston, 1965.

Bloom, G. E., Rudnick, M., and Searless, J. "Some Principles and Practices in the Psychoeducational Treatment of Emotionally Disturbed Children," *Psychology in the Schools,* 1966, 3: 30-38.

Booth, Robert E., et al. *Culturally Disadvantaged: A Keyword-out-of-Context Index.* Detroit: Wayne State Press, 1966.

Clarke, A. D. and Clarke, A. M. "Cognitive in the Feebleminded," *British Journal of Psychology,* 1954, 45: 173-179.

Coleman, James S., et al. *Equality of Educational Opportunity.* U.S. Office of Education. Washington, D.C.: U.S. Government Printing Office, 1966.

Cronbach, L. J. "Programmed Instruction," *NEA Journal,* December, 1962, 142: 45-47.

Crow, Lester D. *Educating the Culturally Disadvantaged Child: Principles and Programs.* New York: David McKay, 1966.

Denny, M. R. and Adelman, H. M. "Elicitation Theory," *Psychological Review,* 1955, 62: 290-296.

Deutsch, Martin. "The Disadvantaged Child and the Learning Process," in A. H. Passow (ed.), *Education in Depressed Areas.* New York: Columbia University Press, 1963.

Deutsch, Martin and Brown, B. "Social Influences in Negro-white Intelligence Differences," *Journal of Social Issues,* 1964, 20: 24-35.

Fowler, W. "Cognitive Learning in Infancy and Early Childhood, *Psychological Bulletin,* 1962, 59: 116-152.

Fowler, W. "The Design of Early Developmental Learning Programs for Disadvantaged Young Children," Supplement to the *IRCD Bulletin,* Yeshiva University, 1967, 3: 1-3.

Fraisse, Paul. *The Psychology of Time.* New York: Harper and Row, 1963.

Frost, J. L. and Hawkes, Glenn (eds.) *The Disadvantaged Child.* Boston: Houghton Mifflin, 1966.

Gordon, E. W. and Wilkerson, D. A. *Compensatory Education for the Disadvantaged.* New York: College Entrance Examination Board, 1966.

Gottlieb, D. "Teaching and Students: The Views of Negro and White Teachers," *Sociology of Education,* 1964, 37: 345-353.

Green, Robert L. "Negro Academic Motivation and Scholastic Achievement," *Journal of Educational Psychology,* 1965, 56: 241-243.

Green, R. L., Hofmann, L., and Morgan, R. F. "The Effects of Deprivation on Intelligence, Achievement, and Cognitive Growth," *Journal of Negro Education,* 1967, 36: 5-14.

Green, R. L., Hofmann, L. J., Morse, R. J., Hayes, M. E., and Morgan, R. F. *The Educational Status of Children in a District Without Public Schools.* U.S. Office of Education Cooperative Research Project No. 2321. Washington, D.C.: U.S. Government Printing Office, 1964.

Green, R. L., Hofmann, L. J., Morse, R. J., and Morgan, R. F. *The Educational Status of Children During the First School Year Following Four Years of Little or No Schooling.* U.S. Office of Education Cooperative Research Project No. 2498. Washington, D.C.: U.S. Government Printing Office, 1966.

Hebb, Donald O. *A Textbook of Psychology.* Philadelphia: W. B. Saunders, 1958.

Hechinger, Fred M. "Head Start to Where?" *Saturday Review* (December 18, 1966), 75: 58-60. (a)

Hechinger, Fred M. (ed.) *Preschool Education Today.* Garden City, N.Y.: Doubleday, 1966. (b)

Hobbs, Nichols. "Helping Disturbed Children: Psychological and Ecological Strategies," *American Psychologist,* 1966, 21: 1105-1115.

Hunnicutt, C. W. (ed.) *Urban Education and Cultural Deprivation.* Syracuse: Syracuse University Press, 1964.

Hunt, D. E. "Adolescence: Cultural Deprivation, Poverty, and the Dropout," *Review of Educational Research,* 1966, 32: 463-473.

Jacobsen, M. (ed.) *An Exploration of the Educational Park Concept.* New York: New York Board of Education, 1964.

Jensen, A. R. "Learning in the Preschool Years," *Journal of Nursery Education,* 1963, 18: 133-138.

Jones, Maxwell. "The Concept of a Therapeutic Community," *American Journal of Psychiatry,* 1956, 112: 647-650.

Jones, Maxwell. *The Therapeutic Community.* New York: Basic Books, 1953.

Karon, Bertram P. *The Negro Personality.* New York: Springer Publishing Co., 1958.

Kellogg, R. "Understanding Children's Art," *Psychology Today,* 1967, 1: 16-25.

Kerber, August F. and Bommarito, Barbara T. (eds.) *The Schools and the Urban Crisis.* New York: Holt, Rinehart and Winston, 1965.

Kimble, Gregory (ed.) *Hilgard and Marquis' Conditioning and Learning.* New York: Appleton-Century-Crofts, 1961.

Kirk, S. A. *Early Education of the Mentally Retarded.* Urbana, Ill.: University of Illinois Press, 1958.

Klineberg, O. "Negro-white Differences in Intelligence Test Performance," *American Psychologist,* 1963, 18: 198-203.

Klopf, G. J. and Bowman, G. W. *Teacher Education in a Social Context.* New York: Mental Health Materials Center, 1966.

Klugman, S. F. "The Effect of Money Incentives vs. Praise Upon the Reliability and Obtained Scores of the Revised Stanford-Binet Test," *Journal of General Psychology*, 1944, 30: 255-267.

Kvaraceus, William. *Negro Self-Concept: Implications for School and Citizenship.* New York: McGraw-Hill, 1965.

Lathen, L. "The Elgin Approach to Special Education for Emotionally Disturbed Children," *Exceptional Children*, 1966, 33: 179-180.

Le Shan, L. L. "Time Orientation and Social Class," *Journal of Abnormal and Social Psychology*, 1952, 47: 589-592.

Levin, E. "Beginning Reading: A Personal Affair," *Elementary School Journal*, 1966, 67: 67-71.

Long, E. R., Jr. *The Effect of Programmed Instruction in Special Skills During the Preschool Period on Later Ability Patterns and Academic Achievement.* U.S. Office of Education Cooperative Research Project No. 1521. Washington, D.C.: U.S. Government Printing Office, 1966.

Loretan, J. O. and Umans, S. (eds.) *Teaching the Disadvantaged: New Curriculum Approaches.* New York: Columbia University Press, 1966.

McCandless, B. "Environment and Intelligence," *American Journal of Mental Deficiency*, 1952, 56: 674-691.

McLoughlin, Q. *"The Current Status of Civil Rights Research," Papers of Michigan Academy of Science, Arts, Letters*, 1966, 51: 333-343.

McPartland, J. and York, R. L. "Further Analysis of Equality of Education Opportunity Survey," in Appendix C1, *Racial Isolation in the Public Schools.* Washington, D.C.: U.S. Government Printing Office, 1967.

Moreno, J. L. *The First Book on Group Psychotherapy.* New York: Beacon House, 1964.

Moreno, J. L. "Psychodrama and Group Psychotherapy," *Sociometry*, 1946, 9: 249-253.

Moreno, J. L., et al., *The First Psychodramatic Family.* New York: Beacon House, 1964.

Morgan, Robert F. "The Adaptational Behavior of Chicks Raised in a Spinning Environment," *Psychological Record*, 1964, 14: 153-156. (a)

Morgan, Robert F. "If You Were a Social Scientist, Would You Let Your Sister Marry an Activist?" *The Guardian* (Mental Health Bulletin of Hawaii), 1966, 3: 5-7. (a)

Morgan, Robert F. *The Muddy Chuckle.* New York: Exposition, 1964.(b)

Morgan, Robert F. "The Patient Evaluation Sometimes Test (PEST): A Monthly Behavior Check for Emotionally Disturbed Adolescents." Unpublished paper, Hawaii State Hospital, Kanehoe, Hawaii, 1966. (b)

Morgan, Robert F. "Temporal Conditioning in Humans as a Function of Intertrial Interval and Stimulus Intensity," *Dissertation Abstracts*, 1966, 27: 6153. (c)

Neill, A. S. *Freedom Not License!* New York: Hart Publishing Co., 1966.

Neill, A. S. *Summerhill* New York: Hart Publishing Co., 1960.

Park, J. S. "'Follow Through' to Follow 'Head Start,'" *American School Board Journal*, 1967, 155: 5-9.

Passow, A. Harry (ed.) *Education in Depressed Areas.* New York: Columbia University Press, 1963.

Pettigrew, T. "Negro American Intelligence," *Journal of Negro Education*, 1964, 33: 6-25. (a)

Racial Isolation in the Public Schools. U.S. Commission on Civil Rights. Washington, D.C.: U.S. Government Printing Office, 1967.

Ratner, Stanley C. and Denny, M. Ray. *Comparative Psychology.* Homewood, Ill.: Dorsey Press, 1964.

Riessman, Frank. *The Culturally Deprived Child.* New York: Harper and Row, 1962.

Rosenthal, R. "Covert Communication in the Psychological Experiment," *Psychological Bulletin*, 1967, 67: 356-367.

Rosenthal, R. and Jacobson, L. "Teacher's Expectancies: Determinants of Pupils IQ Gains," *Psychological Reports*, 1966, 19: 115-118.

Schreiber, D. "Identifying and Developing Able Students from Less Privileged Groups," *High Points*, 1958, 40: 5-23.

Seagull, A. "Sub-patterns of Gratification Choice," *Papers of Michigan Academy of Science, Arts, Letters*, 1966, 51: 344-351.

Shaw, F. "Educating Culturally Deprived Youth in Urban Centers," in A. F. Kerber and B. T. Bommarito (eds.), *The Schools and the Urban Crisis.* New York: Holt, Rinehart, and Winston, 1965.

Smilansky, S. "The Effect of Certain Learning Conditions on Advancement of Disadvantaged Children of Kindergarten Age," *Megamot.*, 1966, 14: 213-224.

Strom, R. D. *Teaching in the Slum School.* Columbus, O.: Charles E. Merrill, 1965.

Wayland, S. "Old Problems, New Faces, and New Standards," in A. H. Passow (ed.), *Education in Depressed Areas.* New York: Columbia University Press, 1963.

Webster, Staten W. *The Disadvantaged Learner.* San Francisco: Chandler Publishing Co., 1966.

Wilson, A. B. "Residential Segregation of Social Classes and Aspirations of High School Boys," *American Sociological Review*, 1959, 24: 836-845.

Wilson, A. B., Hirschi, T. and Ross, A. "Education Consequences of Segregation in a California Community," in Appendix C3, *Racial Isolation in the Public Schools.* Washington, D.C.: U.S. Government Printing Office, 1967.

10 | QUALITY EDUCATION: NEW GUIDELINES

Regina Goff

Dr. Regina Goff is Assistant Commissioner, Office of Programs for the Disadvantaged, Department of Health, Education, and Welfare. She is on the Board of Directors of the United Nations and the Urban League of Maryland, and she has received two fellowships from the Rockefeller Foundation and many awards for public service in education.

Dr. Goff takes a broad look at quality education and examines the positive role which school integration can play in providing quality education. She explores compensatory programs from the preschool level through basic adult education and focuses on the need for increased attention to program evaluation. In view of the large expenditures by the federal government and the urgency of positive results, the discovery of variables which are the most decisive determinants of educational progress and upward mobility is crucial.

Several guidelines for establishing quality education are offered: education from birth, parental involvement in the schools, and a new direction for teacher education.

Because we are unable to state precisely those conditions that determine upward mobility, guidelines must be conceived within a framework of experimentation and flexibility. Ideas must be accepted as hypotheses even as they provide direction for operation. The eventual achievement of quality education requires continued discrimination among data, the testing of correlated ideas, and noncompartmentalization of the related forces upon which growth depends.

Current inquiries in education are of tremendous importance because of the cultural consequences of the answers. After Sputnik, critics of public education presented a picture of comprehensive deficiencies in the school population which transcended idiomatic patterns of any one subgroup. Early criticism paid scant attention to the most glaring travesty of American education—the disadvantaged child and the unskilled adult who is his parent. Although a child's biological equipment is designed so that, barring genetic impairment, interaction with the environment, receptivity and ultimate choice of response are possible, the disadvantaged have been undereducated and unattended for generations.

A dichotomy no longer ignored is the equipotentiality of man as a species and the prevalence of discrepancies in intellectual responses and socioeconomic status among cultural members. The focal point of inquiry is the schools.

Quality education has excellence as its basic characteristic. The new era in education requires excellence in programs designed for all children, especially those whose environments have deficits in stimulation necessary for normal growth. The achievement of excellence for the disadvantaged group depends upon recognition of the intricate system of relationships present in the total subcultural situation. Special characteristics, though not confined to this group, nevertheless identify disadvantaged children and determine the nature of situations associated with them. Despite the fact that modifiability of human behavior is a premise underlying learning, the behavioral patterns and appearance of slum schools are an extension of the culture which surrounds them. The reverse is expected. School impact is expected to alter attitudes and conduct and provide the motivation for optimum individual growth that is consistent with long range social goals of the nation. However, the power of the subcultural environment is so pervasive that traditional school programs have been inadequate as a coping mechanism.

A most salient admission by educators is that traditional, formalized curriculum content, teaching techniques, and materials—when observed in their effect upon disadvantaged children—do not reflect the originally stated goals of education. A major problem involves the systematic ordering of relationships among variables in such a manner as to influence academic and social response. For example, should there be a routinized procedure of morning milk and noon hot lunch for disadvantaged children in ungraded classes? Or is relief from pressure in the more flexible settings sufficient for improved performance?

Current Approaches to Achieve Quality Education

The recent study *Equality in Educational Opportunity* (1966) gives priority to peer group interaction in integrated classrooms. Exposure of low income children to classroom situations where children of more favored socioeconomic level are in the majority is considered a primary source of motivation and achievement for the disadvantaged. The report of the U.S. Commission on Civil Rights, *Racial Isolation in the Public Schools* (1967), supports this finding.

Pettigrew, chairman of the Advisory Commission on Race and Education, has written extensively on the educational park, which many conceive to be a meaningful mechanism leading to classroom integration. The concept provides for alteration of school districts and the creation of wider metropolitan boundaries. The aim is not confined to integration alone but to increasing the total quality of educational experiences. Educational parks built on the periphery of a city would educate all children on a single campus and present the best in curriculum content for all. Equality and quality education are contiguous.

Short of new construction, there are approaches such as the merging of adjacent formerly all-white and all-Negro schools at selective grade levels, the development of "magnate" schools or high caliber schools attractive to all, and interdistrict bussing.

The effectiveness of bussing has been as varied as the schools in which the practice has occurred, and popular reports have emphasized social consequences rather than academic results. Little research is necessary, however, to point out that mere proximity without interaction is futile. In initial efforts, some schools admitted Negro children across boundary lines but assigned them to all-Negro classrooms and instituted Negro recess periods. White parents complained that books and other supplies were insufficient to service the newcomers as well as regular students. Planning in terms of meaningful educational experiences for all children was absent and reflected attitudes of rejection on the part of administrators. In other cities, children traveled as many as twenty-five to fifty miles per day, spent an hour or more in transit to and from school, and attended two and one-half hour sessions with their white peers.

Teachers in integrated schools have found young children very much alike in terms of need, and they have deduced that the most important factor for a successful classroom experience is continual planning and discussion among teachers, supervisors, and administrators. Cole (1968) presents interesting tentative conclusions based on his firsthand observation of bussing situations. Initial reactions of white and Negro children to each other was seen as one of threat, but he observed no physical or psychological harm to either group.

Fears of standards being lowered following integration have not been substantiated. The social class of the majority of the pupils appears the most significant variable influencing academic response. If a majority of disadvantaged Negro children attend a formerly all-white school, the school will reflect the cultural limitations of the new population.

The decision of Federal Judge J. Skelly Wright, in ordering the District of Columbia schools to end discrimination on the basis of race or socioeconomic status, opposes the attitude that school districts have no mandate to overcome unintentional or de facto segregation. This opinion adds a new dimension to liberalism for the urban North which has sanctioned segregation of school districts based on housing patterns. With this decision, civil rights groups envision the possibility of enforcing racial balance in school systems where overcrowded Negro schools could be relieved by bussing across both school district lines and political lines that serve as barriers to integration.

Psychologically, the major deterrent to successful integration is the emotional influence of adults. They utilize residuals of their own childhood training as well as current emotional needs in making decisions on the school question, and they refuse to come to grips with a conflicting morality whose only end is social regression. The projection of a heritage of immaturity means continuing conflict in succeeding generations.

Inasmuch as studies reveal that the quality of school facilities, curriculum content, and teacher qualifications show less influence on school achievement than social class and racial composition of the school setting, and inasmuch as the struggle is still continuing for multi-racial schools and upward social mobility, reality requires fortitude in providing the best possible education within the existing framework of social patterns.

Compensatory Programs

An assumption underlying compensatory programs is that improved instructional practices, improved facilities, and enriched curriculum content will contribute to higher achievement in the disadvantaged school population. Compensatory programs are located in the most isolated settlements of the Navaho sheepherders as well as in the most populated hard-core poverty areas of urban slums. They run the gamut from remedial reading, cultural enrichment, and the use of new educational media through reduced class size, nongraded classes, team teaching, extended school days, summer camp programs, and the use of subprofessionals.

In widely scattered rural areas, as in counties of Idaho and Montana, federal surplus buses have been converted to serve as mobile electronics laboratories, mobile diagnostic educational laboratories, and mobile libraries. Urban areas emphasize remedial reading and, particularly with young children, speech therapy. In speech therapy, much attention is given to encouraging the nonverbal child to speak. In addition to the reading emphasis given in fourth and fifth grades, tasks such as building, disassembling, mixing, and doing are encouraged. Field trips lead to further exploration with books and ideas. Exchanges between urban and rural youth increase understandings and extend knowledge. At the high school level, dropout programs have been emphasized with attempts to inspire hope in the hopeless and trust in the distrustful. The most promising of these programs provide work-study experience and competent guidance toward realistic job placement.

Programs have been designed to help the physically handicapped as well as the socially handicapped. Such programs are directed to the sight-impaired, the hard of hearing, the psychologically and emotionally disturbed, and the educable mentally retarded—children who need the type of help which only special services can provide.

The impressive Head Start program and other preschool programs have received wide acceptance. They offer consistency in physical, social, and psychological need satisfaction as well as attention to health factors including physical examination, eye and dental services, and attention to nutritional needs. The emphasis on preschool education has been accompanied by concern for continuity in services. The desire for effective continuing education has led to legislation to establish Follow Through programs in the early elementary grades.

The traditional classroom is out of step with the technological revolution in education. Some programs sponsor the use of a wide variety of educational media in instruction. The phonoscope, a two-way audio and video communication system, makes communication possible between individuals and classes located at different schools. Students who are widely separated geographically carry on general discussions, debate, and share learning experiences. Teachers in widely scattered areas receive in-service education through this medium.

The area of behavioral technology has directed attention to programmed instruction and teaching machines. For children of deprived environments, well-developed programmed materials have much to offer. Clearly delineated, realistic objectives which are manageable in terms of evaluation are an outstanding contribution to teaching-learning interaction. Also, with learning presented in small increments and with each new step carefully posited on what has gone before, there is an elimination of gaps in understanding and a reduction of misconceptions and nonlearning. In brief, there is needed discipline within a framework of acceptability. Further, as Francis Keppel, former U.S. Commissioner of Education, stated: "Computer technology is color-blind and has no memory of race."

Compensatory programs have emerged under Congressional mandate and represent functional implementation of current critical thinking. Although sporadic attempts have been made by school systems to recognize and meet the needs of deprived children, efforts have been minimal in terms of the immensity of the problem. School districts have been unable to finance supportive programs, and communities have been apathetic. Current federal efforts represent a determination to improve both the process of education through better instruction and facilities and the product of education through a better-prepared individual. For the deprived child, these programs could provide support to a "self" who might otherwise never appear.

Program Evaluation

Although federally sponsored programs are relatively new, the question of evaluation is a major concern. In view of the vast expenditures and the urgency for positive results, it is crucial to discover the variables which are the most decisive determinants of educational upgrading and eventual upward mobility.

One view holds that educational benefits are measured best in terms of increased personal income. The complexity of any question involving human behavior is augmented when placed within a framework of economics which has no socio-psychological coordinate to link nonmarketable attributes or characteristics. Yet self-confidence, a feeling of power in the classroom, and parents' encouragement may be among the most powerful contributors to academic motivation, learning, and later job placement. If, as reports to date reveal, the most potent influence in school achievement is the integrated classroom, energies might best be turned solely to the solution of this problem.

It is interesting to note that prior to federal sponsorship of compensatory programs, projects of this nature had been undertaken in some segregated schools in urban districts. Among these were the Banneker project of St. Louis and the Higher Horizon project of New York City. In both instances, initial gains on the part of Negro children were not maintained through time. Among contributing factors, the racial isolation of the schools cannot be ignored. Despite these findings, instant integration is impossible, and the demands for sound investment "here and now" remain.

A study still in progress (Ribich), a cost effectiveness analysis of five types of improvement programs—compensatory educational programs, preschool progress, increasing the quality and magnitude of resources put into formal education, dropout prevention programs, and job retraining for experienced workers—concludes that job retraining is the most promising. Many studies have dealt with achievement differentials in terms of input and output, including progress attributable to per-pupil expenditures. Perhaps the most exhaustive study of socioeconomic determinants of educational expenditure has been made by Peterson (1963). Kiesling (1965), in his study of New York City, found that in districts with more than 2,000 pupils, additional expenditures of $80 per pupil were associated with an additional month of achievement. In small districts, no perceptible achievement gains accompanied increased expenditures. The study, however, did not identify socioeconomic levels of the pupils.

It remains difficult to draw conclusions about the output derivable from each unit of increased cost per pupil. One view holds that the relationship is negligible. Another view is that only small increases in achievement should be expected per unit of input and that massive spending should be replaced with appropriate combinations of services. Gordon (1966) concludes that the appropriate combinations are not known.

Another attack on the problem includes categorizing program

components as independent variables and selecting particular variables as education inputs for additional funding. An example is the selection of remedial reading, a component of the curriculum, for measurement of achievement gains. Baselines are established for under-achievers and, after program exposure, students are tested for achievement gains. Implicit in the problem, even after determining significant areas of input, is judgment relative to comparative long range benefits as contrasted to immediately measurable benefits which may diminish in the absence of specialized support. Further, there is the danger that one input or subject area—for example, remedial reading—may attain an aura of omnipotence. Thus, emotional conviction may override methodological vigor in the continued testing of hypotheses, and some of the most purposeful and vital aspects of the learning experience may remain unmeasured.

Former Secretary John W. Gardner of the Department of Health, Education, and Welfare stated:

> . . . even in the bleakest frontier community a youngster might be inspired to a lifetime of learning by parents who cared about his education.
>
> This connection between family or neighborhood environment and interest in education must never be forgotten in weighing the achievements of Negroes or members of other culturally disadvantaged groups. . . . the fate of most talented Negro children is sealed long long before college. . .[1]

One of the major assumptions underlying the Great Society is that children from the most humble circumstances may be inspired to a life of worth and productivity. Testing of this assumption and program evaluations in general must involve the composite interpretations of educators, psychologists, anthropologists, and economists.

New Guidelines

Education From Birth

A serious approach posits a relationship between the quality of earliest experience and the quality of ongoing responses. Recent research continues to substantiate the dynamic and powerful role of sensory stimulation and perceptual development. The entire life process is one of activity in an environment.

Rimland (1965) proposes that cortical neurons are responsive to specific patterns of stimulation or sensory input to which they become conditioned, and they *strive* or *want* to discharge when stimulated by their appropriate pattern. From the beginning of life, the organism is sensitive to satisfying input or sensory deprivation. Saul and Werner (1965) state that emotional deficits resulting from an estranged environment during the first six months of life contribute to mental dullness and perceptual distortion. The same study confirms prior assumptions that the earlier the onset of emotional deprivation, the more deep-seated are its effects. A barren environment threatens serious psychopathology and the inability to cope with stress.

A relationship exists between parental provisions for a physically and psychologically hygienic environment and the onset of mental alertness. The potential is as prominent among low income families as among others, but the possibility for achievement is hampered by the exigencies of existence. Economic insecurity, educational limitations, warped self-images, and daily harrassments mingled with a constant search for acceptance and approval of the self as a person may lead to emotional neglect of children and inconsistencies in day-to-day behavior toward them.

An informal survey made by the author among low income mothers in East Baltimore revealed that they took their infants out into the sunlight and the out-of-doors, an average of one hour a week. Working mothers leave infants with whoever is available to attend their physical needs. These persons may be diseased or incapable adults who keep the child's crib in a dark, frequently dank corner throughout the day. Exposure to the out-of-doors may be a function of the mother's inability to find someone to keep the child after work hours while she attends to marketing chores. In such instances, she must take the child along. Other infrequent exposures are short trips to neighborhood friends or relatives.

However, these mothers wish for their children, above all else, the mental acumen which will ensure upward mobility. Riessman (1962) found that over 50 percent of white low income interviewees and 70 per cent of the Negro group, when asked what they missed most in their life and what they wished most for their children, stated "education."

Quality education begins at birth and requires noncompartmentalization of parental education; that is, an approach in parent education which includes, simultaneously, information on child rearing practices and actual practice. A necessary intervention is the establishment of developmental centers in low income communities which include family social services, well-managed baby clinics, other medical facilities, and instruction for parents in child development and home economics. A downward extension of the more successful preschool programs would provide health and educational services requisite to preventing waste of human resources among the disadvantaged.

Parent Involvement

Current philosophy seldom extends to comparable enrichment and compensatory experiences for the head of the family who creates conditions for receptivity in the child's mind—and to whom in the final analysis the child has major loyalties.

At certain age levels, as a matter of fact, cultural enrichment may widen the gulf between the child, with his dawning social awareness, and his near illiterate parent. Around the junior high school years, socioeconomic discrepancies and their meaning are recognized and internalized. Unfavorable comparisons of the self with others sharpens inferiority feelings, and children can and do feel shame and rejection of their home. The influence which low income mothers might have had in creating receptive attitudes and in encouraging school attendance flounders in a morass of confused child attitudes. A major motivational potential is lost. If programs are to be truly compensatory, the circumscribed pupil-teacher emphasis must be broadened to include tangential elements which represent more nearly the human involvements of a child's life. No school program can tap child potential in depth, without attention to totality of elements.

In the past, parents have shunned schools that shunned them. Today, there is a social climate of receptivity to the more vocal parents, and attention is given to the concerns of the more aggressive parents. For example, a random sample of parents living in public projects in low income areas of the District of Columbia were asked this question: "How might the school which your child attends be improved?" The largest percentage of responses (41 percent) was directed to classroom practices including reduction of class size, more teachers, more male teachers, and the improvement of the school plant. The next largest group (16 percent) was concerned with improvements in teacher sensitivity, with particular attention to interaction with pregnant pupils and illegitimate children. Eleven percent favored improved administrative practices ranging from better custodial service to more realistic food items for disadvantaged children. Although nutritionists may not agree, the parents complained that menus contained foods which were rejected by the children because they were foreign to them or outside the range of foods that the children had learned to like. Further, the handling of free meals in settings where some children were able to pay was a source of unremitting embarrassment. Some children had refused to go to school because of the emotional impact of standing in free meal lines.

Eleven percent of the parents favored new parent groups, not dominated by school personnel, in which there would be opportunity for planning school policies and the opportunity for greater interaction between parents and children in school projects. Nine percent of the parents conceded that the home was a major source for learning good manners and for the prevention of delinquency. Suggestions were made for more adult training and work-study programs in vocational education. One mother who was in a work-study program was also a "go go" girl in a local tavern, apparently making use of her best marketable skill while training for something better.

Five percent of the responses favored abolishing both the track system and report cards, stating that whatever a child can do best should determine his evaluation. Two percent of the responses mentioned bussing as a means of educational improvement. A few comments centered on the dominance of white parents in leadership roles, even when they were by far the minority group, and the need for the Negro principal to take a firm stand if proposals are not in the best interest of the school. There were also negative comments on children demonstrating for integration issues during school hours. There were no examples of poor directives from the parents.

More parent participation in school affairs may produce a contingency of responsiveness in the disadvantaged child. The child, who sees his parent as an extension of himself, may awaken to a new dimension of self-importance and find a new avenue to motivation.

Teacher Education

Teacher education has traditionally been an accommodation to the certification requirements of state departments of education. In the past such requirements did not include training to teach special groups. Currently, there is a demand for more realistic exposure to the urban world and its meaning.

The school is conceived of as a major institution furnishing a counterbalance to deprivation. The early school years must contribute to a feeling of belonging and worth, despite the negative forces of the environment. There must be a lessening of uncertainty which may later crystallize into feelings of rejection and hostility.

Traditionally, teacher education has ignored the fact that the child who is a street wanderer develops unique discipline in thought and deduces relationships and insights in his own manner as a result of his own experiences and self-teaching. Riessman (1962) points to the utilization by disadvantaged children of physical orientation in problem-solving. This is observable in their motoric approach to learning, and he encourages its recognition in the classroom. Hunt (1960), recognizing the influence of particular aspects of the environment, speaks of motivation and reinforcement as intrinsic to the organism's interaction with the environment.

Birch (1963) notes the necessity of recognizing that which is primary in the perceptual organization of the learner; that is, "the nature of antecedent experiences necessary for learning to learn" and the conditions under which desired learning will be facilitated. The impact of the social environment on learning is undeniable.

Not all families in poverty expose young children to aggressiveness, sexual learning, abusive language, and constant noise. Unfortunately, many slum neighborhoods do. Under some conditions, organic regulators of sensory input are unable to manage the overstimulation resulting from chaotic street noises and involvement. The result is hyperactivity and distractability in relation to school tasks and demands. Deutsch (1964) points out that noise-packed environments lack incentives for attention. He found, among the disadvantaged, inferior visual and auditory discrimination as well as disability in concept formation attributable to environmental over stimulation.

New orientation may help teachers to understand which pathways of learning are easiest for the disadvantaged child and to provide directives for curriculum content which is not alien to the life of the poor. At the same time, new orientations may develop greater appreciation for the reactions of individuals. As Loren Eiseley states, "structured approaches should be replaced with the freedom which attended the wanderings of the ice-age man who discovered numbers."[2]

Conclusions

It was stated at the outset that the ultimate goal in American education is excellence. The essence of excellence is inquiry—provided the end of inquiry is self-correction toward progress. Guidelines for quality education, as used within the context of this chapter, refer to bases for action. Action should be directed specifically to education from birth, continuity between school, home, and family-related social institutions, and reorientation in teacher education.

Because we are unable to define precisely the conditions in education that are most forceful as determinants of upward mobility, guidelines must be conceived within a conceptual framework of experimentation and flexibility. Ideas must be accepted as hypotheses even as they provide direction for operation. Eventual achievement of quality education requires continued discrimination among data, the testing of correlated ideas, and the noncompartmentalization of related forces upon which growth depends.

Democracy in education requires, beyond opportunity for school attendance, an equal chance for development through quality education—with the ultimate goal being equality of acceptance in the social, political, and economic life of the nation.

Notes

1. J. W. Gardner, *Excellence* (New York: Harper and Row, 1961), pp. 102-103.
2. L. Eiseley, *The Mind as Nature* (New York: Harper and Row, 1962).

References

Birch, H. G. "The Relevance of Learning Theory to Directed Learning in Children," *American Journal of Orthopsychiatry*, 1963, 33: 349.

Cole, Robert. *Dead End School.* New York: Little, Brown, 1968.

Coleman, James S., et al. *Equality of Educational Opportunity.* U.S. Office of Education. Washington, D.C.: U.S. Government Printing Office, 1966.

Deutsch, Cynthia P. "Auditory Discrimination and Learning: Social Factors," *Merrill-Palmer Quarterly*, 1964, 3: 277-295.

Gordon, Edmund and Wilkerson, Doxey. *Compensatory Education for the Disadvantaged: Programs and Practice; Preschool through College.* New York: College Entrance Examination Board, 1966.

Hunt, J. McV. "Experience and Development of Motivation: Some Reinterpretations," *Child Development*, 1960, 31: 489-501.

Kiesling, Herbert. "Measuring a Local Government Service, A Study of Efficiency of School Districts in New York State." Doctoral dissertation, Harvard University, Cambridge, Mass., 1965.

Peterson, L., Rossmiller, R.A., North, S. and Wakefield, H. *Economic Impact of State Support Models on Educational Finance.* U.S. Office of Education Cooperative Research Project, University of Wisconsin, 1963.

Racial Isolation in the Public Schools. U.S. Commission on Civil Rights. Washington, D.C.: Government Printing Office, 1967.

Ribich, Thomas I. *Investing in Education to Reduce Poverty.* Research Report, Brookings Institution, Washington, D.C., 1969.

Riessman, Frank. *The Culturally Deprived Child.* New York: Harper and Row, 1962.

Rimland, Bernard. *Infantile Autism.* London: Methuenand Co. Ltd., 1965.

Saul, A. J. and Werner, S. "Early Influences on Development and Disorders of Personality," *Psychoanalytic Quarterly*, 1965, 34: 327-389.

11 | THE LANGUAGE OF BLACK CHILDREN: INSTRUCTIONAL IMPLICATIONS

Kenneth R. Johnson

Dr. Kenneth Johnson is a specialist in the field of linguistics and language problems of the educationally disadvantaged. He does extensive lecturing and consulting, particularly in urban schools. Dr. Johnson is Assistant Professor of Education at the University of Illinois.

Professor Johnson analyzes the nonstandard dialect which many black students share. He examines the historical origin of the dialect and gives examples of common speech patterns. He looks at the implications of this dialect in educational instruction—for the traditional language program has been a remarkable failure in teaching standard English to disadvantaged black children.

The language barrier that stands between the black child and the educational system must be removed. Johnson proposes a second language approach for teaching standard English—to identify deviations, to contrast standard English patterns to those of the black dialect, and finally to incorporate standard patterns into the black student's speech. If the language barrier can be overcome, disadvantaged black children will acquire a basic tool for social mobility and academic and economic success.

When the black man first landed on American shores, he was denied the opportunity to be fully assimilated into the mainstream of American life. Whites and blacks were denied the opportunity to have emotional, social or cultural interaction. Largely because the black man was not allowed to participate fully in the American cultural experience, unique cultural components emerged in the Afro-American's milieu. Most Afro-American cultural elements differ only in degree from the dominant middle class white culture. However, where unique black cultural traits exist, they may conflict with dominant cultural patterns. Since dominant cultural traits in a society are more highly valued than subcultural components, minority groups are often considered disadvantaged when they possess cultural elements which conflict with those of the larger society.

The language spoken by some black people conflicts with the dominant language in our society. The black man's unique subcultural pattern of speech often interferes with his academic achievement, social mobility, and vocational success. Since one of the expressed goals of the public school is to enhance youngsters' social mobility and vocational success, it has a major responsibility to help black children develop proficiency in standard English. The public school has largely failed in its attempts to help black youngsters attain proficiency in standard English. This chapter will focus on some of the reasons why black children are not developing the needed proficiency in standard English and suggest an alternative instructional program designed to help them become more adept in the dominant language.

Standard English, or the language of the middle class, has been defined as:

> ... the kind of English *habitually* used by most *educated* English-speaking persons in the United States. Thus, "He doesn't want any" would qualify as a sample of standard English—not because some "authority" has certified it as being "correct" but because evidence suggests that educated speakers habitually say "He doesn't wany any" in situations where less-educated speakers might say "He don't want none."[1]

Fries, the noted linguist, has stated that standard English is the variety of English used to carry on the important affairs of our country (Fries, 1945).

Because it is difficult to give an operational definition of standard English, it must be defined normatively. It is usually not difficult, however, to determine what is *not* standard English; the variety of English most often heard in the disadvantaged black subculture is not standard English but a nonstandard dialect of English.

A dialect is the collective speech patterns of one subcultural group as opposed to those of any other subcultural group. A nonstandard dialect is the collective speech patterns of a subcultural group that does not have the prestige of the collective speech patterns (standard English) of the dominant cultural group (the middle class). The variety of English spoken by many disadvantaged black people is called by some linguists the "nonstandard Negro dialect."

Children begin to learn language long before they enter school, and by the time they enter school, they have internalized the features of the particular variety of English spoken in their primary cultural environment. Children born into a middle class culture learn the language of the middle class; children born into a disadvantaged black subculture learn their culture's dialect. This is not the language pattern that often leads to academic, social, and vocational success.

In school, many black children never learn the language of the middle class, the language needed for success. Teachers have generally blamed the children for not learning the middle class language. Perhaps the blame should be placed on the methods and materials used to teach language to disadvantaged black children and on teacher attitudes towards the dialect of disadvantaged black children.

Language is learned during childhood by hearing and then imitating the sounds of models. Repeated imitation of sounds arranged in patterns forms linguistic habits. Thus, language is learned through "out of awareness" processes and informal correction by the models. If the language system the child learns is the language system of the school (standard English), the school reinforces and extends the child's primary language. If the child is disadvantaged and black, however, his primary language is usually a nonstandard dialect of English. If this is the case, the school must teach the disadvantaged black child standard English.

The traditional language program is organized to reinforce and extend standard English skills that middle class children acquire from their cultural environment. That is, the traditional language program emphasizes standard English analysis, descriptions, and written drills. Strangely, the traditional program emphasizes a non-oral approach to instruction. The traditional program has been a remarkable failure in teaching standard English to disadvantaged black children. Many of these children graduate from school speaking the nonstandard dialect they spoke when they entered kindergarten.

The language system of disadvantaged black children has many handicaps. Black children who speak the nonstandard Negro dialect are handicapped academically, socially, and vocationally. Children who cannot speak standard English cannot derive maximum benefits from the total instructional program. They are particularly handicapped in reading (Dawson, 1954). Standard English is the key to academic success; without it, many black children are not able to unlock the shackles of failure imposed by a nonstandard dialect.

Another handicap is that people who speak a nonstandard dialect often evoke negative reactions in listeners who speak standard English. Those who speak standard English make negative judgments about an individual on the basis of how that individual speaks (Lambert, 1963).

Further, many jobs require the ability to speak standard English, particularly jobs that involve contact with the public either in face-to-face relationships or by telephone. An individual can be qualified in every other way for a particular job and be denied the job because he cannot speak standard English (Hernandez and Johnson, 1967).

Origin of the Nonstandard Negro Dialect

Both historical and social factors explain the existence of the nonstandard Negro dialect (Stewart, 1967). Since Negroes are one of the earliest immigrant groups to come to this country, their ancestral origin is frequently dismissed or ignored. When people think of the origin of Negroes, they usually refer to slavery. But Negroes had a previous existence, and the early Negroes spoke African languages, not English.

As with other immigrant groups who had to learn English, the native languages of the Negro slaves "got in the way" of learning English. This "getting in the way" is called *interference.* Interference refers to the tendency of individuals to make a language they are learning conform to the sound and structure of their native language. For example, when the Polish immigrants attempted to speak English, they made English sound like Polish. When German immigrants attempted to speak English, they made English sound like German. The Negro slaves who spoke African languages made English sounds with African inflections. Thus, in the beginning of English development among American blacks, a nonstandard variety was established as the linguistic system of the slaves because of the phenomenon of interference. Further, the interference was compounded because the slaves spoke many African languages. Instead of one foreign language interfering with English, there were many foreign languages within the slaves' social environment.

And, perhaps most significant, slavery did not provide Negroes the opportunity to participate fully in the American culture where the process of correction might have occurred. Negro slaves learned English from overseers who spoke a nonstandard dialect of English.

This has been documented. It is doubtful whether the men who cracked the whip over the backs of the slaves were articulate models of standard English. Thus, Negro slaves undoubtedly had nonstandard linguistic models.

During slavery, then, a nonstandard dialect developed in the slave subculture, and Negroes born into the subculture learned this dialect. Lack of education and social isolation perpetuated the dialect. After the Emancipation Proclamation in 1863, Negroes continued to be isolated socially, and the nonstandard dialect was perpetuated. Undoubtedly, assimilation is the key to acquiring the language system of the dominant culture, as the experience of other immigrant groups has proven. But to this day, most Negroes have yet to be assimilated socially or linguistically into the full stream of American life. Many black children in the schools speak a dialect that has deep roots in their history and in the institution of slavery.

Recognition of the Negro Dialect

Not all educators and linguists agree that there is a nonstandard Negro dialect. Some educators and linguists question whether there is a variety of English spoken exclusively by some Negroes. Phonological and grammatical deviations in the speech of many Negroes are also in the speech of persons who are not Negroes. However, recent research is establishing, quite clearly and conclusively, that there is an aggregate of deviations found in the speech of Negroes. This aggregate comprises the nonstandard Negro dialect (Johnson, 1966; Shuy, 1964; Labov, 1965).

Negroes have known for a long time that they have a dialect of their own, even if educators and linguists were not aware of it. Within the black subculture, there are many ethnic jokes about this dialect. Black people have even utilized this dialect for survival purposes. Often when they didn't want white persons to decode their messages, the dialect proved useful. The dialect has been used by black people as a symbol of unity or brotherhood. Educated black people who speak standard English tend to use the dialect or some features of it when talking *among themselves,* especially about topics which are identifiably and unalterably associated with the black subculture and the black experience.

Black people, whose patience is proverbial and demonstrable, can wait until all educators and linguists agree on the obvious: there *is* an ethnic language spoken by many black people. The reason it is important and necessary for all educators and linguists to agree on the reality of the nonstandard Negro dialect is that black children are not going to learn standard English until there is general agreement on this reality and until instruction in standard English is based on the interference that occurs between the dialect and standard English. Before teachers can effectively teach black children standard English, the interference points between the Negro dialect and standard English must be recognized, and new teaching techniques and materials must be developed that are based on this recognition. This monumental task cannot be accomplished until educators and interested linguists recognize the nature of the problem.

Characteristics of the Nonstandard Dialect

Fortunately, some educators and linguists do recognize the nature of the problem and have begun to describe the features of the non-standard Negro dialect and to illustrate the interference points. On-going research continues to add credence to what black people knew all along—there is, indeed, a dialect of English spoken by black people, especially lower class black people. This research has established phonological and grammatical deviations that operate systematically. To put it shockingly, especially to school teachers, there is a correct way to pronounce words and a correct grammar to be used when speaking the Negro dialect. That's why Negro jokes never sound right when "white folks" tell them—white folks don't pronounce the words correctly and they are ungrammatical when they attempt to talk like black people. (Remember, "correct" is a culturally relative concept.)

The difference between the nonstandard Negro dialect and standard English, however, is not very great, not nearly as great as the differences between dialects in other languages. Chinese and Italian are two examples of languages containing dialects that are unintelligible to those speaking other dialects in the same language.

It may be helpful to illustrate some of the deviations of the nonstandard Negro dialect. One deviation present today in the speech of Negroes may be an example of African influence and inter-ference. The sound represented by the letters *th* that comes at the beginning of such words as *the, this,* and *that* does not occur in the phonological systems of some African languages spoken in West Africa where many of the Negro slaves originated. We also find an absence of this sound in the nonstandard Negro dialect. Many Negroes substitute /d/ in place of /th/ in the initial position. It is interesting, too, that many of these Negroes also substitute /d/ or /v/ in a medial position *(mudder* or *mova* for *mother; brudder* or *brova* for *brother)* and /f/ in the final position *(mouf, souf, wif* for *mouth, south,* and *with)* instead of the standard sound represented by the letters *th.* These substitutions may have originated because of the lack of these sounds in African languages.

Another kind of influence of African languages on Negro speech may be intonation. Many Negroes, instead of using the normal intonation range of English, extend the pitch range. Negro males, particularly, often speak in a falsetto voice which resembles the intonation patterns of some African languages.

Some other phonological deviations or characteristics are: "*r*-lessness," or the tendency to eliminate /r/ in the medial or final positions *(Cal* and *cahpet* for *Carol* and *carpet; dough* and *stow* for *door* and *store);* and "*l*-lessness" in the medial and final positions *(hep* and *fou* for *help* and *follow; too* and *foo* for *tool* and *fool).* Also, /b/ is substituted for the medial /v/ *(seben* and *habing* for *seven* and *having).* Often consonants are eliminated in the final po-sition *(har* for *heart* and *hard; tes* and *tass* for *test* and *task).* These are some of the outstanding phonological deviations from standard English. Further, these deviations tend to operate systematically; that is, they occur in particular and predictable places.

Some of the outstanding grammatical deviations in the non-standard dialect occur in the verb system. For example, the agree-ment morpheme is not included in third person singular, present tense verbs *(He help* and *She go* for *He helps* and *She goes).* The present and past participles of irregular verbs are reversed *(I taken* and *I have took* for *I took* and *I have taken;* or *I written a letter* and *I have wrote a letter* for *I wrote a letter* and *I have written a letter).*

Finally, the verb *to be* is extremely complex in the nonstan-dard Negro dialect—more complex, in fact, than in standard English.

For example, the nonstandard dialect has three structures for one structure in the present progressive tense in standard English *(He running, He be running,* and *He bes running* for the standard *He is running).* These three structures give a different duration to the action, which makes the nonstandard Negro dialect much more precise in this case than standard English. This is ironic because most teachers tend to think of the nonstandard Negro dialect as less precise.

Not only is there a slightly different phonological and grammatical system, but there is a different lexicon used by black people in addition to the words they share with every speaker of English. More accurately, black people have assigned additional meanings to common words, and these additional meanings are culturally relevant. They are referred to as slang words, but often they are the only words black children have for understanding concepts or for communicating their ideas. However, the school does not permit these words to be used inside its four walls. Often these words are untranslatable across ethnic and cultural boundaries because there is no equivalent experience in other cultures to generate the concept which these slang words label. For example, the many synonyms black people have for white people, all with slightly varying meanings, cannot be accurately defined for whites because *it is impossible for white people to have the black experience which has given meaning to these words.* For example, the terms *the man, Miss Ann,* and *Mr. Charlie* refer to certain types of white people. These types are difficult—if not impossible—to define precisely for white people.

The Language Barrier in the Classroom

Thus, the different phonology, grammar, and lexicon of the Negro dialect is a linguistic barrier between white teachers and black children. This barrier can be removed, but its removal will require a number of painful changes for classroom teachers. One of these changes has already been mentioned: the nonstandard Negro dialect must be recognized as a reality. Another change is that second language teaching techniques and materials based on a second language rationale must be the approach for teaching black children standard English (Stewart, 1964). A third change is that standard

English must be taught as an *alternate* dialect rather than a *replacement* dialect (Johnson, 1966; Stewart, 1964). Finally, teachers must not put the "bad mouth" on the language of black children; they must accept both the children and their nonstandard Negro dialect. This will be the most painful change of all for some teachers since an attitudinal change is likely to be the most difficult.

When black children come to school speaking the nonstandard Negro dialect, they are usually told "You can't speak that way" or "Don't use that bad language" or "Please don't speak incorrectly." This type of beratement continues throughout the school career of black children. The question is: What effect does this beratement have on the children? Language is an identity label, a reflection and badge of one's culture. Thus, criticism of an individual's language is really a criticism of the individual's culture and all those who share his culture. In addition, rejection of an individual's language is not likely to help the individual accept the teacher's language—standard English. Finally, telling black children that they can't talk "that way" or that the way they talk is "incorrect" and "sloppy" contradicts reality. The children know very well that they can talk "that way" and, furthermore, they are understood by each other and everyone else in their primary cultural environment. They speak the nonstandard Negro dialect, their parents speak it, their neighbors, friends, preachers, relatives, and almost everyone else with whom they come into contact speak it—except teachers. Thus, the beratements of teachers are tuned off because they are false.

The teachers are not to blame for their attitudes toward the nonstandard Negro dialect. They have been trained to hold this negative attitude. Also, the literature is filled with negative descriptions of the language of disadvantaged black children. Their language has been described as "sloppy speech." If teachers would note the frequency, consistency, and linguistic environments in which the deviations from standard English are made, they would discover that black children are systematic in their deviations from standard English. Therefore, "incorrect" and "sloppy" are the wrong labels to describe their language.

The literature is also replete with inaccurate statements, such as disadvantaged black children have "lazy tongues and lazy lips." This statement is unfortunate and it also defies distribution probabilities:

it is simply improbable that the great number of black children who speak the nonstandard Negro dialect could all possess "lazy tongues and lazy lips."

Another reason frequently given to explain the language of disadvantaged black children is that they have poor auditory discrimination skills. Neither is this rationale supported with research. Again, it is improbable that so many children are affected in this way. But there is a better argument against the claim that these children have poor auditory discrimination skills: If their auditory discrimination skills are poor, how did they all learn the uniform variety of English that they speak? If their auditory discrimination skills are poor, wouldn't each black child have his own speech pattern? Wouldn't the deviations differ from one child to the next? Instead, these deviations are systematic, which indicates that their auditory discrimination skills are *different.* Just as speakers of English cannot reproduce some of the sounds in Chinese or Russian because the speaker of English does not have the auditory discrimination skills to hear the sounds, these children cannot produce some of the sounds of standard English because their auditory discrimination skills are different from those who speak standard English. It was pointed out that white people sound affected when they imitate the nonstandard Negro dialect. Is this because all white people have poor auditory discrimination skills? Or is it because their auditory discrimination skills are different from the black speakers they attempt to imitate?

Teachers must modify their erroneous notions about the language of disadvantaged black children. They must recognize that these children speak a dialect that is different than standard English in its phonology and its grammar. Until teachers recognize this, they can do little—as they have already demonstrated—in teaching standard English to black children. Also, teachers must accept the Negro dialect and avoid embarrassing minority children with beratements, negative judgments, and criticisms of their dialect.

This change of attitude is especially important for elementary teachers. It is important for young children to express their ideas and to interact with the environment, the teacher, and with each other while using the language system that is most natural. Constant correction will retard their verbal development. Many important concepts developed in the elementary grades can be understood and expressed in the children's dialect. The important thing is to encourage children to talk, especially in the primary grades. They can be taught standard English later. It may be futile to teach primary disadvantaged black children standard English. They are just becoming confident and proficient in their own dialect, and it is unreasonable and unprofitable to expect them to juggle two dialects of English. Also, standard English probably will not be reinforced in their primary cultural environment.

This leads to the question of when the schools should teach standard English. Certainly, instruction in auditory discrimination should begin in the early grades because the children must hear standard English sounds before they can read them. Also, children in the early grades should be exposed to standard English that has been carefully composed to include those grammatical patterns that are lacking in or in conflict with their dialect.

Formally teaching the children standard English—that is, helping them to develop the ability to speak standard English—probably should not begin until the later grades, most probably not until the junior high school grades. These children must recognize a need to learn standard English, and elementary children are not likely to recognize the need. They seldom have an opportunity to participate in a cultural environment where standard English is operable, and they can function very well in their own cultural environment speaking their nonstandard dialect. Thus, it is doubtful whether black children will acquire standard English until they realize that they will have to function in the dominant culture where standard English is the dialect that is used for communication.

The program to teach standard English to disadvantaged black children must be based on the rationale of teaching English as a second language. These children should learn standard English as a second, or an alternate, dialect. The methods and types of materials will be similar to those used in teaching English as a second language.[2]

An examination of the reasons the traditional English program has failed with black children will reveal the approach that should be taken to teach these children standard English. The traditional language program treats deviations from standard English as if these deviations are speech idiosyncrasies of each black child who utters them. Teachers recognize that black children are uniform in these deviations, yet the language program does not treat these deviations as systematic speech occurrences characteristic of a social group. When these deviations occur, the traditional program corrects them "on the spot" ("Don't say it like *that*, say it like *this*"). This, in a nutshell, is the traditional language program. There is no rationale to deal with the systematic deviations from standard English.

A second language rationale recognizes the system in the nonstandard Negro dialect. These deviations are isolated, and the children are given instruction which contrasts their deviations with standard English. Instruction focuses on the particular interference points, and children are given drill and instruction utilizing second language techniques to help them acquire standard English patterns. These techniques include pattern practice drills (the students repeat standard English patterns which are equivalent to the dialect patterns); slot drills (the students supply standard English patterns or forms left out of sentences); auditory discrimination drills (the students discriminate between standard English phonology and their dialect— e.g., *mouf, mouth*); pronunciation drills (the students practice pronouncing words with sounds that are in conflict with their dialect or lacking in their dialect). These second language techniques can be adapted to fit disadvantaged black children trying to learn standard English. The crux of this approach is that instruction is focused on the points of interference between the nonstandard Negro dialect and standard English.

Another reason the traditional approach fails is that audiolingual techniques for teaching language are not used. Students are given little opportunity to practice standard English patterns orally. The emphasis of the traditional program is on written and analytical activities, instead of oral and functional activities. Children must be given more opportunity to practice language orally, and they must be given more opportunities to practice standard English. The schools must arrange activities that permit black children to interact with persons outside their subculture. If this cannot be done, or if it can be done only on a limited basis, then role playing is an effective technique to give black children an opportunity to participate in situations that require standard English.

Summary

A second language approach for teaching standard English to disadvantaged black children can be divided into steps: (1) The deviaations must be identified. (2) The children must hear the standard English pattern being taught. (3) The standard English pattern must be contrasted with the corresponding deviation in the children's dialect. (4) The children must discriminate between the standard English patterns and the corresponding pattern in their dialect. (5) The children must be given oral drills which require them to reproduce the standard English pattern. (6) The children must be given drill and practice that requires them to use the standard English pattern in their speech. (7) And, finally, the children must incorporate the standard English pattern in their speech when they are in situations requiring standard English (Johnson, 1966). The instructional emphasis throughout these steps must be on oral language drills, rather than written language drills, for reinforcement.

Second language techniques should be incorporated into the reading program for disadvantaged black children. Presently, these children are required to read words containing sounds which are either lacking in their auditory repertoire or are in conflict with the phonological system of their dialect. Black children must be given special instruction on certain phonological features. For example, the sound represented by the letters *th* that occurs at the beginning of words like *the, this, them,* and *those* is substituted with /d/. When the letters *th* occur in the medial position of a word *(brother),* many disadvantaged black children substitute either /d/ or /v/. When the letters *th* occur at the end of words, many black children substitute /f/. These deviations imply that the instruction given to black children to learn the sounds of *th* must be different from the instruction given to children who already speak standard English.

Yet, no teacher's manual for teaching reading points this out, and reading teachers seldom deal with the phonological deviations from standard English that are in the dialect of black children. The reading program must place more emphasis on interference between standard English and the nonstandard Negro dialect.

Finally, standard English must be taught as an alternate dialect rather than a replacement dialect. The traditional program encourages black children to discard their dialect in favor of standard English. As long as these children live in segregated communities and confine most of their interpersonal relationships to others who speak the nonstandard Negro dialect, they will not discard their functional dialect. The school, in attempting to teach standard English as a replacement dialect, is attempting the impossible. Black children (or anyone else) will not give up their primary language system as long as it is functional and as long as they are prevented from participating in a cultural environment where standard English is functional. The reality of segregation requires that standard English be taught as an alternate dialect to be used in appropriate situations.

In conclusion, the language barrier that stands between the teacher as instructor and the disadvantaged black children as learners must be removed before the education process can operate fully. Removal of the barrier requires both a change in the teacher's attitude and a change in the teacher's techniques for teaching standard English. If these changes occur, the language barrier will topple and disadvantaged black children will acquire the basic tool for social mobility and academic and economic success.

Notes

1. Virginia F. Allen, "Teaching Standard English as a Second Dialect," *Teachers College Record* (1967), 68: 355-356.
2. See Golden, 1960; Johnson, 1966; Lin, 1965; and *Teaching Standard Oral English,* 1966.

References

Dawson, Mildred A. "Interrelationships Between Speech and Other Language Arts Areas," in *Interrelationships Among the Language Arts.* Champaign, Ill.: National Council of Teachers of English, 1954.

Dillard, J.L. "The Urban Language Study of the Center for Applied Linguistics," *The Linguistic Reporter,* 1966, 8: 1-2.

Fries, Charles C. Teaching and Learning English as a Foreign Language. Ann Arbor: University of Michigan Press, 1945.

Golden, Ruth I. Improving Patterns of Language Usage. Detroit: Wayne State University Press, 1960.

Hernandez, Luis F. and Johnson, Kenneth R. "Teaching Standard Oral English to Mexican-American and Negro Students for Better Vocational Opportunities," *Journal of Secondary Education,* 1967, 42: 151-155.

Johnson, Kenneth R. "Improving Language Skills for Culturally Disadvantaged Pupils," in *Teaching Culturally Disadvantaged Pupils.* Chicago: Science Research Associates, 1966.

Labov, William, Cohen, Paul and Robins, Clarence. "A Preliminary Study of the Structure of English Used by Negro and Puerto-Rican Speakers in New York City," *Cooperative Research Project No. 3090.* New York: Columbia University Press, 1965.

Lambert, Wallace E. "Psychological Approaches to the Study of Language, Part III—Bilingualism," *Modern Language Journal,* 1963, 47: 114-121.

Lin, San-Su C. *Pattern Practice in the Teaching of Standard English to Students with a Non-standard Dialect.* New York: Columbia University Press, 1965.

Loban, Walter D. *Language Ability.* Office of Health, Education and Welfare. Washington, D.C.: U.S. Government Printing Office, 1966.

Loflin, Marvin D. "A Teaching Problem in Non-standard Negro English," *English Journal,* 1967, 56: 1312-1314.

Pederson, Lee A. "Some Structural Differences in the Speech of Chicago Negroes," in R.W. Shuy (ed.), *Social Dialects and Language Learning.* Champaign, Ill.: National Council of Teachers of English, 1964.

Shuy, Roger W. (ed.) *Social Dialects and Language Learning.* Champaign, Ill.: National Council of Teachers of English, 1964.

Stewart, William A. (ed.) *Non-standard Speech and the Teaching of English.* Washington, D.C.: Center for Applied Linguistics, 1964.

Stewart, William A. "Sociolinguistic Factors in the History of American Negro Dialects," *The Florida F.L. Reporter,* 1967, 5: 1-4.

Teaching Standard Oral English. Los Angeles: Los Angeles City Schools, 1966.

12 | SEPARATISM: A REALITY APPROACH TO INCLUSION?

Barbara A. Sizemore

Barbara A. Sizemore presents a comprehensive analysis of separatism, particularly black separatism, as it relates to gaining full participation in American society. She draws parallels between the black minority and other excluded groups—the early immigrant groups, the Irish Catholics, the Amish. She also analyzes the Black Muslim movement within the context of separatism.

Rejecting the "supply and demand" paradigm that permits the inclusion of individuals in the mainstream of American life, Mrs. Sizemore presents a five-stage power-inclusion model for excluded minority groups. First is the Separatist Stage during which the excluded group defines its identity. Second is the Nationalist Stage in which the excluded group intensifies its cohesion by building a religio-cultural community of beliefs around its own history and development. Related to this cohesion is the rejection of others.

The third phase is the Capitalistic Stage during which the group cohesion developed in earlier stages makes it possible to build an economic base for the minority group. In the Pluralistic Stage, the group utilizes its cohesion-rejection powers and its economic base to form a political bloc. Fifth is the Egalitarian Stage in which the interests of the group have just as much chance as other groups at this level of participation.

Separatism has resulted from the acute awareness that power and initiative must originate in the black community. In this regard, separatism may be a constructive step toward the full inclusion of black Americans in society. The author sees the necessity of an excluded group taking the initiative itself to develop a structure which will lead to meaningful inclusion.

Mrs. Sizemore is Director of the Woodlawn Experimental Schools Project District in Chicago, Illinois. Mrs. Sizemore is also an instructor in Education at Northeastern Illinois State College. Formerly she was principal of Forrestville High School in Chicago. She is also a consultant to Project Follow Through, U.S. Office of Education.

In this chapter, the separatist movement will be discussed as a special form of power-oriented movement to win a position of advantage for a minority group and its members. Black Americans have been involved in the struggle for position in the social order since 1619, and the nature of this involvement has been given many names. Among these have been: pluralist, assimilationist, secessionist, and militant (Turner and Killian, 1957). To be militant is to be aggressive and vigorously active; consequently, because of the constraints imposed by the caste system, any black struggle would be militant. Other names have been given to the goal of black Americans: integration, inclusion, and separatism.

Separatism as a black movement was catapulted into prominence by the fiery oratory of Malcolm X. He used "black nationalism" and "separation" interchangeably but defined black nationalism to include non-separatists. In Malcolm X's final months, he sought to describe his philosophy more precisely and more completely than black nationalism alone (Breitman, 1965).

Black nationalism has given impetus to the rise of black consciousness, black power, black heritage, and black pride. This new mood has been discussed widely in the journals and the newspapers. On the one side, many have fears that the separatists' militancy may lead to a greater polarization of the races; yet others feel that these beliefs deal constructively with the reality of separation.[1]

To develop an understanding of the relation between separatism and education, this chapter will: review the effects of integration and racism; study concepts related to group participation in American life; consider separatism as a possible route to participation; and indicate the implications for quality education.

Integration and Racism

The conclusions of the Kerner Report stress black power as a response to the frustrations, hopes, and expectancies provoked by the failure of the civil rights movement to deliver the promises of its judicial and legislative victories. This posture has been generally accepted and appears frequently in the literature.[2] The Kerner Report accuses separatists of retreating from a direct confrontation with American society on the issue of integration and of functioning as an accommodation to white racism.

But there are other ways to view the conclusions of the Kerner Report. First, confrontation, in a sense, implies the act of bringing together two ideas or cultures for examination or comparison. The black community—through separatism and its emphasis on political, social, economic, and cultural programs—has submitted the declared white Anglo-Saxon Protestant value system to rigorous examination and comparison with its actual accomplishments (Carmichael and Hamilton, 1967). Second, the great demand for housing in the black communities of major metropolitan cities has forced black people to initiate desegregation. This is a direct confrontation with American society on the issue of integration. The white response has been separation or resegregation.

Cruse (1967) may offer some insight into the view that blacks are "functioning as an accommodation to white racism." He discusses the American group reality as a struggle for democracy among ethnic groups rather than between two races and describes the civil rights struggle as such a contention. Cruse argues that the three most apparent minorities in this "nation of nations" are white Anglo-Saxon Protestants, African-Americans, and Jewish-Americans. The Jewish people, strong allies in the fight for integration, reject integration for themselves. They cling tenaciously to the Jewish right to a separate cultural existence and fight fiercely for a special kind of nationalism called Zionism.

Moreover, Cruse says that ethnic groups in the United States constitute a "motley collection of refugees from Fatherland poverty who worship daily at the altar of white Anglo-Saxon Protestant superiority."[3] As a result of such collective worship, this has become a nation of minorities ruled by a minority of one. He charges the white Anglo-Saxon ideal with effectively dissuading, crippling, and smothering the development of democratic cultural pluralism in this country. Cruse questions the policy of integration through the imposition of this ideal which stigmatizes the cultures of other ethnic groups. This policy makes the choice of integration impossible. Considering this argument, one could say that any group which integrates on these terms would be "functioning as an accommodation to white superiority."

Handlin (1965) asserts that the civil rights movement has never made a clear choice between available alternatives, and herein may lie the test of the "white Anglo-Saxon ideal." Handlin gives two definitions of integration. One refers to the openness of society, to a condition in which every individual can make the maximum number of voluntary contacts with others without regard to qualifications of ancestry. If this alternative were effected, all barriers to association would be leveled except those based on ability, taste, and personal preference. The other definition refers to integration as racial balance, which means that individuals of each racial or ethnic group are randomly distributed throughout the society so that every realm of activity contains a representative cross-section of the population. The former definition indicates free choice to equals; the latter makes no such assumption. For Handlin, the only barriers left in his "open society" would be taste, ability, and personal preference. For Cruse's "ethnic pluralism," the remaining barrier is culture, based on one's personal taste and preference. Neither one of these positions precludes separatism.

Despite these views, most planning for integration has been based on the concept of racial balance with desegregation of black people as the first step.[4] This goal-decision is probably due to the lack of well-defined means for achieving integration as an open society. Therefore, the liberals, determined to correct segregation and armed with the decision of the Supreme Court, have chosen alternatives best suited to already defined goals and interests but which fail to correspond to the interests of the black masses. The differing goals and interests of middle class white liberals and Negroes have obscured the real issues and obstructed critical analysis. A closer look at the social arrangements would have revealed the patterns of white resegregation and raised a more relevant question: How does one desegregate whites? This question might have led to a new set of definitions and alternatives.

As a result, many blacks have refused to support the concept of racial balance. They argue that eighty percent white and twenty percent black is also racial imbalance. They decry the assumption that a school is bad because it is predominately black or poor. Carmichael and Hamilton declare this position:

> Clearly, "integration"—even if it would solve the educational problem—has not proved feasible. The alternative presented is usually the large-scale transfer of black children to schools in white neighborhoods. . . . Implicit is the idea that the closer you get to whiteness, the better you are.[5]

They propose a course of self-determination for better black definitions of social arrangements and more productive solutions for black
people. In their proposal there is a rejection of belief in the "universal
rightness of the white Anglo-Saxon ideal."

Myrdal (1962) explored this belief and the psychic resistance
which it caused. His work indicated that the legitimate task of education is to correct the "crudely false but popular beliefs" concerning
the blacks and their relation to the larger society by subjecting these
beliefs to careful examination. This educational objective would have
to be achieved in the face of psychic resistance mobilized by people
who feel an urgent need to retain their biased beliefs in order to justify their way of life.

Moreover, this psychic resistance has crippled seriously whatever
chances exist for a genuine open society. The flight to the suburbs
curtails opportunities for open housing, open enrollment, bussing,
pairing, and transfer. As the core cities become blacker and blacker,
the number of available voluntary contacts between the races decreas-
es. Thus, it would seem that "psychic resistance" and the manifestation of racism are real problems with which the desegregation of
blacks simply does not deal.

Consequently, to say that black power is a withdrawal policy of
frustration and hopelessness seems to oversimplify a much more basic
issue. Racism and its attendants—poor education, poverty, and unemployment—create a situation unable to sustain life. Black people,
then, must find a way to survive. The black man searches for this
way—by a careful study of his history, an agonizing analysis of the
data from empirical studies, a critical examination of circulating
myths, and an ongoing evaluation of the great welfare programs.
More than ever, he attempts to create his own definitions and develop
his own concepts.

Concepts Related to Group Participation

The concept of identity appears frequently in the literature of the
black separatist movement. Elijah Muhammad (1965) discusses it
within the framework of "Original Man." He urges his followers to:
"Know thyself, love yourself, understand self, help self, get knowledge to benefit self and use knowledge of yourself." He also deals
with what the so-called Negro must do for himself.

Essien-Udom subtitled his report on the Muslim community "A Search for an Identity in America":

> The tragedy of the Negro in America is that he has rejected his origins—the essentially human meaning implicit in the heritage of slavery, prolonged suffering, and social rejection. By rejecting his unique group experience and favoring assimilation and even biological amalgamation, he thus denies himself the creative possibilities inherent in it and in his folk culture. This "dilemma" is fundamental: it severely limits his ability to evolve a new identity or a meaningful synthesis, capable of endowing his life with meaning and purpose.[6]

Erikson (1968) develops the concept more fully and arrives at three different identities: personal, ego, and group. Personal identity is the perception of the continuity of one's existence in time and space and the perception of the fact that others recognize one's sameness and continuity. Ego identity concerns the quality of that existence or the awareness of the fact that there is a selfsameness and continuity to the ego. Group identity is the group's basic way of organizing experience, which is transmitted through child training to the foundation of the ego.

Erikson argues that man has survived as a species by being divided into pseudospecies:

> First each horde or tribe, class and nation, but then also every religious association has become *the* human species, considering all the others a freakish and gratuitous invention of some irrelevant diety. To reinforce the illusion of being chosen, every tribe recognizes a creation of its own, a mythology and later a history: thus was loyalty, to a particular ecology and morality secured.[7]

Therefore, the development of the pseudospecies becomes a program of group cohesion and group solidarity to protect the group from other pseudospecies. Concomitant to such cohesion is the rejection of others, which Erikson explains as negative identity. The negative identity of other pseudospecies is "perversely based on all those identifications and roles which are most undesirable" and "dictated by the necessity of finding and defending a niche of one's own."[8]

So it becomes necessary for the well-defined pseudospecies to project its negative identities toward the other tribes. Erikson says that for this reason the pseudospecies is one of the more sinister aspects of group identity, for "this projection in conjunction with their territoriality gave men the reason to slaughter one another." He questions whether or not:

> ... identity, can be said to be a good thing in human evolution since it has vastly overburdened the system of mortal divisions with the need of reaffirming for each pseudospecies its own superiority.[9]

Notwithstanding this universal position and all-human ethic, such divisions do exist in American group reality so that one group's identity is relative to another's. The desire for emancipation from a more dominant group identity may be the central dynamic in groups of stigmatized individuals.

Stigma is a useful concept in understanding the dynamics of negative identity. Moreover, various kinds of racial discrimination are devised on this assumption:

> We construct a stigma-theory, and ideology to explain his inferiority [the minority member] and account for the danger he represents, sometimes rationalizing an animosity based on other differences, such as those of social class.[10]

For Goffman, personal identity is the means available to differentiate an individual from all others by a single, continuous record of intertwined and entangled social and biographical facts. Social and personal identity are part of other persons' definitions regarding the individual while ego identity is a subjective reflexive matter that is felt by the individual.

Using these concepts, Goffman presents an analysis of group alignment and ego identity. Emphasis is placed on the dilemma of the stigmatized individual who finds that the "in" group and the "out" group each present an ego identity for him. Society tells him that he is a member of the larger group, which means that he is a normal human being, but also that he is "different" in some degree and that it would be foolish to deny this difference.

Goffman proposes several solutions to the stigmatized black man: (a) to support a norm but be defined by himself as outside the relevant category, to realize the norm, and put it into practice personally; (b) to alienate himself from the community which upholds the norm, or refrain from developing an attachment to that community; or (c) to pass and cover as a member of the "in" group.

Goffman and Erikson deplore alienation and argue its faults for an integrated society; yet Goffman realizes that the support of such a norm shifts the burden from society to the victim:

> It is said that if he is really at ease with his differentness, this acceptance will have an immediate effect upon normals, making it easier for them to be at ease with him in social situations. In brief, the stigmatized individual is advised to accept himself as a normal person because of what others can gain in this way, and hence likely he himself, during face-to-face interaction.[11]

This line clearly absolves the wider society of any responsibility for the unfairness and pain of the society-imposed stigma; therefore, society can remain relatively uncontaminated by intimate contact with the stigmatized and relatively unthreatened in its identity beliefs. Consequently, the stigmatized black who cannot pass or cover must decide to assume responsibility for the sin or alienate himself from the community of the sinner.

In fact, Grier and Cobbs submit that it is necessary for a black man in America to develop a profound distrust of his country and of his white fellow citizens because he must be on guard against physical hurt. This condition promotes a cultural paranoia in which every white man is a potential enemy unless proved otherwise and every social system is set against him unless he personally finds otherwise. Adaptive devices are developed in response to this environment.

> They are no more pathological than the compulsive manner in which a diver checks his equipment before a dive or a pilot his parachute. They represent normal devices for "making it" in America, and clinicians who are interested in the psychological functioning of black people must get acquainted with this body of character traits which we call the Black Norm.[12]

The stigmatized black man fights for survival by synthesizing his personal and ego identities, weaving them into an "inner self" that is usually in conflict with the external world, which can be fought only by the self-determination of his group.

Interestingly, Erikson argues that self-determination is an integral part of ego identity:

> For the American, group identity supports an individual's ego identity as long as he can preserve a certain element of deliberative tentativeness, as long as he can convince himself that the next step is up to him and that no matter where he is staying or going he always has the choice of leaving or turning in the opposite direction.[13]

Parsons states that a strong ego, secured in its identity by a strong society:

> ... does not need artificial inflation for it tends to test what feels real, to master what works, to understand what proves necessary, to enjoy what's vital, to overcome the morbid, and to transmit its purpose to the next generation for the creation of a strong mutual reinforcement with others in the group.
>
> A weak ego does not gain substantial strength from being persistently bolstered.[14]

The choice of alternatives remains difficult for the black man in America. He is victim of a stigma which is so highly visible that passing or covering is almost impossible. If he supports the norm, he supports his own inferiority. In his separated status, he has created a black norm. This black norm has made the drive for integration impotent. This black norm may lead toward black nationalism.

The concept of nationalism has been discussed by Parsons (1965) in the framework of "societal community." Societal community refers to the total society as a system which forms a Gemeinschaft— a focus of solidarity or mutual loyalty of its members and a consensual base underlying its political integration. Such a Gemeinschaft may not exist for the total American society but only for the religio-ethnic-kinship groupings which form a network of associations. If so, it is necessary to establish a common core of values which Parsons discusses as follows:

> ... the associational structure must be in accord with the common values of the society: members are committed to it because it both implements their values and organizes their interests in relation to other interests. In the latter context it is the basis for defining rules for the play of interests which make integration possible, preventing the inevitable elements of conflict from leading into vicious circles radically disruptive of the community. It is also the reference base of the standards of allocating available mobile resources in complex communities.[15]

He argues that societal community is linked with political organization in all advanced societies but is also differentiated from it. However, that political organization (or government) is not identical with the community in American society today, and it is when the two are in conflict that revolutionary situations arise. Such a conflict exists at present between the political organization and that part of the black community which is not committed to the values of white supremacy and European superiority.

The central concept in Parsons' explanation of the emergence of nationalism is the differentiation of societal community. Three aspects of this emergence are: the differentiation of criteria for belonging to the nation in contrast to membership in the religio-ethnic-kinship group; the differentiation of the nation from its government; and the differentiation of the societal community as a nation from the integration of community, ascriptive bases and government to a synthesis of citizenship and territoriality.

Parsons defines inclusion as the process by which previously excluded groups attain full citizenship or membership in the societal community, and he classifies the components of citizenship as civil or legal, political, and social. Parsons feels that inclusion must be linked intimately with the process of differentiation to produce an increasingly pluralistic social structure. Inclusion should guarantee multiple roles and full participation with the maintenance of distinctive ethnic or religious identity.

Parsons analyzes the process of inclusion by using a model similar to the "supply and demand" paradigm of economics. With more control in the hands of those who are "in," there are demands for inclusion from the excluded group and from the elements already "in." In addition, there is a supply which operates from both sides of the exclusion line. Supply refers to the excluded groups' qualifications for membership, a matter of their cultural and social structures. Demand depends on the attitudes of both the group "wanting in" and important sectors of the group already "in." Much of the process occurs inconspicuously without much movement, but such movements gain strength as the strain of conflict between the normative requirements for inclusion and the actual limitations are translated into pressures to act. Parsons comments finally that the ultimate social grounding of the demand for inclusion lies in commitment to the values which legitimize it. However, the intensive strain to increase mobilization of such commitments encounters a problem deriving from the fact that value-commitment is only one of the factors necessary for successful inclusion. Parsons summarizes in this way:

> Strengthening this factor without likewise strengthening the others may lead not to promotion of the "cause" but to a disproportionate activation of the always-present factors of resistance, and hence to setbacks.[16]

Parsons' goal is inclusion, which needs value and association commit-ment and political power and influence for fruition. For excluded blacks, the reality base or starting point consists of the "always present factors of resistance," the absence or presence of a strong economic base, and the necessity for the excluded group to fight its way in. In assessing the alternatives available for decreasing the dis-tance between the blacks and their goal of inclusion, there is a need for power. This presents a major problem for Parsons' inclusion para-digm, for he applies the principle of supply and demand to a situa-tion demanding power.

Parsons strongly repudiates those who would achieve integration by power, emphasizing, instead, the mobilization of political and economic interests at the expense of value emphasis, acceptance, and willingness. He believes that only a balanced combination of ideal and real factors provides the formula for success. He indicates that the inclusion process is not synonymous with becoming white Anglo-Saxon Protestant. This process would hardly produce a new "in" group but rather a carbon copy of the group already "in." Conse-quently, the "in" group would continue to perpetuate itself because it constructs the qualifications for membership, restructures the insti-tutionalized "slots," and rearranges the basic citizenship patterns. Such a condition would be rife with difficulties for a group whose major disqualifying factor is unchangeable.

The weaknesses in the "supply and demand" paradigm for the in-clusion of black people seem numerous. The demands for inclusion from certain elements already "in" may be too small, silent, or power-less: the supply of those qualified for membership may be limited due to the unacceptability of blackness or of non-occidental values and cultures; the creation of institutional "slots" may be exclusively exploitative according to the basic citizenship patterns prevailing in the community; and the mobilization may rest almost entirely in the hands of the excluded group (the black people).

Assuming that the mobilization of factors for inclusion rests predominately with the excluded group, a model should afford that group with the initiative and the power. The black man needs a power model for many reasons. He is discriminated against because of color, which can never be altered to fit the requirements of the "supply " dimension. He has to fight for his legal-political rights. He has lost his religio-ethnic-kinship origins and heritage. He has rejected his adaptive and acquired plantation culture and lost the record of his gifts and contributions to the country. Parsons recognizes this condition:

> Even as the victim of the most radical discrimination of any group, the Negro has not only been forced to be subservient, but has also failed to develop, or bring with him from his southern rural past, sufficient ingredients for socially effective self-help. A question not merely of individual qualities and initiative, but of collective solidarity and mutual support at many levels, particularly the family and the local community.[17]

In fact, the "supply and demand" paradigm is much more suitable for individual mobility than for group inclusion because of the group's need for solidarity and collective support, power dimensions which spring from a separated condition. Although Parsons, Goffman, and Erikson discuss the dangers of separatism for America, they offer no viable alternatives which dignify blackness.

Erikson argues that the oppressor often has a vested interest in the negative identity of the oppressed because it is a projection of his own unconscious negative identity—a projection which makes him feel whole. It would seem highly likely, then, in view of this reality, that most excluded or stigmatized groups would actively adopt separatism.

But the decision to separate requires some degree of collective solidarity and mutual support. This has never occurred on a large scale in the black community. Grier and Cobbs explain:

> Thus the dynamics of black self-hatred are unique. They involve the child's awareness that all people who are black as he is are so treated by white people. Whatever hostility he mounts against white people finds little support in the weakness and the minority status of black people. As it is hopeless for him to consider righting this wrong by force, he identifies with his oppressor psychologically in an attempt to escape from his hopeless position. From his new psychologically "white" position, he turns on black people with aggression and hostility and hates blacks and, among the blacks, himself.[18]

Unity cannot be achieved because too many opportunists, who are anxious to be on the side of the winner, join the oppressor. Parsons suggests that the healthiest line of development for the black man would be toward group solidarity and cohesion and the sense that being a black man has positive value. Although he fears the danger of cultivating separatism, he feels that the pluralistic solution is "neither one of separatism, with or without equality, nor of assimilation, but one of full participation combined with the preservation of identity."[19]

One consideration from Carmichael and Hamilton, Cruse, Goffman, Parsons, and Erikson, then, is that group solidarity and cohesion may be best acquired from a separated condition or vantage point.

Separatism: A Possible Route to Inclusion

There are several explanations which support the assumption that separatism is a normal step up the sociological ladder to full participation in society. One argument compares black nationalism to the separatist approach of the early Christians, who tended to exaggerate their own importance and to reject all others. Carroll explores this proposition:

> . . . the early Christians by no means had the universal love for men that Christ spoke about. They appear to have gone through a definite phase; they had universal love for the *brethren*—and a universal pity for the rest of mankind. The brethren were the "in" group, the ones who knew Christ and His way and were on the road to salvation. The pagans were the "out" group, and the Christians pitied them and wished to convert them.[20]

The early Christians considered the lives of the pagans worthless, evil, and fit for damnation.

There is also a parallel between black separatism and the newly-arrived ethnic groups who were extremely nationalistic and entertained a contempt for all other groups, both racial and religious. Nationalism was used by the Irish in their attempts to participate more fully in American life:

> Irish nationalism was the cement, not the purpose of Irish American organization. Essentially they were pressure groups designed to defend and advance the American interests of the immigrant. Nationalism gave dignity to this effort, it offered a system of apologetics that explained their lowly state, and its emotional appeal was powerful enough to hold together the divergent sectional and class interests of the American Irish. This nationalism was not an alternative to American nationalism, but a variety of it. Its function was not to alienate the Irish immigrant but to accommodate him to an often hostile environment.[21]

This nationalism, which gave structure to the Irish working class resentments, often produced political radicalism in other groups. In addition, the Irish "negative identity" operated in other ways during the Civil War:

> The divergence between liberal Protestant and Catholic views in New York grew when Catholics generally declined to support the movement for the abolition of Negro slavery. In July, 1863, the New York Irish rioted against the newly enacted draft. For four bloody, smoke-filled days the mobs ranged the city. They attacked Negroes everywhere, lynched some, and burned a Negro orphanage.[22]

Moreover, the Catholic Church was opposed to the issues of social reform during the post-Civil War period and alert to the perils of socialism.

A comparison also can be made between black separatism and the separation of colonial nations from the master countries. Clark (1965) first defined the dark ghetto as an economic colony, and Carmichael and Hamilton use this definition:

> At all times, then, the social effects of colonialism are to degrade and to dehumanize the subjected black man. White America's School of Slavery and Segregation, like the School of Colonialism, has taught the subject to hate himself and to deny his own humanity. The white society maintains an attitude of superiority and the black community has too often succumbed to it, thereby permitting the whites to believe in the correctness of their position.[23]

Nothing meaningful has been done about institutional racism because the black community has been the creation of, and dominated by, a combination of oppressive forces (imposed stigma) and special interests in the white community. Carmichael and Hamilton stress the need for the black community to redefine itself, to set forth new values and goals, and to organize around them (vis-à-vis Erikson's pseudospecies declaration).

In each of the three instances described above, an increase in group cohesion (pseudospecies declaration) seems to result in an increase in rejection of other groups (negative identity). Fanon describes this as follows:

> The naked truth of decolonization evokes for us the searing bullets and bloodstained knives which emanate from it. For if the last shall be first, this will only come to pass after a murderous and decisive struggle

between the two protagonists. That affirmed intention to place the last at the head of things, and to make them climb at a pace (too quickly, some say) the well-known steps which characterize an organized society, can only triumph if we use all means to turn the scale, including, of course, violence.[24]

Fanon concludes that one cannot decide to turn any society upside down unless one decides from the start to overcome all obstacles that intervene. Fanon's ideas apply to any society where a group is excluded—in this case, the colonialism of the ghetto.

In order to overturn all obstacles, reality demands that black men deal effectively with negative identity, with their social identity, with their group identity, with their personal identity, and with their ego identity.

The Black Muslim movement endeavors to do exactly this. Elijah Muhammad continually emphasizes the need for group identity and unity. He urges black men to love one another and to pool their resources for the common good. This social identity is forged into the Community of Islam, an international brotherhood of Asiatics (since Africa is a part of Asia). The name "Negro" is discarded. A new name, given by Allah, is presented to each new member to re-place his slave name. The quality of existence is enhanced by certain teachings. Arabic and the civilization and religion of the black man are taught in Muslim schools. The people are encouraged to obey rules and regulations that are more stringent than those of the Prot-estant Ethic, moral codes similar to those of the New England Puritans.

Muhammad's major critics arise out of the protest against racial and religious hate. They expect Negroes to be patient:

> White society assumes that the Negro will almost always act in accordance with the stereotypes of behavior which it has evolved. Thus, in its view, the Negro will always act as a paragon of almost supine patience and reasonableness; he will not be subject to the human emotions of hatred, anger and love, nor of personal and group pride.[25]

White society does not want the Negro to be bitter. White society does not want to feel responsible or guilty about its actions. The Negro is expected to take the punishment for an uncommitted crime and to love the criminal in return.

On the other hand, Elijah Muhammad does not expect his

followers to shoulder the blame for their treatment in the larger society. He puts the blame squarely on the shoulders of white society, charging that such a society must be one of devils and beasts. This is his black norm. Having freed his people of the burden of blame, the dilemma is resolved. They are free to decide what is to happen to them. He provides new identities and new motivations.

Although Erikson deplores the division of mankind into pseudo-species because it interferes with world identity and the oneness of mankind, it was such a division which promoted the cohesion of the black community and its concomitant rejection of whites. This shift toward separatism, led by Malcolm X through the teachings of Elijah Muhammad, is reflected now in the messages of nonviolent and violent Christian leaders.

In a plan outlined for the Chicago public schools, Rev. Jesse L. Jackson, director of Operation Breadbasket, said:

> Black children, preyed upon psychologically, destroyed spiritually and confined physically, are victims of America's sickness bent upon devastating all hopes of innocent black boys and girls. . . . A new order is going to reign in the black community. Whites who remain in the ghetto schools will find it very hot. In fact, white principals must go. White engineers must go. White glaziers must go. White imagery must go.[26]

This position has been stated by others. The Inner City Parents' Council, under the leadership of Rev. Albert B. Cleage, Jr., presented a program to the Detroit Board of Education in 1967. Their report made the following recommendation for quality education in the inner city schools:

> We propose that all administrative vacancies (Counselors, Department Heads, Supervisors, Assistant Principals, Principals, Administrative Assistants and Junior Administrative Assistants, Assistant Directors, Divisional Directors, Assistant Superintendents and Field Executives) be filled with Afro-Americans until such positions have been filled with Afro-Americans in proportion to the number of Afro-American children and young people in the Detroit school population.[27]

This posture is not unlike the position of earlier ethnic groups. In his study of the Irish and Italian minorities of New Haven, Dahl (1961) called this nationalistic phase "the stage of socioeconomic homogeneity and ethnic solidarity." He hypothesized that an ethnic group passes through three stages on the way to political assimilation, from a highly homogeneous stage to a highly heterogeneous stage. He described an ethnic group member in the first stage as a ghetto resident, a member of a family with low and uncertain income, a victim of unemployment, a person of little prestige, or an object of discrimination by middle class Anglo-Saxon citizens.

Dahl explained that the public school system is an important instrument to the ethnic group. The acquisition of education provides the first step on the economic ladder, and the attainment of a teaching position affords a higher step.

> Jobs in the school system have been one of the main avenues of assimilation. When an ethnic group is in its first stage, some of its members become janitors in the schools. Later, as the ethnic group moves into its second stage, school teaching is a wedge that permits the group to expand its white collar segment. Then, in the third stage, members of the ethnic group begin to receive appointments as school administrators.[28]

Two prerequisites are necessary for this process of assimilation: (1) the training required for teaching must be inexpensive and easily available; and (2) teachers from immigrant backgrounds must be free to enter teaching without discrimination.

The petitions of Cleage and Jackson differ from those of the Irish and the Italians of New Haven in only one respect. The latter groups did not publicize their take-over.

Examples of separatism are abundant in the literature, but much ambiguity surrounds the concept because a confusion of bases exists. Separatism can be either a means or an end. When it is a means, the end is group mobility expressed as one of the following: assimilation, acculturation, inclusion, integration, or full participation in an open society. It is not within the scope of this chapter to discuss all ends. This chapter is concerned with integration and with inclusion or full participation, as discussed by Carmichael and Hamilton in this passage:

> The concept of Black Power rests on a fundamental premise: Before a group can enter the open society, it must first close ranks. By this we mean that group solidarity is necessary before a group can operate effectively from a bargaining position of strength in a pluralistic society. Traditionally, each new ethnic group in this society has found the route to social and political viability through the organization of its own institutions with which to represent its needs within the larger society.[29]

The Muslim community's attempt to deal with this goal may be prompted by the atavistic impulse to take the nationalistic tribal route. In this sense, as Carroll argues, nationalism in itself is a phase of growth common to all segments of mankind.

The maintenance of distinctive ethnic and religious identity may require separation in order to gain group solidarity and collective support to fight negative identities and stigma. Group solidarity and collective support are power dimensions which the "supply and demand" paradigm does not guarantee. The black man must have a power-inclusion model.

A Power-Inclusion Model

The power-inclusion model discussed here has been used by excluded groups for the achievement of group mobility and full citizenship in the American social order. This model has possibly five stages of progression toward inclusion. (See Figure 1.)

The first stage is the *Separatist Stage* during which the excluded group defines its identity. This process includes the manifestation of the pseudospecies declaration, "We are the chosen people." It is during this stage that social or group identities are carefully delineated and religion is used to emphasize the "we" or "in" group feeling from which cohesion results.

The identity-separation phenomenon is difficult to analyze, for it is an ongoing process. The stages of identity formation probably occur before the inclusion process but provide the necessary impetus for movement into it. The process cannot begin until identity is defined; once this definition occurs, cohesion can develop.

The second stage is the *Nationalist Stage* in which the excluded group intensifies its cohesion by building a religio-cultural community of beliefs around its creation, history, and development. The history, religion, and philosophy of the nation from which the group comes dictates the rites, rituals, and ceremonies utilized in the proselytization of the old nationalism. Because of rejection by the white Anglo-Saxon Protestant and the ensuing exclusion from full participation in the social order, the excluded group rejects that social order and opts for its former nation. For the Irish Catholics, it was Ireland; for the Polish, it was Poland. This intense nationalistic involvement led to increased separation.

Figure 1 — Power-Inclusion Model for Excluded Groups

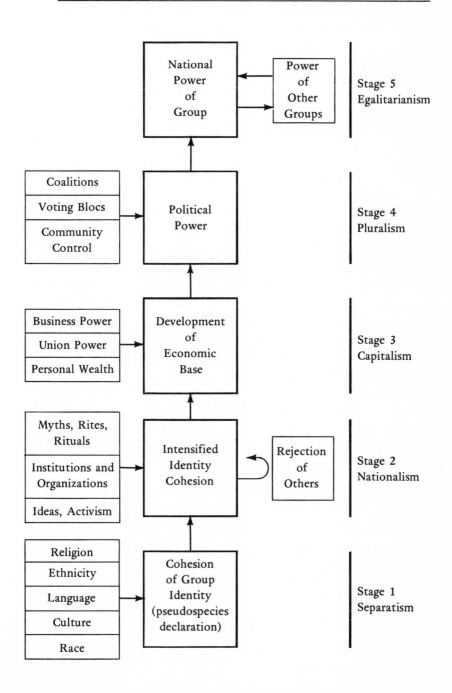

Accordingly, in the United States many groups are still separated. In some ways, the Jews are separated from gentiles; the Irish Catholics are separated from the Polish Catholics. Each ethnic, racial, social class, and religious group seeks voluntary association with its own members in one or more ways. Ethnic groups plug their form of nationalism into Americanism (the common core of myths and language provided by the white Anglo-Saxon ideal) and become Irish-Americans, Italian-Americans, German-Americans, and so forth. The nationalism of these groups is paraded annually on holidays such as March 17. So intense was the involvement of the nationalistic stage that such vestiges still remain. As group cohesion and solidarity increased, the development of negative identity occurred, resulting in the rejection of others.

The third stage of progression toward inclusion is the *Capitalistic Stage.* The cohesion developed in the Separatist Stage and magnified in the Nationalist Stage, added to the rejection of others created in the second phase, produces a need which can be developed into an economic base for the ethnic community founded on its active nationalism.

Such programs were discussed both by W. E. B. DuBois (1940) and by Booker T. Washington. In fact, one of the accusations of the Kerner Report criticizes the "Booker T. Washington rhetoric" of the black separatist's economic programs. Glazer and Moynihan (1963) discuss the implications of the lack of a black business class, as proposed by Booker T. Washington, on job opportunities for black people.

Although there are many explanations for the lack of black businessmen, other ethnic groups obtained footholds in business by serving their own. This also provided jobs for their own people.

Glazer and Moynihan demonstrate that the best jobs demand skills and training which tend to be kept within the "in" group. Therefore, the problem is not simply discrimination against the blacks or any one group but against all outsiders. In other words, there are Irish and Italian skilled workers, in part, because Irish and Italians were prominent in contracting and construction and they dominated the unions. With other groups, then, nationalism and separatism have contributed toward an ethnic base for business and jobs.

The fourth stage is the *Pluralistic Stage* during which the group utilizes its cohesion-rejection powers to form a political bloc on its economic base in order to thrust its interests into the foreground of the political arena (Carmichael and Hamilton, 1967). It is this stage which gives the illusion that integration is real.

For example, in the black man's drive for integration in housing, the white response was separation. At first sight, it would appear that whites were opting for separatism. On the other hand, since identity cohesion is an important variable in three stages of the power-inclusion model, the particular ethnic group involved in desegregation could be responding to the need for identity cohesion.

If an ethnic group is approaching or in the nationalistic phase when identity cohesion is great, the rejection of others will be intense. Resistance to desegregation may be fierce and violent. If the ethnic group is approaching or in the capitalistic phase, when identity cohesion and rejection have formed a strong economic base, resistance may be immediate but nonviolent. In desegregation of housing, for example, this group could afford to relocate or to prevent the invasion.

When a group enters the pluralistic stage, desegregation may be a threat to their cultural institutions, but the group's high degree of participation in decision-making offers abundant opportunity for control of the rate of desegregation. Resistance might be delayed and nonviolent. Once in the egalitarian phase, the group has the power to control the conditions which provide impetus for desegregation. Bachrach and Baratz (1962) call this the silent face of power.

Carmichael and Hamilton indicate that coalitions are not viable when blacks are not equal partners. In this capitalistic society, no partner without capital is equal. In summarizing the experiences of the Mississippi Freedom Democrats, they write the following:

> The major moral of that experience was not merely that the national conscience was generally unreliable but that, very specifically, black people in Mississippi and throughout this country could not rely on their so-called allies. . . . Black people would have to organize and obtain their own power base before they could begin to think of coalition with others.[30]

In Carmichael's opinion at that time, it was imperative to form an independent base of political power *first*. The failure of the Lowndes County Freedom Organization in Alabama indicates the omission of a step in the progression—the economic base. Simply, candidates cost and need money. Any candidate who must be supported by another group has a bifurcated allegiance and can serve neither master.

The fifth stage is the *Egalitarian Stage,* sometimes called democratic, in which the interests of the group have as much chance of winning as those of other groups at this level of participation. This is utopian, yet in the American social order. For example, power is still held by white Anglo-Saxon Protestants but both Jews and Catholics are trying to get in. The Irish Catholics, through coalitions with other Catholics and blacks, managed to elect a president after some thirty years. Until recently, the Irish Catholics have been generally ineffective in gaining government assistance or support for their service programs, even though they save money for the taxpayers in educational facilities.

As Cruse says, this American world:

> ... manages to reflect the social aspirations of the WASP, Catholic and Jewish groups above all others. ... Among these three there is intense competition for recognition and group status, which, for political and propaganda reasons, is called fighting discriminatory practices. As long as the WASPS rule the roost, charges of discrimination will never cease until Catholics or Jews achieve more power and privileges than any "minority" could ever hope for in Rome or Israel.[31]

According to Cruse, American culture is sick because there is an American identity problem. If there is no American identity, what is the identity which is called American? If the so-called American identity is WASP, who are the people who are not WASPS? To solve these questions, Cruse calls for complete democratization of the national cultural ethos.

Implications for Quality Education

The ultimate goal of inclusion for excluded or stigmatized groups depends upon self-respect and identity. Wheelis (1958) says that identity is founded on value, specifically, on those values at the top: "beliefs, faiths and ideals which integrate and determine subordinate values." Any development of positive identities for members of excluded groups would require, then, a redefinition of Americanism in pluralistic terms and a revision of the common core values. For black people, stigma results from racism—the belief that race is the primary determinant of human traits and capacities and that racial differences produce an inherent superiority of a particular race. This belief may be firmly entrenched in the core values of American society.

Separatists say that this value has destroyed the concept of the black man as homo sapiens. Wheelis suggests that modern man cannot recapture an identity out of the past because the old identity is not only lost but outgrown. He says that identity is not to be found but to be created and achieved.

Erikson prefers Vann Woodward's term "surrendered identity" because it does not assume total absence but something to be rediscovered. This must be emphasized because what is latent may become an actuality and a bridge to the future. He argues, moreover, that what is at stake is the realization of the fact and the obligation of man's genus. Separatists call this the struggle for survival.

As Grier and Cobbs say, there are no more psychological tricks that blacks can play upon themselves to make it possible to exist in dreadful circumstances. "No more lies can they tell themselves. No more dreams to fix on."[32]

With survival, then, as his goal, the separatist plans to rediscover his "surrendered identity" through black history, black literature, black myths, black models, black heroes and heroines, black teachers, black principals, and black religion. Such a process seems to repudiate the preservation of certain common core values. But to insure a pluralistic democracy, the common core of values should be common to each "nation" in this nation. Some common core values could be: love, peace, industry, honesty, democracy, humanity, and knowledge. Others, that are now common core values, could become alternates: property, western civilization, conformity, white male superiority, and Protestantism.

Donald A. Erickson (1968) explores this issue in his account of the struggles of the Amish people against the State of Iowa. They had been accused of violating the law by staffing their private schools with uncertified teachers. His research corroborated numerous other studies in showing that the Amish educational approach had served the ethnic group well—and probably better than conventional schooling serves the larger society. The Amish ways are strange and their nonconformity is intransigent. Furthermore, they do not reinvest their earnings in the local economy because they are forbidden to purchase appliances and equipment, but they are skillful farmers, industrious, self-reliant, and humane. Erickson concluded that the action against the Amish was prompted not by the concern for the welfare of their children but by a bitter antagonism toward the Amish people and their common core values. He describes this Anglo-Saxon posture as "cultural arrogance."

The Community of Islam suffers from the same kind of religious discrimination. Muslim ways are also strange and their nonconformity is intransigent. In addition, they do not hide their conformance to the black norm.

Studies that have investigated separated groups with differing core values reflect some light on this difficult problem. Greeley and Rossi (1966) found two ways by which Catholics could succeed markedly: the path of alienation from the Catholic community and the path of integration into the Catholic subculture. The latter was the most successful in leading to achievement, much more desirable from the Church's viewpoint and not dysfunctional for the larger society. The most likely explanation offered by Greeley and Rossi is that the religious community provides emotional support.

Erickson, in his review of the same study, observed that attending Catholic schools and participating in Catholic friendship cliques may promote well-being seldom experienced by adolescents who must function as members of a minority. He raised several provocative questions with regard to this observation.

> Will it turn out that the assimilationists are defeating their own purposes in attempting to outlaw Amish, Hutterite and Black Muslim schools? In the push for racially-integrated education, is the Civil Rights movement sometimes imposing a handicap on Negro youngsters by making them function as a minority at a time when they are most in need of emotional support? [33]

Being educated in the emotionally supportive setting of a school operated by one's own religious or ethnic group may promote more self-acceptance and security and render the individual more capable of full social participation. Erickson says it is possible:

> ... despite folklore to the contrary, that if more Catholics were educated in Catholic schools, more Lutherans in Lutheran schools, more Jews in Jewish schools and more Amish in Amish schools, there would be more national unity rather than less. [34]

Moreover, there is limited evidence to suggest that many graduates of Black Muslim schools continue their education in reputable colleges and universities and find niches in solid middle class vocations (Vontress, 1965).

Other studies have been concerned with the core values of early ethnic groups. Handlin (1951) wrote much about the conflict between the public schools and the early ethnic groups. The schools were alien to the immigrants who thought of them as "sore spots" from which "might spread a hostile influence that could undermine the health of the whole immigrant community." One alternative was to devise voluntary schools that would serve to strengthen rather than weaken the coherence of the group. Although these attempts were judged unsuccessful by Handlin, the school was only one of several means of education utilized to build cohesion. The ethnic newspaper was another.

In addition to content, today's separatists are interested in the teaching-learning process and the use of school resources. Allison Davis (1948) pioneered the study of the effects of school resources and the teaching-learning process on children from different social classes. It was largely his work, and that of his colleagues, which changed the concept of intelligence and introduced the notion of cultural effects.

The Coleman Report (1966) also attempted to study the effects of school resources on the achievement of various ethnic groups. With some exceptions, mainly Oriental Americans, it found that the average minority pupil scored lower on tests at every level than did the average white pupil. However, the white group included many religio-ethnic-kinship groups. The Coleman Report might have yielded more information regarding the effects of ethnicity and religion had it separated Jewish, Catholic, and other ethnic groups from the white majority.

Stodolsky and Lesser (1967) have investigated this issue and confirmed the findings of Davis (1948) and Sexton (1961) that children from lower classes with less income do less well on tests than children from the middle classes. But, the most striking finding of the study by Stodolsky and Lesser is that ethnicity does affect the pattern of functioning on intelligence tests, and once the pattern specific to the ethnic group emerges and is reinforced by the environment, social class variations within the ethnic group do not alter this basic organization. The other important finding is that social class influence is more powerful for the black group than for the other ethnic groups.

The test scores of middle class children from various ethnic groups (Chinese, Jews, Negroes, Puerto Ricans, Irish Catholics) resembled each other more than the scores of different social classes within an ethnic group. For example, the verbal ability scores of middle class Negroes were more like the scores of middle class Jews than lower class Negroes. Significantly, the Irish-Catholic group failed to produce an ethnic group pattern:

> In short, there are at least two plausible explanations for the failure to replicate our results on other ethnic groups with the Irish-Catholic children: poor sampling of middle class and lower class Irish-Catholic families (due to their unexpected unavailability in Boston) or a real difference between Irish-Catholic children and those from other ethnic groups tested.[35]

A third explanation in terms of the power-inclusion model is that the Irish-Catholic group is now in the pluralistic stage of the inclusion process, vying for a place within the "in" group. Consequently, the original thrust has been dissipated by success.

Stodolsky and Lesser argue that providing a lower class family with what a middle class family has—better jobs, education, and housing—will produce levels of intellectual functioning resembling those of middle class children. This action will provide equal education and social opportunities for equal development. Then, since ethnic groups differ in patterns of ability, the problem becomes one of providing equal educational opportunity to all ethnic groups to maximize their development even at the expense of magnifying differences among the groups.

Stodolsky and Lesser conclude that recognizing the particular patterns of intellectual strength and weakness of various ethnic groups and maximizing the potential power of these patterns (by matching instructional conditions to them) will make the intellectual accomplishments of different ethnic groups more diverse and provide gains in pluralism within the society.

These findings chart directions for the development of separatism in the teaching-learning process. When the group is cohesive enough to create jobs from a strong economic base (which will change the milieu), additional income, education, and housing will lessen the effect of poverty on the learner. This will accelerate the process of equalization, for the disparity between the mental ability scores of middle class black children and lower class black children is greater than any other ethnic group tested.

A curriculum should be designed to expedite the maximum positive development of any combination of individual strengths and weaknesses. Such a curriculum would need to support pluralistic values at the common core, and separatist values as alternates, in order to provide emotional support for all learners and to develop their personal, ego, and group identities. Necessarily, teacher-training institutions must be changed, and other social, governmental, and private agencies must be committed to correcting income deficiencies which prohibit learning in stigmatized groups.

Most minority groups in the United States desire full participation in American life. The majority of black people are not different. Grier and Cobbs believe that the black masses will rise with a demand that white Americans "get off our backs!" They argue that the solution will be to simply get off!

> This is no oversimplification. Greater changes than this in the relations of peoples have taken place before. The nation would benefit tremendously. Such a change might bring about a closer examination of our relations with foreign countries, a reconsideration of economic policies, and a reexamination, if not a redefinition, of nationhood.[36]

On the other hand, Elijah Muhammad and his followers do not share their faith in the white society. The black norm is far more evident in his approach:

> I have taught for years that you cannot demand the white man to accept you as his equal or as his brother, because he is intelligent enough to know that you are not his equal, that you are not his brother. Even if you go back to Adam—he is not the black man's father. We are not all compatible.[37]

Elijah Muhammad believes that the education of so-called Negroes has been a failure because it was designed by the slavemasters to keep Negroes in their place. He wants his people to acquire an education that will make them better able to use their knowledge for themselves.

Grier and Cobbs argue that the family prepares the child through its training to be free or slave and that "in spite of the yammering of naive observers, education has never offered a significant solution to the black man's dilemma in America." But their solution is still dependent upon the white man's initiative, upon his decision to act on this problem. Elijah Muhammad insists that this is folly:

One hundred years up from slavery. You still today feel that you have been schooled. You have a few diplomas and degrees. You can do little things educationally, but that does not yet even get you justice in America. You still suffer injustice with an armful of diplomas and degrees from colleges and universities . . .[38]

The objective of Muslim education, then, is to reeducate the so-called Negro: to attain his rightful place in the sun as a black man; to develop a feeling of dignity and appreciation of his own kind; to observe the daily Moslem duties; to learn Arabic; to observe the dietary laws; and to develop a sound moral character.

Elijah Muhammad directs his educational program toward group ends. This has not been the usual thrust of the educational institution in the United States. Janowitz explains that the American school system is adapted to facilitating the mobility of individuals rather than dealing with the problems of group mobility:

But the contemporary requirements of social progress mean that the school system must also become concerned with group mobility, that is, with the transformation of the slum as a social entity.[39]

The option for separatism is neither new nor revolutionary. In fact, it seems to be the basic route to full participation chosen by excluded groups because it gives the initiative to the excluded group. For black people, this choice may be both a response to the failure of the whites in America to do anything and a reaction to their intransigence. But, more important, separatism has resulted from the acute awareness that this initiative must originate in the black community. This initiative may be beneficial to race relations in this country. The prospects are exceedingly good for the black people to "make it" but:

. . . if this phase is inhibited by doting politicians or do-gooders, it may never come to be and a whole segment of mankind may be pushed deeper and deeper into immaturity.[40]

Notes

1. For a full discussion of this rationale, see L. Wirth, "Types of Minority Movements," and R. Linton, "Nativistic Movements," in R. H. Turner and L. M. Killian, *Collective Behavior.*
2. Martin Luther King, Jr., takes important notice of this and also offers a searching analysis of the white backlash in *Where Do We Go From Here: Chaos or Community?* (New York: Harper and Row, 1967), pp. 12, 18, 94, 117-118.

3. H. Cruse, *Crisis of the Negro Intellectual* (New York: William Morrow, 1967), p. 456.
4. See the literature on the Evanston, Ill., school desegregation and G. Coffin, "Moving Toward Integration," *Illinois Education* (November, 1968).
5. S. Carmichael and C. V. Hamilton, *Black Power* (New York: Random House, 1967), p. 157.
6. E. U. Essien-Udom, *Black Nationalism* (Chicago: University of Chicago Press, 1962). Reproduced by permission.
7. E. H. Erikson, *Identity, Youth and Crisis* (New York: W. W. Norton, 1968), p. 41. Reproduced by permission.
8. *Ibid.*, p. 175.
9. *Ibid.*, p. 41.
10. E. Goffman, *Stigma* (Englewood Cliffs, N.J.: Prentice-Hall, 1963), p. 4.
11. *Ibid.*, p. 119.
12. W. H. Grier and P. M. Cobbs, *Black Rage* (New York: Basic Books, 1968), p. 178. Reproduced by permission.
13. E. H. Erikson, *op. cit.*, p. 67.
14. T. Parsons, "Full Citizenship for the Negro American?" in T. Parsons and K. B. Clark (eds.), *The Negro American* (Boston: Houghton Mifflin, 1965), pp. 709, 750. Reproduced by permission of *Daedalus*, Journal of the American Academy of Arts and Sciences.
15. *Ibid.*, p. 710.
16. *Ibid.*, p. 722.
17. *Ibid.*, p. 740.
18. Grier and Cobbs, *op. cit.*, pp. 198-199.
19. T. Parsons, *op. cit.*, p. 750.
20. J. J. Carroll, "A Second Look at Black Nationalism," *America* (July 22, 1967), p. 84.
21. T. N. Brown "Social Discrimination Against the Irish in the United States," in N. Glazer and D. P. Moynihan, *Beyond the Melting Pot* (Cambridge: MIT Press, 1963), p. 241. Reproduced by permission.
22. N. Glazer and D. P. Moynihan, *Beyond the Melting Pot*, p. 233.
23. Carmichael and Hamilton, *op. cit.*, p. 31.
24. F. Fanon, *The Wretched of the Earth* (New York: Grove Press, 1963), p. 30. Translated from the French by Constance Farrington. Copyright 1963 by Presence Africaine.
25. Essien-Udom, *op. cit.*, p. 23.
26. Rev. J. L. Jackson, *Chicago Defender* (March 8, 1968), p. 10.
27. "Inner City Parents Present Program for Quality Education," a report of the Inner City Parents' Council, Detroit, July, 1967.
28. R. A. Dahl, *Who Governs?* (New Haven: Yale University Press, 1961), p. 153.
29. Carmichael and Hamilton, *op. cit.*, p. 44.
30. *Ibid.*, p. 96.
31. Cruse, *op. cit.*, pp. 451-452.
32. Grier and Cobbs, *op. cit.*, p. 213.
33. D. A. Erickson, "Contradictory Studies of Parochial Schooling," *School Review* (1967), 75, pp. 425-436.
34. D. A. Erickson, "Nonpublic Schools in Michigan," *School Finance and Educational Opportunity in Michigan* (Michigan Department of Education, 1968), p. 276.
35. S. S. Stodolsky and G. Lesser, "Learning Patterns in the Disadvantaged," *Harvard Educational Review* (1967), 37, p. 576-577.
36. Grier and Cobbs, *op. cit.*, p. 203.
37. Muhammad, *Message to the Blackman in America*, p. 233.
38. Essien-Udom, *op. cit.*, pp. 254-255.
39. M. Janowitz, "Institution Building in Urban Education," in D. Street (ed.) *Innovation in Mass Education* (New York: John Wiley and Sons, in press).
40. Carroll, *op. cit.*, p. 85.

References

Bachrach, Peter, and Baratz, Morton S. "Two Faces of Power," *American Political Science Review*, 1962, 56: 947-952.

Breitman, George (ed.) *Malcolm X Speaks.* New York: Grove Press, 1965.

Carmichael, Stokely, and Hamilton, Charles V. *Black Power.* New York: Random House, 1967.

Clark, Kenneth B. *Dark Ghetto.* New York: Harper and Row, 1965.

Coleman, James S., et al. *Equality of Educational Opportunity.* U.S. Office of Education. Washington, D.C.: U.S. Government Printing Office, 1966.

Cruse, Harold. *Crisis of the Negro Intellectual.* New York: William Morrow, 1967.

Dahl, Robert A. *Who Governs?* New Haven: Yale University Press, 1961.

Davis, Allison. *Social Class Influences Upon Learning.* Cambridge: Harvard University Press, 1948.

Davis, Allison, Gardner, Burleigh B., and Gardner, Mary R. *Deep South.* Chicago: University of Chicago Press, 1965.

DuBois, W. E. B. *Dusk of Dawn.* New York: Harcourt, Brace, 1940.

Erickson, Donald A. "The Plain People and American Democracy," *Commentary*, 1968, 45: 36-44.

Erikson, Erik H. *Identity, Youth and Crisis.* New York: W. W. Norton, 1968.

Glazer, Nathan and Moynihan, Daniel P. *Beyond the Melting Pot.* Cambridge: MIT Press, 1963.

Greeley, Andrew M. and Rossi, Peter H. *The Education of Catholic Americans.* Chicago: Aldine Publishing Co., 1966.

Grier, William H. and Cobbs, Price M. *Black Rage.* New York: Basic Books, 1968.

Handlin, Oscar. "Goals of Integration," in T. Parsons and K. B. Clark (eds.), *The Negro American.* Boston: Houghton Mifflin, 1965.

Handlin, Oscar. *The Uprooted.* New York: Grosset and Dunlap, 1951.

Muhammad, Elijah. *Message to the Blackman in America.* Chicago: Muhammad Mosque of Islam No. 2, 1965.

Myrdal, Gunnar. *American Dilemma.* New York: Harper and Row, 1962.

Parsons, Talcott. "Full Citizenship for the Negro American?" in T. Parsons and K. B. Clark (eds.), *The Negro American.* Boston: Houghton Mifflin, 1965.

Report of the National Advisory Commission on Civil Disorders. U.S. Riot Commission Report; also called the Kerner Report. Washington, D.C.: U.S. Government Printing Office, 1968.

Sexton, Patricia C. *Education and Income.* New York: Viking Press, 1961.

Stodolsky, Susan S. and Lesser, Gerald. "Learning Patterns in the Disadvantaged," *Harvard Educational Review*, 1967, 37: 546-589.

Turner, Ralph H. and Killian, Lewis M. Collective Behavior. Englewood Cliffs, N.J.: Prentice-Hall, 1957.
Vontress, Clemmon E. "The Black Muslim Schools," Phi Delta Kappan, 1965, 47: 86-90.
Wheelis, Allen. The Quest for Identity. New York: W. W. Norton, 1958.

13 EDUCATIONAL LEADERSHIP AT THE CROSSROADS

Neil V. Sullivan

Dr. Neil Sullivan, eminent scholar and educator, is Commissioner of Education, Commonwealth of Massachusetts. He is widely known for his contributions to education and especially to the education of the disadvantaged. He has been Superintendent of Schools, Berkeley, California, and of the Free Schools of Prince Edward County, Virginia, a member of President Johnson's U.S. Civil Rights Commission Advisory Committee, and a member of the U.S. Educational Development Program for Navajo Indians.

Dr. Sullivan asks an important question in this chapter: Where do the schools stand as they are confronted with society's racial dilemma? Educational leaders have not been willing to meet this problem head-on. Today's educational leader must face the crucial issue of race and education. Dr. Sullivan believes that at least one answer to the problem of race and education is clear: racial balance in the school population must be achieved if the schools are to prepare all young people, blacks and whites, for first-class citizenship. He provides convincing legal, academic, psychological, and sociological reasons to support his viewpoint.

The Berkeley, California, public schools provide a case study of the process of achieving desegregation. Dr. Sullivan takes a close look at some of their programs for achieving a multiracial school population.

The author analyzes the role of the superintendent—who must be the chief agent for educational change in the community. He warns that if superintendents continue to abdicate their executive responsibilities, they will become clerks. The superintendent and his staff should spearhead the policies, programs, and services of the school to meet the urgent needs and demands of the community at this crisis period in history.

Whatever our class, caste, color, or the condition of our purse, we do not have to look far to see the critical realities of our time. Our wide world seeks an alternative to the sweeping threat of atomic war. The nation copes partially with a multitude of human and technological problems which defy the artificial boundaries of states and localities. Our century has urbanized the hard, unplanned way. The industrial revolution is getting into full swing. The acceleration of change piles up and proliferates the problems of individuals and community. Within this setting, too many superintendents of schools sit behind closed doors and hide from the modern facts of life, as the need and demand for solutions intensify.

The City Today

A look at today's city reveals magnified problems of urban living—the birth rate increased, the death rate in decline, megalopolis inundated by new immigrants who congregate in modern ghettos known as inner city slums. The black immigrant too often is deprived of housing in other parts of the city or suburbs, remains jobless, shut out from the main economic, social, cultural, and educational stream. There is de facto separation, segregation, second class citizenship—and consequent alienation.

The by-product of anger and violence in poor communities matches the traditional white violence against those minority group members who impolitely demand or take their rightful places as first-class citizens. All of these elements join to complicate the festering problems of the metropolis. Can you imagine the year 1976 when there could be more than twenty million Negroes living tightly packed in uniracial neighborhoods, attending segregated schools? To allow this process to continue could lead to a Revolution of 1976 that would make the Revolution of 1776 look like a tea party.

There is among separated and segregated white youth in cities and suburban communities a growing preoccupation with despair, a retreat from the "world of the establishment." They are marked by the unusual hairdo, unconventional dress and behavior, and the use of debilitating narcotics. Initially, teachers, parents, and the adult community feel self-righteous rage and shocked, helpless sorrow. The end, unless all of us bestir ourselves, can only be self-destruction, as varieties of alienation and hostility break into violence in the city and the suburbs.

In some respects, the nation is one neighborhood and the world is one vast community. Each reflects the highly mobile, unstable family of our time. As technology takes hold and the computer plays an almost overwhelming role in many areas of life, the individual of every class and race tends to become depersonalized, lost, unimportant in the scheme of things. This is equally true of career, school, and community pursuits. The television "darling" is a natural candidate for president. The competition of ideas, the platforms, and the issues of this time are distorted and blunted by the artists in communications who will work for any master if the price is right.

Increasingly, the individual becomes a cog in a machine-centered, computerized world. His entire life may become an open book, courtesy of the computer. The inalienable rights of personal privacy are threatened as never before. The upshot is a pressure to conformity which could bear out George Orwell's grim, foreboding prophecy of doom.

Educational Leadership Today

Where do the schools stand as they are confronted with the educational aspects of society's dilemma?

By and large, there has been and is a vacuum in leadership, both at the state and the local level. Although there are notable exceptions, too many superintendents act as if they were operating in the good old days—when the superintendent was, in fact, a clerk for the board of education and a pawn of the business-oriented community. Too many feel that their hands are tied by the realities of the power structure which, in fact, is not the solid, one-directional, single-dimensional structure it once was. Too many prefer to pass the buck of inaction and unconcern to boards of education that also find safety in "do nothing" administrative leadership.

Today, de facto segregation is more a way of life in northern school systems than it was in 1954. The vacuum in leadership is paralleled by outdated programs and teaching styles more appropriate to Old Bailey than to a twentieth century classroom. Organization is immaculately hierarchical in the image of the nineteenth century industrial establishment which was its model. Obtaining sufficient staff—let alone interracial staff—trained to cope with modern needs is a dilemma of critical proportions. As school systems are integrating, the staffing crisis deepens. The perennial shortages in plant and equipment continue to be critical, especially in light of new needs and new technologies. Financing the public schools, normally a problem, has reached crisis proportions as loads, needs, and demands multiply and costs continue to spiral.

Now is hardly the time to continue the traditional pattern of educational leadership, whether in the classroom, the superintendency, or the university. With evidence of educational, social, and economic blight at every hand, the time is past when superintendents can blithely overlook commitment to the basic essentials of change to meet the human crises of this generation.

The Quest for Solutions

So public education continues to fight for its life, but in a tremendously more complex setting that demands a strong sense of urgency. There are superintendents, perhaps more than a few, who see today's social and educational issues clearly. They stand committed to meet these issues head-on and to act in a leadership capacity in order to find solutions.

Some superintendents, like those in San Antonio, Englewood, Rochester, Syracuse, Pittsburgh, and Sacramento, have seen the issue of de facto segregation clearly and are working toward desegregation of their schools. Others, in Berkeley and Evanston, have accomplished desegregation. School integration remains a critical ultimate goal for all.

Some speak out for fair housing. They are rough on realtors, for they know the critical and important role which the real estate business has played nationally in perpetuating segregated neighborhoods and the uniracial school. Some have dared to question the wisdom of the Vietnam War and its acceleration. They know that not only are lives being lost on the battlefield, but billions of dollars are being wasted, the very billions which could win the war on poverty and the struggle for excellent, equal education in racially-integrated schools.

A very few recognize the dangers of book-burning and witch-hunting and not only speak out but support the victims. Some speak out continuously against the archaic neighborhood school, the outdated teaching programs in most fields, the tired teaching styles employed so widely, and the "quiz kid" approach to learning. These leaders continuously advocate the principles, platforms, and programs to which they are professionally and personally committed.

The Overriding Problem

One domestic problem overshadows all the others, North and South. The specter of segregation in schools and housing haunts this land more than ever. Fifteen years after the Brown decision, the overwhelming mass of Negro children in the South still attend predominantly black schools. The North has not done well, for fifteen years after the Brown decision, schools in northern centers of population are more segregated than ever. Most urban centers are rapidly becoming solid racial communities. Urban public schools have increased in population and decreased in quality as immigrants from the South, both black and white, have enrolled and emigrants from these schools have fled to the suburbs. Accompanying the emigration of white students from poor schools, there has been an outflow of teachers, special services, consultants, textbooks, and per pupil expenditures.

Educational leaders, pressured by community groups of segregationists and integrationists who advocate either maintaining the uniracial neighborhood school and providing quality education within this structure or closing the segregated school and integrating its students into more advantaged schools, are torn by the alternatives. Should they seek racial balance in their schools, or should they concentrate on providing equal educational opportunity within the urban segregated school?

Today the educational leader faces no more crucial problem than the issue of race and education. However, the answer is clear: racial balance must be achieved, and sooner rather than later, if the schools are to prepare all young people, black and white, for first-class citizenship. The reasons for this position are many and varied—legal, academic, psychological, and sociological. Only when balance has been accomplished will the schools fulfill their commitment to the individual and to the community.

Legal Reasons for Integration

The 1954 decision in Brown vs. the Topeka Board of Education was based on de jure, not de facto, segregation. However, from the standpoint of the individual child, its conclusions—that segregated schools are inherently inferior for the minority and the majority—

are valid for any kind of segregation. School administrators *must* be concerned with the harmful effects which segregation imposes if they are to conform to the spirit of this landmark decision.

In many states the courts and other governmental agencies have gone considerably farther than the 1954 decision. Massachusetts, for example, has made satisfactory desegregation a condition for state aid to local districts and has gone the farthest in its legal and financial support of racial balance.

In California, the State Board of Education officially declared as a matter of policy that:

> . . . persons or agencies responsible for the establishment of school attendance centers or the assignment of pupils thereto shall exert all effort to avoid and eliminate segregation of children on account of race or color.[1]

The attorney general gave an opinion as follows:

> The governing board of a school district may consider race as a factor in adopting a school attendance plan, if the purpose of considering the racial factor is to effect desegregation in the schools, and the plan is reasonably related to the accomplishment of that purpose.[2]

Most recently, the State Board of Education has specified that every local school district must seek a racial balance in its schools within 15 percent of its overall racial mix.[3] In theory, both State Superintendent Max Rafferty and Governor Ronald Reagan talk integration to some audiences, but in practice they idealize the neighborhood school and the small, educationally inferior and financially costly school district. They pose as revolutionists but are, in fact, revolutionists in reverse.

The intent of the law is clear throughout the nation. But there have been many cases, with differing results, bearing on the question of *how far* school officials are compelled to go in combating de facto segregation. Regardless of how far they are forced legally, there are many reasons why school officials should *want* to take action to improve racial balance.

Academic Reasons for Integration

The bulk of available evidence, although admittedly not exhaustive, tends to support the hypothesis that students drawn from minority groups or a lower socioeconomic class (black or white) achieve more academically in schools with mixed student bodies than they do when segregated. This conclusion is supported by several studies (Havighurst, 1967; Wilson, 1967; Coleman, 1966). More recent assessments (1967) of the Riverside and White Plains experience underscore those findings.[4] This should not be a surprise to anyone who has been exposed to low income segregated schools. Historically, segregated schools have had inferior teachers, buildings, textbooks, and equipment—in short, a totally inferior opportunity for minority youngsters (Green, 1966). Poor schools are, in fact if not always in theory, the result of segregated economic, social, and cultural "disprivilege."

Children are stimulated by contact with those of differing backgrounds. In the case of the minority youngster, such contact frequently results in raising his aspirations. However, the benefit is not all one way. The white boy or girl is stimulated and his learning enriched and made whole by exposure to the ideas and attitudes of students of different backgrounds. In this day, segregated education spells inferior education for the white student separated from the human relations mainstream of his community and his world.

Psychological Reasons for Integration

Crucial to an individual's academic success and his general effectiveness as a citizen is the development of a positive self-image. Segregation has traditionally carried with it a symbolic rejection by society. In the case of de jure segregation, this rejection is more than symbolic. It has blocked the South's economic, social, and cultural development, keeping it the semi-feudal captive of the North. However, even the de facto segregated school symbolizes rejection. Even if educators are not involved in residential discrimination, the school symbolizes society's rejection. The same holds for all forms of discrimination—real and fancied, overt and hidden. And we have reaped a harvest of backlash in every urban segregated neighborhood.

The Coleman study (1966) stresses the importance of the individual student being able to feel that he has some control over his own destiny. This feeling can hardly be engendered in a school that symbolizes society's rejection of a child's race. The psychological effects of segregated schools make it impossible to accept "separate but equal" schools. Segregation within desegregated schools through rigid ability grouping is just as damaging and psychologically equally unacceptable.

Sociological Reasons for Integration

The mobility of population within our country has helped to create cultural diversity in our communities. If our young people are to be educated for living in this multi-cultural world, they need contact with other ethnic groups at a very early age. This need applies to all groups—majority as well as minority. Indeed the education of the segregated white child for full participation in today's world is as shoddy as the segregated education provided so many minority children in urban neighborhoods.

Much stereotyped thinking about ethnic groups comes through lack of contact with members of other groups. Racial balance in a school provides an opportunity for personal associations to be formed across ethnic lines. Students can learn by actual experience to make judgments of other people on an individual basis and not in terms of the group to which they belong. This is important in both directions. The stereotypes which majority youngsters have of minorities, and vice versa, make a sham of the democratic society to which we aspire.

Myths Concerning Integration

Educators who express interest in improving the racial balance of their schools can expect to be barraged with several myths. The first myth is that segregation is not a problem for educators but rather a problem of housing patterns and employment discrimination: "We professionals must mind our own shop." I hope that this myth can be put to rest by the legal, academic, psychological, and sociological reasons mentioned and by the ominous reality of urban blight.

The second myth is that the education of white students will suffer because of desegregation. Berkeley's experience indicates that this does not happen. The Coleman Report and *Racial Isolation in the Public Schools* (1967) concur after in-depth investigation of the national experience. When desegregation is carefully planned and administered, substantial gains are made in the achievement of minority youngsters—*without* the predicted dire consequences to white boys and girls.

The third myth is that white youngsters will be subjected to increased violence at the hands of minority youngsters. We must face the fact that there has been some violence among students. All of us must accept the responsibility for working against student violence— educators, police, parents, lay citizens, and especially the students themselves. However, the records show that, over the years, blacks have been on the receiving end of the violence more often than whites. The black student's violence is a by-product of traditional white violence, disrespect, and disregard. Administrators in desegregated schools have stated that most violence does not have racial overtones. Again, Berkeley's experience has shown a substantial improvement in the educational environment offered to minority youngsters *without* a corresponding deterioration in the school environment for whites.

The fourth myth is that school desegregation will be followed by a mass exodus of whites. Berkeley's experience contradicts this. Our city had a long-standing pattern of gradually declining white enrollment dating back to the early postwar years, long before any significant action was taken to desegregate. In 1964, after intensive study and discussion by citizens' committees, the school staff, and the community at large, de facto segregation was eliminated at the secondary level. Later, a token bussing program was instituted with ESEA funds. The student racial census taken in the fall of 1967 revealed that, not only had the steady decline of white students stopped, but there had been an *increase* both in the number and percentage of white students over the preceding year. Desegregation leading to integration can take place without the dismal consequences predicted in these myths if the action is well planned and executed and if the public is convinced that the quality of the schools will not suffer. Actually, with staff commitment and public, political, and financial support, the quality of education for all of the children will vastly improve.

Berkeley, California, Case Study

Berkeley, California, where the author served as superintendent of schools from July, 1964, to February, 1969, is a medium-sized interracial city of 121,500. Its school enrollment of 15,700 is approximately 50 percent white, 41 percent black, 8 percent Oriental, and one percent other races. In recent years it has sought to deal directly and to solve realistically the problems of "locked in" de facto segregation. It succeeded in desegregating and reorganizing its secondary schools, grades 7 to 12, by fall, 1966. By September, 1968, the desegregation of all Berkeley elementary schools was completed. Berkeley has integrated its staff and improved its counseling. In the process, it has pioneered the ungraded school, team teaching, intergroup education, new math, new social science, an integrated preschool program, Head Start, compensatory education, a new and intense reading program, Negro history, and a developmental health education program. You name it, we tried it.

Before total desegregation, ninety-one separate experimental projects were underway in this relatively small school system. Most dealt with the problems of poor schools and the youngsters who had been crippled and scarred by the ghetto experience. After four years, we found, as in *Equality of Educational Opportunity* (1966) and *Racial Isolation in the Public Schools* (1967), that education of races and social classes in isolation is inherently mis-education. Compensatory education in the setting of slum disinheritance and destitution is a waste of talent, money, and time. We found that the emasculated, separate, and bookish education in the silken isolation of the "hill schools" of Berkeley was inferior and unreal in this problem-ridden world.

The Berkeley community—partially desegregated, its total educational program improving, its thrust experimental—had made snail-like progress toward total racial desegregation during the years 1964 to 1968. This was Berkeley, pioneer in the push toward equality and excellence. This was the Berkeley of the Ramsey Plan, which desegregated all secondary schools. The elementary schools were partly desegregated, but four of seventeen schools and kindergarten-primary units were racially separate.

To those who would see, it was increasingly clear that as long as this school system continued to be "half-slave and half-free," all students would suffer educationally. Minority students would continue to bear personal humiliation and degradation. White students, ignorant of the interracial world around them, would blossom into falsely smug and superior adults, as generations had before them. The "uptight" community would deny them—much as it denies the racial minorities—an education relevant to their needs in this century. All would be prepared by rote to follow the leader and vent full hate on the man or the child who is different or out of step. Thereby the cult of superiority and the culture of violence would be safeguarded. It was indeed clear to many people in Berkeley that segregation by race, separation of students from the mainstream of the community, coupled with irrelevant, lockstep education, could destroy both the schools and the community.

In the spring of 1967, the Board of Education set September, 1968, as the deadline for the complete desegregation of Berkeley public schools within a framework of quality education. This was a Board-staff answer to the eloquent, insistent demands of organized citizens from Berkeley's ghetto area and to the two teacher organizations. This decision was made after full public airing of the issue. The demand was for desegregation now, not a year from now. Nevertheless, planning and programs were essential, and the process of timing each major step began immediately:

> These schools shall be totally desegregated on September 10, 1968, and we might make history on that day.

A staff task group immediately began screening proposals from the staff, community organizations, and individuals. Within two weeks, on urgent recommendation of the original task group on organization, a second group was at work on how to tailor the instructional program to racially mixed classrooms. The recommendations of both task groups were presented widely to the community and the staff for critical analysis and recommendations. The administration submitted its recommendations to the Board, and then a period of Board and community deliberation followed. In January, 1968, the Board of Education adopted *The Berkeley Plan,* which became operative on September 10, 1968.

The Berkeley Plan, inspired by the Princeton matched school approach, had the merit of simplicity. All of Berkeley was divided into four zones, west to east, cutting across the racial and class housing pattern of the city—from "flatland" through "foothill" to "hill." The large predominantly black neighborhood school in each zone became the intermediate school, grades 4 to 6, for every student in the new enlarged attendance area. The predominantly white neighborhood schools became the primary schools, kindergarten to grade 3, for each zone. Children in kindergarten to grade 3 who lived in the black area were bussed up the hill to the primary schools. Children in grades 4 to 6 who lived in the white area were bussed down the hill to the intermediate schools. A total of 3,500, or 40 percent of the city's elementary school children, were transported about 20 minutes to and from school. Bussing was the mechanism whereby all Berkeley's elementary school children were mixed racially and socioeconomically by school and by classroom. Heterogeneous ability grouping was the primary objective.

Yes, Berkeley made history on the 10th of September, 1968, as predicted a year and a half before:

> I am happy to report that every boy and girl in Berkeley is enrolled in a desegregated classroom . . . . The Berkeley plan is unusual in that it involves bussing white children to schools in black neighborhoods as well as the other way around. Many districts across the country have achieved partial integration by closing schools in black neighborhoods and bussing the children to previously all white schools.[5]

Berkeley was acclaimed nationally as the first school system in a city of 100,000 to totally desegregate its schools and to accomplish this by bussing majority as well as minority children. Despite general anxiety, the schools were desegregated with minimal disorganization, classroom disruption, or interracial incidents.

All of this was accomplished within the realistic framework of available financing and school plant capacity. The additional cost of desegregation amounted to $530,300, or about 2.5 percent of a total budget of $21,967,300. Of that amount, about $37,500 was spent for teacher training; $14,000 to move books, furniture, and equipment; $57,750 to purchase modular classroom units and to renovate buildings; and $205,000 to meet safety requirements in the primary schools. Bussing costs were $202,000, or .9 percent of the total budget, at least half of which will be reimbursed under a special aid for transportation program.

Most important were the educational provisions for desegregation. Each intermediate school was provided with a student center for children who might be so disturbed, frustrated, or angry that they disrupted the new classroom. Individual, personal, and educational help was provided for them, as needed. All of the schools were in the process of developing learning laboratories. These were multimedia centers for individual learning projects and activities of the widest variety. Teacher aids, paid and volunteer, from all communities were on hand to help teachers and students in each classroom, meeting a wide variety of individual needs within the mixed group. Special programs funded primarily through special state, federal, and local grants totalling $2,000,000 were focused on the mixed classroom: Follow Through, Head Start, a new science program, new math, new reading—both developmental and remedial, new music, new social studies, and teacher and community aid programs.

Finally, the whole process of desegregation was built upon strong Board and administrative leadership that was self-confident enough to build continuing community, staff, and student involvement into the whole process. A comprehensive and tight organization was welded together in the face of insistent hard-core opposition from segregationists, tax protestors, citizens, and parents who were fearful that their children might be hurt academically by the change.

D-Day, 1968, has passed and the desegregated elementary schools are very much in business. New principals and new teaching staffs are adjusting, not without pain, to their racially mixed classes and student bodies. Students from differing cultures are together for the first time and are developing a realistic appreciation of each other. Several thousand parents from all parts of town are learning to collaborate as volunteers in school programs. PTA's are desegregated. An after-school activities and recreation program is developing slowly and · unevenly. The bussing program is meeting schedules and providing late buses for children engaged in after-school programs.

Many teachers, whose previous experience had been in predominantly white schools, have had great difficulty relating to and meeting the needs of black children. Others, whose previous experience had been in predominantly black schools, are having difficulty teaching effectively in mixed classrooms. Consequently, the district will embark on a broad-scale in-service training program to develop a staff capable of top quality teaching in the new classroom environment. Since the white staff, even with the best of intentions, is often ignorant and unperceptive of the feelings, needs, and heritage of minority people, the district has begun a mandatory in-service training program in minority history and culture for all members.

As the Berkeley schools prepared for and accomplished elementary school desegregation, the issue of resegregation of the secondary schools came to a head. Although desegregated in 1964, the persistent tracking by ability in the junior and senior high schools and the lockstep curriculum and requirements tended to resegregate the students by race within each school. Pressure from the minority community, students, and teachers persuaded the Board of Education to reorganize the secondary schools in fall, 1969. The process of task group study and community involvement parallel to the desegregation study of 1967-68 is now in process. When school convenes in September, 1969, classes will be heterogeneously grouped wherever possible, flexible scheduling will have been introduced, and programs and requirements will have been made more relevant to the needs of this generation of students. Thereby, the total desegregation of the Berkeley public schools will have been protected and preserved.

The superintendent's prime task will be to exert the leadership that will move the school system from the interim period of desegregation to the integration of students, staff, programs, and community. That must be the goal if public education and our community are to survive and flourish. It is the most arduous task of all as the racial minorities seek their rightful, equal place in a stubbornly resistant, predominantly white Christian community.

In the long run, the new Berkeley school-community for modern education might best be served by educational parks and community educational centers. The community centers, way stations to the city-wide educational centers, might provide twenty-four hour service for citizens of every age. Educational services could be joined with the spectrum of human services essential to an urban-suburban people. Then the integration of races, classes, programs, services, and technology might be achieved in our children's time, in our city. This would indeed be utopia.

Dimensions of the Superintendent's Role

The good old days of the city superintendency were not that good. But the great difference today is in the complexity of problems in the urban setting, the increase in social and educational needs and demands, and the enlarged resources in knowledge, technology, and human experience that are available.

It may be that modern educational tasks are too large for the educational establishment to be separate and distinct from community government. There may be need for an "educational executive." But whether or not the superintendent should be subsidiary to community-wide executive leadership is debatable. Nevertheless, a special role of professional leadership in education is realistic within the complexity of the modern scene. And there is logic in viewing the superintendency as an evolving position in the context of a society and an educational system in continuous transition.

Surely, the superintendent as clerk to the board of education and a mere transmission belt of teacher wishes and demands (a common proposal of teacher organizations) must be rejected today as it was in the beginning of the superintendency. Today it has less relevancy. However, should many superintendents continue to abdicate their executive responsibilities, resign from the struggle, bend with each wind that blows, avoid the critical issues of this day, they will, indeed, become clerks.

The city superintendency must be considered primarily a position in education, featuring executive functions in community education. While maintaining the classic advisory relationship to the policymaking board of education, the superintendency is a leadership function. The superintendent and his staff should spearhead policies, programs, services, and technologies tailored to cope with educational change at this crisis period in history.

The Ideal Superintendent

With these factors in mind, then, what are we looking for in a superintendent of schools? He must have the personal and temperamental graces which the books on personnel all document. He must be committed to the fulfillment of the American dream for the variety of children and adults who typify America—racially, religiously, occupationally, politically, and economically. His commitment must bridge the gap from words to action. He must take a forthright and continuing stance on critical local, state, national, and international issues of the day which affect the educational welfare of the community's children and adults. He must continuously and publicly stand up and be counted on the issues, making America's unique concept of democracy a living factor in our time for all the citizenry.

The superintendent needs a unique and broad education across the disciplines as well as in the technical aspects of administration. As with the children, the approach should be toward critical problem-solving and discovery rather than bookish gospel. The superintendent needs the tools of general management and administration. He must be sensitive to the varied and subtle dimensions of communications, community relations, and community organization. His education should involve an internship and apprenticeship in a city school system, a work-study program at the graduate level. It should include work in community, city, educational, and regional planning as prime prerequisites. It could eschew the traditional courses in educational methods and curriculum, but it must include training in interpersonal relations.

The city superintendent should bring to his position solid experience in the critical areas of administration, planning, community relations, community organization, communications, and human relations. This experience should be demonstrable. As for classroom experience, the mythology that the superintendent must have been a teacher and a principal, coming up through the instructional ranks, to function effectively in the superintendency should be put away once and for all. Such experience, although helpful, should not be the critical requirement it is today. Finally, there should be an alternative para-professional route to the superintendency. It should recruit the cream of our nation's talent into the field of education and provide opportunities for advancement and training, from rudimentary to advanced.

The superintendent should be a warm, responsive human being, direct in his relationships with staff and public alike, able to delegate but equally quick to require performance commensurate with responsibility. He should set an example to his staff in consistency, honesty, sincerity, dedication, and commitment. He must treat his staff with patience and understanding but also with firmness, insisting on their best effort at all times. He should expect them in return to emulate the best behavior in their relationship with the student in the classroom. He must know his board members. They are the policy makers, but he should make strong recommendations in areas of policy, never casually waiting for the board to take the lead.

The best school system has a strong board and a strong superintendent. It is possible to have a fine system with a weak board of education if you have a strong superintendent. But you can *never* have a strong system with a weak superintendent as leader.

The superintendent must be the forceful influence in the education family. He must be definite in his decision-making. He must be a dynamic leader of his staff, respected by a majority of the citizenry. He must lead the community—by involving them—ever mindful of his goals. He cannot be weak, he cannot vacillate, he cannot procrastinate. He must have insight into the future. He must be strong.

An Agent for Educational Change

The modern educational leader must be the chief agent for educational change in his community, able to insure involvement, participation, and impact of staff at every point of the way in policy-making, program development, and evaluation. He must also be the leader, able to bring each element of the public and the student body into the whole process of change. This requires exceptional ability in human relations and in management.

The superintendent must understand the many languages of the people. He must move around the community and not be tied to the Rotary Club or to the American Legion or to the National Association for the Advancement of Colored People. He must open channels of communication between divergent groups. He must bring the community to the "action table," not the conference table. He must develop a "multilogue" approach rather than dialogue. He must be perceptive of human needs and give them top priority in the educational program. He must understand pressure politics and be able to redirect pressure groups toward the *common* goal. He must be willing to admit the many weaknesses of the public school system and enlist the support of *all* hands to correct these inadequacies. He must never talk "off the record" nor become "one of the boys." He must make no deals with any group—he must treat them all with fairness. And he must work constantly to bring equality of educational opportunity to everyone in the community.

Conclusion

Public education is a specialized social institution dedicated to the preparation of children and youth primarily, but also adults, for effective individual and group participation in the changing community of work, play, and politics. Education is the keeper of the culture. It is the teacher, guardian, and guide of society's children as they experience the reality that is today and enter the wonderland or wasteland that may be tomorrow. But public education is caught in the critical human dilemma of this world as atomic power, the computer, and space technology move to the forefront. If coping with change and managing change for human ends is critical to survival on this planet, then the role of education in preparing our young for this staggering task must be a crucial one.

The fate of public education depends on the ability of the men who lead, and those men, whether we like it or not, are our school superintendents. The literature is replete with profiles of the ideal professional superintendent. The details of the job have been analyzed and presented on innumerable occasions. The headaches of the position have been noted by professors and practitioners. That the position has evolved into the strategic one in local education cannot be denied as one notes the size and responsibility of the educational establishment in this century. In this era, the superintendent's professional competence and expertise are not enough. The crux of the matter is: Where does the superintendent stand on vital educational and social issues? Can he make his position felt? Or is he still, as he has been traditionally, the prisoner of his background, his board, and the community power structure? Is he no different from the clerk of the mid-nineteenth century who was a pawn of his board? Or the vulnerable business leader and representative of the business community in the 1930's? The superintendent is at the crossroads in his professional career.

In educational leaders, we want boldness instead of softness; we want creativity instead of rigidity. We want men who are up to the challenge; we want fearless men who will lead the way. They must lead the establishment back to excellence in public education through innovative and creative programs, directed dynamically by committed, fearless individuals. If they must disagree publicly with vacillating boards of education, so be it. If it means that their careers might be cut short in some board room in the wee hours of the morning, so be it. If it means that they and their families may be abused publicly by those who want to retain the status quo, so be it. If we are serious about providing equal educational opportunity and educating all of our children to participate effectively in a multiracial society, then this is the price we must be willing to pay.

Notes

1. *Administrative Code, Title 5,* Sections 2010 and 2011, State of California.
2. *Opinion of Stanley Mosk, Attorney General,* No. 63/101, August 15, 1963, State of California.
3. Leonard Kreidt, "State Board of Education Defines Racial Imbalance, Urges Balance," California Educational News Service, News Release No. 828, February 17, 1969.
4. *A Progress Report—A Study of Desegregation in the Public Schools of Riverside, California,* Riverside Unified School District and University of California, Riverside, 1967; *A Three Year Evaluation of the White Plains Racial Balance Plan,* White Plains Public Schools, 1967.
5. Neil V. Sullivan, *Integrated Quality Education,* Berkeley Unified School District, 1968.

References

Coleman, James S., et al., *Equality of Educational Opportunity.* U.S. Office of Education. Washington, D.C.: U.S. Government Printing Office, 1966.

Green, Robert L. "After School Integration—What? Problems in Social Learning," *Personnel and Guidance Journal,* 1966, 44: 704-710.

Havighurst, Robert J. and Neugarten, B.L. *Society and Education.* Boston: Allyn and Bacon, 1967.

Racial Isolation in the Public Schools. U.S. Commission on Civil Rights. Washington, D.C.: U.S. Government Printing Office, 1967.

Wilson, Alan. "Educational Consequences of Segregation in a California Community," in *Racial Isolation in the Public Schools,* Vol. 2. Washington, D.C.: U.S. Government Printing Office, 1967.

14 THE THRUST TOWARD COMMUNITY CONTROL OF THE SCHOOLS IN BLACK COMMUNITIES

Preston Wilcox

Preston Wilcox is at the center of the movement for community control of the public schools in New York City. He is President of Afram Associates, a consultation service which deals with the educational problems of "less chance" communities. He is chief consultant to the Intermediate School 201 Community Education Center in East Harlem. Mr. Wilcox is also Chairman of the National Association of Afro-American Educators.

He has been a member of the educational affiliate of the Bedford-Stuyvesant Educational Development and Service Corporation. At Columbia University School of Social Work, he taught courses in community organization and trained Peace Corps and VISTA volunteers.

Mr. Wilcox presents an articulate examination of the relationship between the larger white-run school systems and the schools located in the black areas of our cities where the residents are demanding greater community control. He suggests that the American Dream has not been developed to include the black American. He argues that the black American must build his own dream since he can no longer entrust his dream to white society and particularly to the white school system. The minority group student is being miseducated by a school system that represents everyone's interests but his. Urban black schools have become an arena where the white-oriented middle class teacher can salve her guilt by steadily fulfilling prophecies of failure.

The thrust for control over urban schools represents a shift in emphasis. Black people and poor people have turned from replicating that which is white and middle class to reshaping the schools to reflect their concerns. This represents at its deepest level a desire by the black and the poor to become effective contributors to the common good. The school system must no longer be a racist tool; it must be a liberator of the human conscience, intellect, and spirit.

So far as Mr. Washington preaches Thrift, Patience and Indus-trial Training for the masses, we must hold up his hands and strive with him, rejoicing in his honors and glorying in the strength of this Joshua called of God and of man to lead the headless host. But so far as Mr. Washington apologizes for injustice, North or South, does not rightly value the privilege and duty of voting, belittles the emasculating effects of the caste system and opposes the higher training and ambition of our brighter minds—so far as he, the South, or the Nation, does this—we must unceasingly and firmly oppose them. By every civilized and peaceful method we must strive for the rights which the world accords to men, clinging unwaveringly to those great words which the sons of the Fathers would fain forget: "We hold these truths to be self-evident: That all men are created equal; that they are endowed by their creator with certain inalienable rights; that among these are life, liberty and the pursuit of happiness."[1]

W. E. B. DuBois

This observer suspects that the egalitarian ethic deriving from our Judeo-Christian values, although viewed as a force to protect and promote the right of all Americans, has, in fact, been employed against black Americans. They have subscribed to the melting pot thesis and the American Dream more than most ethnic groups, and they have been induced to long for opportunities and experiences which are systematically denied to them. The dream is more frequently a nightmare. Brotherhood has more frequently meant "big brother" and "little brother."

The essence of the struggle at Intermediate School 201, which is described in the following pages, was to actively communicate to the black and poor residents in Harlem that they had to build their own dreams and that the system, in the last analysis, was organized for the protection of others—not black Americans. Intrinsic to the struggle was the potential for convincing the students at I.S. 201 that they could be black *and* successful!

In a meeting with members of the New York City Board of Education in April, 1966, the I.S. 201 activists, a group of parents and community leaders, sought to elicit the Board's agreement to conduct an experiment in community control. Their proposal suggested that the principal be selected by the parents and not by the school system. Beyond the Superintendent of Schools, the interest was minimal or nonexistent, as indicated by the evasive and perfunctory responses. One member raised a question which has not escaped memory. He wondered how one could bring about change in an entire system by selecting one piece of that system for special treatment.

This Board of Education, appointed by the Mayor and expected to represent *all* of the people, has an established and unwritten policy which requires a consensus; for example, its publicly announced decisions have reflected a minority position in only three instances known to this observer. A consensus, in most cases, guarantees that the interests of the poor will be overlooked. The exceptions are those instances when an issue of particular significance to the poor has been entertained. Only one of the nine members of the Board is black; none is Puerto Rican. The pupil population is over 50 percent black and Puerto Rican.

In July, 1966, a reply to the proposal for a "new approach to relations between the community and the educational system" was written. The proposal and the reply appeared in the same edition of *Urban Review*. A key point in the proposal for an experiment at Harlem's I.S. 201 was:

> In the viewpoint of the ghetto, the problem is stated in terms of a fact: the present system has failed, and is failing, in its task of enabling minority group youth to seize the opportunities America holds out to its other citizens.[2]

The reply questioned how a principal, a professional who applies independent judgment and skill in the discharge of his tasks, could be "accountable to the parents and also accountable under the law to the district superintendent and the Board of Education." The respondent continued:

> The claim that this would be an "experimental program for . . . at least one school in one community" raises questions that Professor Wilcox should be most sensitive to, as a community organization specialist. A good social experiment is one that can be *widened* eventually to fit the total community.[3]

On a subsequent date, the I.S. 201 activists carried their fight to the Mayor's office. They wanted his support as a last ditch effort to achieve school integration in Harlem. The Mayor, in very measured and somewhat professorial tones, told them after a lecture on the tax base of the city that school integration might stimulate an escalation of the white exodus.

A trip to Washington to see the Commissioner of Education, Harold Howe, was next on the agenda for the activists. Howe was cordial, concerned, committed to principle, but he was helpless to act—at least if measured by what he was able to do.

I.S. 201 and its four feeder elementary schools were one of three school units to receive a Ford Foundation grant. But even when the Ford Foundation was granting funds to multischool units "in which parents, other neighborhood residents, and teachers would have an unprecedented voice in the management of the public schools,"[4] the Board limited its participation to a promise of "speedy review of detailed plans." The resources, talents, and presumed "good intentions" of the Board were held in abeyance.

On November 9, 1967, the Mayor's Advisory Panel on Decentralization transmitted their plan for decentralization of the entire New York City school system to the Mayor. The panel included the following statements in its report:

> A system already grown rigid in its negative powers has been called upon to meet the unexpected challenge of an extraordinary immigration of impoverished citizens whose children have special needs for the very best our schools can offer, and the system has not effectively met this challenge. The new needs of large numbers of Negro and Puerto Rican students from low-income families may be the most dramatic, but *they are not the only group which now needs better schools. No plan of government can be successful if it aims only at the particular needs of particular groups.*[5]

The panel included one Negro and one Puerto Rican among its five members; it was more representative than the Board of Education.

The activists from I.S. 201 had been called upon to provoke a controversy at their home school. The confrontation began when the schools opened in September, 1966. The activists' thesis was that the system was failing to educate black and poor students. They had to expose the system's unwillingness or inability to deliver quality integrated education, both as a means to mobilize community support and in order to engage the issue of local community control. Paradoxically, no meaningful efforts had been made to involve local parent or community leaders in improving the caliber of segregated education which had become their children's destiny. The failure to integrate was an indication of the Board's inability to live up to its promises. The failure to undertake the responsibility to turn back to the community the responsibility of guarding the educational aspirations of their own children was more than a broken promise. It was professional disregard measured by the *failure to educate.*

The respondent quoted above, the members of the Board, the Mayor, and his panel tended to define public education in terms of white America. Phrases such as the "entire system," "widening" the experimentation, "they are not the only group which needs better schools" and the "white exodus" were presumed to include the legitimate interests of black Americans when, in fact, such broad and general considerations effectively exclude them. It is fair to surmise that the concept of America as understood by the actors above includes black Americans not as full participants and beneficiaries but essentially as a group to be considered after the interests of others are attended.

The ultimate test as to whether America will achieve its goals resides not in white suburbia but within the black communities. However, school programs draw heavily upon white middle class assumptions. It was this tendency to deliver *generalized* white products into *specialized* black communities which set the stage for the thrust by black communities to take control of the schools set up to serve their children.

The issue engaged at I.S. 201 has spread to at least four other sites in New York City and to Washington, Columbus, Ohio, and Boston. And it can be expected to occur in the South. In every instance a confrontation between the black and poor and the school system has been engaged. This thrust—unlike the middle class-oriented drive for quality integrated education outside the ghetto—is based within the "less chance" communities and builds its hope on a constituent group of parents and community leaders.

Middle class blacks participate, to be sure; but they differ from their black bourgeoisie forerunners. The middle class blacks discern that their destinies are tied directly to the plight of the black poor. Their predecessors tended to value being held accountable by the white middle class.

Leslie Campbell observed the cleavage between the black bourgeoisie and the black poor. In discussing the confrontation between the black masses and the public school system, he submitted the following opinion:

> Seemingly [the black parents] had won a victory for improved education in the black ghetto. Then the establishment turned to its secret weapon, the Negro professional. The Negro teachers at I.S. 201 helped transfer victory into defeat.[6]

Tilt of the Schools Against the Black and Poor

The public school system, while not the manufacturer of the system described herein, has become a sophisticated purveyor of the pattern. It has been established fairly conclusively that on the basis of ethnic composition, performance, scores, per capita expenditures, teacher turnover and assignments, and the effective upgrading of minority group staff, many large urban complexes have dual school systems: one white and one black but both controlled by whites. Beyond this, an expanding body of evidence suggests that residential segregation, the track system, and dropout patterns are less the accident of good intentions gone sour than they are deeply ingrained "gentlemen's agreements" which are stacked against the best interests of black and poor youth.

Jonathan Kozol has recorded with eloquence how the Boston school system (both staff and procedures) operated to influence him to identify with the system and to turn black kids off. At one point he pondered how a country which daydreamed about exporting democracy has so little left for its own people. "It is certain that we do not have a great deal of it to spare for Negro children."[7] Kozol ran into a problem because he considered black and poor students to be *people*.

When Elliott Shapiro, at one time Harlem's best loved principal, allowed himself to become a hero to his charges, he simultaneously earned the status of outcast within the system (Hentoff, 1966a,b). Other Harlem principals treated him as though he were rocking the boat.

The *Hobson v. Hansen* court proceeding in Washington, D.C., brought to public visibility the deliberateness with which black students were assigned to the slower track, often on the basis of visual evidence alone. Skin color was used to teach black kids to learn slowly. The judge ruled that the track system deprived:

... the poor and the majority of the Negro students in the District of Columbia of their constitutional right to equal educational opportunities. Children are classified in the tracks not according to ability to learn but according to color and class factors extraneous to innate ability.[8]

The minority group student finds himself in the curious position of being miseducated by a system that represents everyone's interests but his. Such students are ordered to attend school under compulsory education laws, seemingly for the express purpose of being convinced of their ineducability. One observer has intimated that the system helps such youth to *feel* that they cannot learn. When board members and their staffs mouth a belief in the opportunity for people to be equal but listen with greater clarity to protagonists of the white racist "neighborhood concept" in school integration struggles, they render the frustrations of minority students appropriate.

Under-utilization of white schools frequently has been kept from public view while over-utilization of black schools has often been used to justify the failure to educate. Teacher authority has been employed to discipline and blunt rather than to unleash and channel potential. Ghetto schools have a prison atmosphere. Concern for the "safety of the children" has a secondary meaning for teachers who are terrified of ghetto children. Controlled children and teacher security are viewed as being synonymous.

Black students who are able to negotiate the schools often have to adopt the views of their oppressors. They have to behave toward their teachers in a fashion that helps the teacher to alleviate her "unknown" fears. They have to listen to discussions of slavery that highlight the honesty of George Washington but conveniently overlook his ownership of plantation and household slaves. The white WASP model is substituted for one with which black students could identify more readily.

Ghetto schools are becoming "teacher orientation centers"; they serve as stepping-stones to lily-white schools. Somehow, the "democratic" assignment policies find few experienced or competent teachers being assigned to the predominantly black schools and a limited assignment of black teachers (one by one) to white schools. Teachers have a good thing going; the institutionalization of mediocrity gives them a sense of security (economic and professional). New York City is an example:

Of 54,235 teachers in the system, in the last five years, only 170 regular teachers and only 82 substitutes have been given unsatisfactory ratings, and in the last five years, the tenure of only 12 teachers was discontinued.[9]

Perpetuating the System—"Dropout Expectations"

Vintner and Sarri (1965), in the study of malperformance in high schools, suggested that the dropout problem was mainly a fault of the system—not of the students who quit. The system responded most effectively to white middle class students; it tuned out the black and poor. Factors such as the sanctioning procedures, the record systems, and teacher perspectives converted black and poor students into "pushouts." Once defined as a "malperformer," the student had an indelible label. And the white-oriented middle class teacher could salve her guilt by steadily fulfilling the prophecy of failure for black and poor youth.

Kenneth Clark has observed:

> Once one organizes an educational system wherein children are placed in tracks or that certain judgments about their ability determine what is done for them or how much they are taught or not taught, the horror is that the results tend to justify the assumptions.[10]

The decision in the *Hobson v. Hansen* case in Washington, D.C., documented that, in this instance at least, the system was indeed organized on the basis of "certain judgments."[11]

It is to Robert Rosenthal, a Harvard social psychologist, that Clark should turn for substantiation of his position. In a study of teacher expectations, Rosenthal demonstrated that, as he succinctly expressed it:

> The difference between special children and ordinary children, then, was only in the mind of the teacher.[12]

Rosenthal found that children falsely labeled as potential "bloomers" tended to bloom with extraordinary frequency—without any special tutoring or crash programs. He wrote:

> Even before a teacher has seen a pupil deal with academic tasks, she is likely to have some expectations for his behavior. If she is to teach a "slow group" or children of darker skin color or children who are "on relief," she will have different expectations for her pupils' performance than if she is to teach a "fast group" of children of an upper-middle class community.[13]

Rosenthal's findings confirm the relationship between teacher expectations of student achievement and the student's ethnicity. Of the total group studied, two subgroups showed the most improvement:

a) The average students who were neither at the top or bottom of the school's ranking system and those Mexican-American children who looked most like Anglo-Saxons.

b) The boys who looked most Mexican showed the least improvement, reflecting the teacher's prejudices.[14]

A person's potential may, like beauty, be in the eye of the beholder.

Control Over Information

Black and poor students are generally *without advocates* within the school system. Those who advocate for them outside the school face all kinds of barriers. A strong barrier is the lack of access to information on which to construct action and improvement programs.

On February 17, 1967, Leonard Buder of the New York Times published the reading scores of the New York City system. To this observer's knowledge, it was the first time in the history of the city that such data had been released publicly via the press. Buder had to follow a circuitous route to obtain the information. Word has it that Adam Clayton Powell, Harlem's dethroned Congressman, requested the data from the New York City Board of Education. When Powell received it, it was passed on to Buder via a third party. Buder prepared his story, checked it with the Board of Education for validity, and then published it. (EQUAL, an educational activist group, has published the most complete record of reading scores. They credit Adam Clayton Powell with obtaining the data.)

Buder's story revealed that:

Pupils in schools in middle class neighborhoods are often three, four, and sometimes five years ahead of youngsters of the same grade in predominantly Negro and Puerto Rican schools.[15]

This news release served to heighten parental interest in the quality of education their children were receiving—and raised a question as to why the Board maintained an aura of confidentiality over essentially public information. The same information had been made available to social researchers in the past but was not easily accessible to parent or community leaders.

There are other forms of control over information. After a boycott of Manhattan's P.S. 125 ended in March, 1967, the teachers were warned against discussing the boycott in the classroom with their students. The students who participated in the boycott had been fully informed of the rationale behind it by volunteers at the West Harlem Liberation School, the interim school developed during the boycott. Discussion, role playing, written papers, and even drama were used to project the idea.

When the same students returned to school, their respective teachers remained silent about the most acute social issue in the lives of their students. Instructions from the school superintendent to the school staff read: "Make no references in our classes to the happenings of the past week." Teachers were advised to reply *in private* if the students themselves brought up the events. Class discussions were to be tabled and avoided "today or subsequently."

The wisdom of this action is not being questioned as much as the *right* of anyone to make such a decision without consulting the parents of the children involved. This unilateral action by school officials had the impact of rendering community actions "illegal" and "unconstitutional." Embedded within such official actions were the seeds for encouraging community reactions to unilateral school actions.

Teacher Power

The "beholders" in the New York City system, organized into a professional union by the United Federation of Teachers, have, in a presumed search for quality education, displaced the power of the Board with their own. Gittel (1966) noted that the UFT was among the system's major policy-makers. She further observed that the Board of Education was, in fact, a political subsystem.

The interests of the teacher and the system (white middle class America) are well protected by practices and procedures. Residential segregation, the track system, the self-fulfilling prophecy of failure, and the push-out policies function as insurance. The teachers often serve as insurance agents on the system's behalf. They condone its dysfunctioning by remaining decent and silent.

In fact, the school system has benefitted economically from its failures. Title I and Title III grants to educational systems to intervene into the problems of the so-called "disadvantaged" are based on the premise that the disadvantaged are to be blamed for their own short-comings. The disadvantaged qualify for such programs by revealing a shortcoming. The position of this observer is that such programs compensate educational systems for their failures rather than providing *equity* to consumers to work on their own behalf. The irony of it all is that the very institutions that have shown themselves to be incapable of educating such youths receive special grants to do so at higher pay.

The School as a Manpower Allocation System

Whitney Young observes:

> Fifteen percent of [the] population is Negro, seventy-five percent of [the] welfare recipients are Negro, seventy-five percent of [the] crime is committed by Negroes. It costs $3,000 a year to keep one family on welfare.[16]

Orshansky (1965) notes that nonwhites suffer a poverty risk three times as great as white families do.

The school, when viewed as a manpower allocation system, is a key social determinant: one's life chances can be enhanced, minimized, or wiped out. Black people are proportionately over-represented in Vietnam; 14.5 percent serving are black. They are over-represented among those served by the Office of Economic Opportunity; 31 percent of those living below the poverty line are black. Considering the correlation between the ingrained tendencies of the school and their impact on the black and poor, it is difficult to ascertain whether the schools have failed or succeeded!

Voluntary Segregation—By Whom?

It may be of interest to note that the malperformers and the push-outs have had more interracial experiences in jail, in Vietnam, and on the relief rolls than in school. After all, school integration has presumably failed because residential segregation has succeeded. Tilly, Jackson and Kay (1965) studied the relationship between race and residence in Wilmington and determined that residential patterns were produced by a combination of four factors: land use, external controls, resources, and the criteria of choice. They posited that residential segregation amounted to an *organized defense of the advantages of whites and of the barriers whites maintain to keep them from having to acknowledge others as their equals.*

Taeuber (1965) identified three principal causes of residential segregation: "choice, poverty and discrimination—the third is by far the strongest."

In alluding to the plight of black Americans, Whitney Young sought to appeal to the white conscience: "It costs $3,000 a year to keep one family on welfare." Tilly, Jackson and Kay appealed to the *group self-interests of black people* when they wrote:

> It is curious how often whites think of themselves as subsidizing Negroes through their expenditures, via taxes, for schools or public services. In Wilmington's housing market the opposite is true: Negroes subsidize whites. They do so (unwillingly, to be sure) by paying more for an inferior grade of housing, and by not competing for dwellings in the all-white sections of the city.[17]

Recognition that the same forces which urge *gradual* school integration also engineer *instant* residential segregation has increased the likelihood that the black and the poor would begin to promote their own self-interests.

The Rationale of Community Control

The thrust for control over ghetto schools represents a shift in emphasis by black and poor people from a concern with replicating that which is American to a desire for reshaping it to include their concerns. There is less concern with social integration than there is with effective education. Recall that blacks have been the major proponents of school integration; whites have been the major opponents. The conflict around school integration is only another example of the distorted configuration of black-white relations. Blacks have sought quality education via school integration; whites have assumed that this was a ruse leading to intermarriage or residential integration. Even as blacks sought to be brothers to their white counterparts, whites feared that blacks wanted to become their brothers-in-law.

On the other hand, blacks have begun to recognize that the educational system probably has no intention of educating black Americans to promote their own agendas. The system's preference is for Americans of color to develop pride in white America. What is really feared is collective action by blacks in the economic and political spheres.

The underlying thread is white paranoia about racism. While there is a great deal of interest in softening its impact, there is great reluctance to employ the reality of racism as a premise on which to organize and develop black communities. White Americans benefit from the realities of racism; blacks suffer its consequences.

The incarceration of black people behind the "colored curtain" and the failure of "good intentions" to lead poor blacks anywhere but toward hell has provided the evidence around which black Americans have begun to organize. It is up to black people to remove white profit from black ghettos. To assume leadership of institutions serving the black community, to develop an advocate system for blacks, and to develop the political strength of its social fabric is the ultimate challenge facing black Americans. Interestingly enough, the integration of essentially white institutions will arise less from the expression of social commitment by whites than by pressure from the black community.

The shift in group self-interest is occurring on several levels:

1. From a *one by one* approach (i.e., Jackie Robinson and Kenneth Clark) to efforts *en masse*.
2. From an appeal to white conscience to an appeal to black consciousness.
3. From reliance on white leadership to the exercise of effective black leadership.
4. From excessive identification with the values of the white oppressor (the melting pot, American idealism) to a redefinition of these values appropriate to the aspirations of black people.
5. From entrapment as economic consumers to an elaboration of roles as economic producer.
6. From political dependence to political interdependence.
7. From the role of victimized plaintiff to that of articulate participation-proponent for specific changes to benefit blacks directly.

The dilemma of white Americans relates to how they can continue to make democratic and egalitarian pronouncements in the face of rampant racism. Not that they are moved by the injustices of racism; it's that they somehow have to develop the verbal, social, intellectual, and emotional skill to justify why it exists. The dilemma for black people is different. How do they become an *effective minority* without at the same time becoming victims of the system they are attempting to change? The civil rightists perceived themselves as victims and glamorized their roles accordingly. The black power theorists are more critical of themselves for believing that whites would or could liberate them.

Black people believe their time has come. "No army can withstand the strength of an idea whose time has come," as Victor Hugo said. Resistance to the black power ethos provides it with a kind of validity that would disappear if white America recognized black power.

Alexander Dumas once observed that every human advance is opposed at its outset by ninety-nine percent of humanity:

> But this is of no importance, seeing that the hundredth to which we belong has, since the beginning of the world, made all reforms for the ninety-nine others who are well pleased with them, but who nevertheless go on protesting against those which still remain to be carried out. . . . Majorities are only the evidence of that which is, whereas minorities are often the seed of that which will be.[18]

Alexis de Tocqueville noted this same expectancy when he visited America in the nineteenth century prior to the Emancipation Proclamation:

> If ever America undergoes great revolutions, they will be brought about by the presence of the black race on the soil of the United States; that is to say, they will owe their origin, not to the equality, but to the inequality of condition.[19]

The patterns of duplicity and concealment exercised on the race issue by white Americans of northern vintage is not really a reaction to avoid handling guilt. It is much more a need to perpetuate the myth of equality undergirded by white supremacist policies. The reluctance to teach black history has existed because of a fear of developing black hatred of whites. The reluctance to release test scores has been explained as fear of negative reaction that could arise among parents.

One wonders whether blacks should *respect* whites solely because they are white; whether black communities should respect white-controlled schools which fail to educate their children. Or should they respect whites who also respect them and advocate on behalf of their children?

The thrust, then, for control of schools serving black communities is essentially a surge by black people to have their concerns incorporated into this society's agenda. Any honest examination of the school system will reveal that social class and social caste factors operate to keep black and poor students uneducated. Poor whites, however, often benefit from the racism that demeans poor blacks. In addition, a majority of blacks belong to poor economic groups. A minority of whites belong to such classes. Poor whites join their ethnic counterparts whenever blacks introduce their own agenda, even though in many cases poor whites would benefit from the positive changes that take place.

The school has been singled out as the institution to engage in battle because of its social and economic utility. It lends itself to becoming the unit around which community planning takes place. The governing board of the schools could focus or evaluate all other services, public and private, within a geographic area in terms of their impact on education. Welfare programs should be evaluated on dual criteria: how do they aid families economically and how do they enhance the school attendance and performance of the children? Job training programs should be judged on the degree to which employment is provided for the parents or guardians of school children. School-based programs should be evaluated on the degree to which they transmit skills in the three R's *and* the degree to which the social fabric of the surrounding community is impacted. As a consequence, school-related organizations should not exist for the sole purpose of creating new schools within black colonies. They should also aid in the effort to remove the community from its colonialistic state.

Education should be viewed as a total experience within the community. It should not be limited to what happens in the classroom. Students should be educated about the nature of slumlords, police corruption, consumer exploitation, and absentee decision-making. PTA's have served as tools for the control of parents, as forces to eliminate the roles of community leaders who are not parents, and as platforms for principals. PTA's should be declared obsolete and replaced by dues-collecting parent unions which hire professionals—lawyers, psychologists, social workers, sociologists, social psychologists—as advocate-technicians to work on behalf of the black and poor, not only against them.

Suppliers of goods and services should be canvassed to learn how many local black and poor residents they hire and whether or not they can develop work-study or job training programs for local students and parents.

University researchers should be expected to provide para-professional jobs and scholarships for local students. Such research should be geared toward providing data out of which action can be taken—action formulation, not mere Ph.D. accreditation.

An important asset of the locally-controlled school would be its accessibility to local parent and community leaders and, hopefully, its function as a tool for family education. Parents who have easy access to the school would be urged to function as teachers; that is, they would be called upon to develop the teaching aspect of the parent's role. The school would be required to help parents acquire skills to support and enhance the learning potential of their children. Hopefully, teachers would lend their efforts to this end also. Modification of the relationship between the school and the community encompasses a predisposition toward greater parental involvement. The content of this involvement would be based on the elaboration of teaching roles for parents in their own homes. Lower class parents have tended to delegate the total responsibility for education to the schools; and, then, they have incurred the blame for not carrying it out in the home.

Community residents—parents, local influentials, and the like—should be viewed as resources, not as irrelevant people. The decision to drop a child from school should be made only after community people have full and complete understanding of the reasons for it. Such action should be taken only when all efforts are exhausted. Local residents, because they live side by side with the disruptive children every day, might be helped to save these children, rather than be urged by a negative school system to support the oppressors.

Teachers ought to be evaluated on the basis of their efforts to adjust the school system to the student. The school exists for the students, not for the system. Teachers who care about black and poor youth will teach them the art of manipulating their environment. Teachers should legitimate student actions by attempting first to manipulate the student's environment for him. Such teachers should enable families who reside in poor housing to initiate rent strikes, to file complaints, and to develop political know-how.

A ghetto school is not a middle class school. A teacher in the ghetto has to *enjoy* the hostility of middle class America in order to free herself to help her charges decide whether they, too, want to become middle class. She also has to be concerned about the *extraschool life* of the student. Teaching in middle class schools is a profession; in ghetto schools it is an art. A teacher in a ghetto school has to be a cynic and a realist about the nature of our society. He has to recognize and accredit *functional anger;* he has to risk himself on behalf of his students.

Summary

The thrust for control over ghetto schools by local residents represents at its deepest level a desire by the black and poor to become effective contributors to the common good. This view may be surprising to some, but it is a reasonable and democratic response to the record of failure of school systems across the country. This dissatisfaction is not a reaction to the failure to integrate but to the *failure to educate.* It is a recognition of the forces that sanction the memorialization of a middle class system and society. This is less a criticism of the form of society than it is of its functioning.

Black and poor students are asked to behave like the middle class without being guaranteed the opportunities and resources for becoming middle class. They are asked to ignore their extraschool experiences, while the same experiences are demeaned by the schools. They are called upon to promote teacher comforts, while the same teachers fail to hold out high expectations for them. They are barred from the informal channels of influence and opinion, while such communications define them in negative terms. Black and poor children are asked to identify with their oppressors—a pattern of behavior which middle class Americans, black and white, have skillfully mastered. Middle class Americans reap secondary economic benefits for doing so. Black and poor Americans have not been able to visualize rewards at the other end of the rainbow.

The movement for local control is a challenge to America to become "truly American," to include the black and the poor as people. More than that, it is an effort by a group that has the most to gain by participating in that process. When parent and community leaders, whose apathy has become an American legend, mobilize themselves for their own self-advancement, one wonders why the school system reacts so negatively and in such an organized fashion. One suspects that the skeleton in the school system's closet may be a major reason: it may be the trained incapacity of white-oriented middle class teachers to effectively educate black and poor students. A white-oriented middle class teacher is one who reacts instinctively and negatively to black and poor students, even if covertly. This includes the black bourgeoisie.

Restructuring the relationships between school and community is the key to the thrust for change. It is an attempt to modify the role of the school from that of prosecutor of black and poor students to that of defender and advocate for black students. Two *inseparable* outcomes will mark the success of this venture: the degree to which black and poor kids *invest* themselves in the learning process (instead of allowing themselves to be taught that they are slow learners) and the degree to which the local school unit becomes an agent for local community change (not just changing students).

The *struggle* in which the black and poor have engaged has had its positive consequence. Conflict and controversy and the bumbling of the systems which are the targets of their rage have produced a new level of understanding of their rights to hold the public accountable in a democracy (Simms, 1966). Poor people, too, have a right to "blow the whistle." Public edict or legislation alone could not have convinced the black and the poor that the school system could *not* educate their children without their sustained interest. The shame of the nation is that, had the struggle not erupted, school systems across the country would have gone merrily along giving tenure to teachers for *not* teaching their students.

As one with a sense of fair play, my omission of any of the school system's assets in this chapter does not plague me. Rather, it reaffirms a deeply held conviction that the rationalization of deprivations is fair only to the rationalizers. My calling is to ensure fair play for the illegally deprived.

In the last analysis, the performance of school systems cannot be evaluated solely against the backdrop of the number of its Ivy League candidates. Nor is the school a riot control vehicle nor a builder of mediocre men for menial jobs. In the fullest sense, it must come to be a liberator of the human conscience, intellect, and spirit—to the limits of the student's capacity. The human potential which has been blunted within the ghettos has within it the seeds of its own development or the dehumanization of our cities. The choice made by the black and the poor is obvious.

Notes

1. W.E.B. DuBois, *The Souls of Black Folk* (New York: Fawcett Publications, 1953), pp. 53-54. Reproduced by permission.
2. P. R. Wilcox, "One View and a Proposal," *Urban Review* (July, 1966), pp. 13-16.
3. R. A. Dentler, "In Reply to Preston Wilcox," *Urban Review* (July, 1966), p. 17.
4. *News from the Ford Foundation* (New York: Ford Foundation, July 6, 1967), p. 1.
5. *Reconnection for Learning: A Community School System for New York City* (New York: Mayor's Advisory Panel on Decentralization of the New York City Schools, 1967), p. 2. Italics are the author's.
6. L. R. Campbell, "The Difference," *Negro Teachers Forum* (December, 1966), p. 3.
7. J. Kozol, *Death at an Early Age* (Boston: Houghton Mifflin, 1967).
8. "The Washington, D.C. School Case," *Integrated Education* (1967), 4, p. 49.
9. F. M. Hechinger, *New York Times*, April 8, 1967.
10. K. B. Clark, *Clash of Cultures in the Classroom* (Washington, D.C.: Tutorial Assistance Center, 1966), p. 6.
11. See "U.S. Appeals Court Judge J. Skelly Wright's Decision in the District of Columbia's Track System," in *Congressional Record*, pp. H7655-H7700. Also, S. O. Jacoby, "National Monument to Failure," *Saturday Review* (November 18, 1967).
12. F. M. Hechinger, "Bright Ones Spurt Ahead," *Youngstown Vindicator* (August 13, 1967), p. A9.
13. *Ibid.,* p. A9.
14. W. M. Young, "To Be Equal: Slum Schools Get Failing Grades," *Buckeye Review* (October 27, 1967), p. 4.
15. L. Buder, "Fifth of City Pupils Found Two Years Behind in Reading," *New York Times* (February 17, 1967), p. 1.
16. D. Halberstam, "Whitney Young's Way with Executives Gains Jobs for Negroes," *New York Times* (January 8, 1967), p. 54.
17. C. Tilly, W. D. Jackson, and B. Kay, *Race and Residence in Wilmington, Delaware* (New York: Columbia University Press, 1965), p. 97.
18. R. Michels, *Political Parties* (New York: Dover Publications, 1959), p. 50.
19. Alexis de Tocqueville, *Democracy in America*, Vol. II (New York: Vintage Books, 1945), p. 270.

References

Gittel, Marilyn. *Participants and Participation: A Study of School Policy in New York City.* New York: Center for Urban Education, 1966.

Hentoff, Nat. *Our Children Are Dying.* New York: Viking Press, 1966. (a)

Hentoff, Nat. "The Principal," *New Yorker,* May 7, 1966, p. 51. (b)

Orshansky, Mollie. "Counting the Poor: Another Look at the Poverty Profile," *Social Security Bulletin,* U.S. Department of Health, Education and Welfare, January, 1965.

Simms, Gregory. *Elements of Democracy: A Paper on the Principle of Public Supervision of Public Goods and Services.* Trenton: New Jersey Community Action Training Institute, 1966.

Taeuber, Karl E. "Residential Segregation," *Scientific American,* 1965, 213: 11-19.

Tilly, Charles, Jackson, Wagner D., and Kay, Barry. *Race and Residence in Wilmington, Delaware.* New York: Columbia University Press, 1965.

Vintner, Robert D. and Sarri, Rosemary C. "Malperformance in Public Schools," *Social Work,* 1965, 10: 9-11.

INDEX